The Life and Teachings of

(Nitya-lila-pravishta Om 108 Shri)

Krishna Das Baba

(Madrasi)

# of Radhakund

Karunamayi Das
(Zakrent Christian)

Second Edition

Edited and introduced
by
Neal Delmonico

Blazing Sapphire Press
715 E. McPherson
Kirksville, Missouri 63501
2012

ISBN: 978-0-9817902-7-5 (0-9817902-7-5)

Library of Congress Control Number: 2012941022

Published by:
Blazing Sapphire Press
715 E. McPherson
Kirksville, Missouri 63501

Available at:
Nitai's Bookstore
715 E. McPherson
Kirksville, Missouri, 63501
Phone: (660) 665-0273
http://www.nitaisbookstore.com
http://www.blazingsapphirepress.com
Email: neal@blazingsapphirepress.com

Contents

Blessings v

Editor's Preface vii
Editorial Approach xxv

Author's Preface xxix
Auspicious Invocations xxix
Expression of Gratitude xxxiv
Radhakund xxxv

1 The Life and Times of Shri Krishna Das Baba 1
1.1 The Holy Land 23

2 Teachings and Practices (I) 25
2.1 Baba's Favorite Recitations 25
2.2 Shishir Kumar Ghose 27
2.3 *Bhajan* 28
2.4 Dust of Vrindavan 28
2.5 Baba's Treasure 29
2.6 His Room 31
2.7 Hope 32
2.8 Cowherd Women of Vraja (*Gopis*) 33
2.9 Love-in-separation (*Vipralamba*) 33
2.10 Humility 34
2.11 Offenses to Vaishnavas 34
2.12 The Residents of Vraja (*Vraja-vasis*) 36
2.13 The *Manjari* Identity 40
2.14 Sakhicharan Das Baba and his Bead-bag 43

2.15 Chanting the Holy Names 44
2.16 The Names of Radha 45
2.17 Radha 49
2.18 To Radha for Love 51

3 Teachings and Practices (II) 53
3.1 The Sampradayas (Communities) 53
3.2 Color of Clothes 55
3.3 The Guru 56
3.4 Passionate *Bhakti* 62
3.5 Gates to *Bhakti* 63
3.6 Service of the Guru 64
3.7 External Symptoms of *Bhakti* 65
3.8 Real Renunciation 66
3.9 Ajamila 68
3.10 Guidance in the Holy Sites 69
3.11 Hearing Discussions about Krishna (*Krishna-katha*) 70
3.12 Wondrous Radhakund 71
3.13 Vaishnava Marriage 72
3.14 Dowry and Women's Rights 74
3.15 Humility 75

4 Teachings and Practices (III) 77
4.1 Shri Radhakund 77
4.2 Bathing in Shri Radhakund 79
4.3 Service of the Vaishnavas 79
4.4 The Path-showing Guru 80
4.5 The True Nature of the Living Being (*Jiva*) 80
4.6 Song of the Cowherd Girls (*Gopis*) 83
4.7 The Krishna Initiation *Mantra* 84
4.8 The Two Gopal Mantras 84
4.9 Worship of the Sacred Image 85
4.10 Eligibility for and Responsibilities of Worship 86
4.11 A Christian at Radhakund 87
4.12 Absence of Pride 87
4.13 Grace 89
4.14 Diagrams for Visualization 90
4.15 Snakes 90
4.16 Spiritual Patrimony 90

4.17 The *Vyashti* and *Samashti* Gurus 91
4.18 The Guru in Succession 91
4.19 Abandoning the Guru 93
4.20 Baba's Personal Habits 94
4.21 Baba's Miraculous X-ray Image 94
4.22 In the Winter 95
4.23 Visions and Ecstasies 96
4.24 Poor Man's Guru 97

5 Teachings and Practices (IV) 99
5.1 Remembering (*Smaran*) 99
5.2 Passionate and Passion-pursuing *Bhakti* 101
5.3 Levels of Meditation 104
5.4 The *Rasas* 105
5.5 Success (*Siddhi*) 109
5.6 The Stages in the Cultivation of *Bhakti* 110
5.7 Obstacles to Progress 112
5.8 The Seven Day Recitation of the *Bhagavata* 114
5.9 The Stature of the *Bhagavata Purana* 114
5.10 Baba's Blessings 117
5.11 Baba's Letters 117
5.12 Parting Submission 118

A Shri Sakhicharan Das Babaji 119
A.1 Foreword 121
A.2 The Life of Srila Sakhicharan Das Babaji 122

B Images 137

C Glossary of Terms and Names 143

Bibliography 159

Blessings

[From Pandit 108 Shri Ananta Das Babaji Maharaja (Mahanta of Radhakund)]

Shri Shri Gaura-vidhur Jayati!

Shri Shri Krishna Das Madrasi Baba, who has now entered the eternal abode, was a great worshiper and a great devout and a high-souled Vaishnava. He had achieved in his life profound devotion to the lotus feet of Shri Shri Radharani. We were friends for many long years. He helped me greatly with the books I have written and I am very deeply obliged to him for this. I am very glad to learn that his beloved disciple, Shriman Karunamayi Das, is publishing his biography. Many, many thanks to him. I pray that his desires will be fulfilled.

Well wisher,
Shri Ananta Das
17-05-2006
Radhakund

Editor's Preface

It is a great pleasure for me to be able to present, at last, Shri Karunamayi Das's hagiography of his guru, Shri Krishna Das (Madrasi)[1] Baba of Radhakund, whom I, too, had the good fortune of meeting and getting to know during the period I lived in Vraja (1974-6). Shri Krishna Das Baba would often visit me at the place I was staying in then in Vrindavan and on those occasions we would have long and interesting discussions about Chaitanya Vaishnavism and the hopes and aspirations of those who regard themselves as members of that tradition. That period of my life was one of turmoil and indecision, and Krishna Das Baba was like a kindly uncle to me then. He gave me much solace, guidance, and encouragement during that difficult period, drawing on the wisdom he gained from his many years of practice and experience in the tradition, and from contact with many of the great Chaitanya Vaishnavas of an earlier period.

Seeing Krishna Das Baba's humble and self-effacing demeanor, those who met him were drawn ineluctably to the conclusion that he had progressed far in the process of cultivating love (*preman*) for Krishna. As I got to know him better I came to understand how much he had suffered for his faith, and how much he had gained from his sufferings, as well. When he visited me, he unfortunately often had to face abuse from those with whom I was staying at the time. He took such arrogant rudeness calmly, humbly, and without agitation. Nor did he stop coming to visit me. We not only talked about the tradition; on occasion he read me

[1]The word Madrasi distinguishes Krishna Das Baba from the many other Krishna Das Babas who live in Vraja and other places. Madrasi means "from Madras," now called Chennai, in South India. Actually, Krishna Das Baba was not from Madras but from Kerala. Since most North Indians do not distinguish between Madras and Kerala, Madrasi here just means "from South India."

passages from some of the tradition's sacred texts. He told me how much he enjoyed guiding Western followers of the Chaitanya tradition around the sacred sites of Radhakund when they came for a visit. His English was excellent and thus he was able to communicate well with any English-knowing visitor who happened, by intent or accident, to wander into Radhakund.

On one of his visits Baba told me about a time when he suffered a terrible fever caused by malaria and how he came very near to death. Only the kind nursing of one of his companions at Radhakund helped him survive. As a result, Krishna Das Baba was never quite able to pronounce certain sounds again. The malaria had permanently damaged some parts of his nervous system. To demonstrate, he recited some Sanskrit verses from the *Bhagavata*, the *Chaitanya-charitamrita* and the *Radha-rasa-sudha-nidhi*, verses that he had memorized and had been able, prior to his illness, to recite flawlessly. Sure enough, at some point in each verse the otherwise nicely pronounced and melodic recitation broke down into a stammer or a stutter as Baba struggled to pronounce a particular word or syllable. I realized then how hard a life he and others like him, who had given up everything to worship Radha and Krishna full time, lived. It humbled me and increased my admiration for him and the other *babajis*.

If Krishna Das Baba suffered much for his faith, he seems to have gained much from it as well. I remember another occasion when he visited me. He began to read from a section of the *Chaitanya-charitamrita*. After so many years I no longer recall what passage he read. Whatever it was, he had read for only a few minutes, reading out loud the Bengali and Sanskrit and then translating for me, when he was suddenly swept away by a deep emotional reaction to the text. Tears poured out of his eyes, his body shivered, the hairs on his arms stood erect, his throat choked up, and he was no longer able to proceed. We sat there silently for a few minutes and I wondered, somewhat alarmed, what, if anything, I should do or say. After a while he recovered himself, obviously embarrassed. He apologized to me and said that he was very sorry, but he could not continue the reading at that time.

What Baba seems to have experienced on that occasion are some of a group of autonomous, physical reactions referred to by members of the Chaitanya tradition as the eight *sattvika* conditions. They are becoming stunned [immobilized], profuse sweating, the standing of one's hair on end, the cracking of the voice, violent trembling, losing or changing one's physical color, tears, and fainting. They are regarded as outward physical manifestations of powerful, inner religious emotions. Those emotions when heightened, enhanced, and relished, become known as *bhakti-rasa*, or sacred rapture.[2]

Many religious traditions around the world recognize physical conditions like the *sattvikas* as signs of divine grace or presence. A prime example, of course, is the "gifts of the spirit" recognized in Christianity (following Mark, Chapter 16, verses 17-18: "And these signs will follow those who believe: ..." and Acts, Chapter 2: "There appeared to them tongues like flames ..."), which are important to many of the charismatic forms of modern Christianity. Gifts of the spirit are things like expelling demons, speaking in tongues, prophesy, being immune to snake bites and poisons, and curing the sick by touching them. In medieval times and even today signs like uncontrollable trembling and crying, being struck dumb, fainting, the appearance of stigmata on the body, and so forth are often seen as signs of grace. In many religious traditions that involve possession, similar signs indicate the "living" presence of a god or goddess who "possesses," that is, abides within and controls the body of the votary.

Stevan Davies in his *Jesus the Healer* has suggested that possession experiences were important in the life of Jesus and in early Christianity. I think a similar argument can be made in the case of Chaitanya and in Chaitanya Vaishnavism. The experience of the *sattvikas* may be regarded as a kind of routinization or institutionalization of Chaitanya's own possession experiences. The Chaitanya tradition already recognizes the validity of being possessed by divine power. This is referred to as a type of descent (*avatar*) called the *shaktyavesh avatar*, the descent of the power of deity into a person. That kind of descent is generally regarded as occurring to accomplish some great or extraordinarily difficult task. The Chaitanya tradition, for instance, regards Vyasa as an example of a *shaktyavesh avatar*, and this allowed him to write so many of the sacred texts of the Hindu tradition (the *Mahabharata*, the *Puranas*, and the *Brahma-sutras*). Theologically, of course, the infusion of such power only applies to ordinary living beings, and Chaitanya is not regarded as an ordinary human being. He is considered by the tradition to be the Supreme Person himself and thus the source of that power. Nevertheless, all agree that he was playing the role of the model *bhakta*.

---

[2]See the discussion of the *sattvika-bhavas* in the glossary.

The *sattvikas* may, thus, also be regarded as signs of the infusion of a divine power, the pleasure-giving power (*hladini-shakti*) of Krishna, into a person such that that person is transformed into a lover of Krishna.

Possessed states also involve peculiar physiological phenomena. As Davies writes, summarizing various studies of possession in different traditions:

> Physiological aspects of the possession experience tend to be similar wherever the experience occurs. Those possessed usually have considerable muscle rigidity and loss of control of gross motor movements. In the initial phases of the possession experience, people often move jerkily, shake uncontrollably, fall and have difficulty rising. The labels "shakers," "quakers," and "holy rollers' for Christian charismatic groups arose from observation of those behaviors by outsiders. They will often speak in a babbling "abbababab" fashion (Gal 4:16), or, with practice, in more rhythmic cadences of glossolalia (1 Cor 14:18), or they might utter powerful groans, shouts, barks and other inarticulate sounds.[3]

At least three of the *sattvikas* seem to be represented here as the results of possession.

While in the case of Chaitanya Vaishnavism, the physical reactions have been "civilized" (i.e., named, counted, organized, categorized, and so forth) there is still something of their original, numinous wildness about them. The divine love that Rupa says overruns the mind and causes the *sattvikas* to appear in the body is not thought of as a product of nature. It is believed to be a supernatural or other-worldly entity, power, or presence that comes into the mind of the practitioner from outside of the material world. Thus, the development of love for Krishna can be understood legitimately as a case of possession. That love is understood by Chaitanyites to be a special kind of pure goodness or pure being (*shuddha-sattva-visheshatman*), and thus it is different from all worldly or material forms of goodness or being which are always regarded as mixed or composite. It enters the mind of advanced practitioners from the transcendent realm of Krishna, becomes united with it, and remains there, transforming profoundly the practitioners' perception of the world and their relationship to it.

---

[3]Davies, *Jesus the Healer*, pp 33-34. (New York: Continuum, 1995)

Krishna Das Baba seemed to have experienced at least six of the *sattvikas* when he recited those passages from the *Chaitanya-charitamrita* in my presence long ago. Though such signs are not necessarily indicators of someone who has developed love for Krishna, they can be taken as lending support to Karunamayi Das's major thesis in this work, which he describes as a "hagiography." He seeks to show that Krishna Das Baba of Radhakund had reached the level of having genuine love for Radha and Krishna and thus that he deserves to be recognized as a "saint" by the members of the tradition. But what exactly is a saint in the Chaitanya tradition and how does one recognize one? Once we have a better understanding of these phenomena we will be better able to understand what Karunamayi Das has tried to do in this book.

In the Indic religions there is no word comparable to the English word "saint." The word saint is from the Latin word *sanctus*, which means "sacred." *Sanctus* is the past participle of the Latin verb *sancīre*, "to make sacred," and thus it means one who is "sanctified or made sacred." In the Western religious traditions, especially in Catholicism, which seems to have developed the idea of the saint the most fully, a saint is one who is believed to have entered heaven after death. Thus, sanctified in this case means ascended or one who has ascended into heaven according to Catholic beliefs. The Catholic church has also developed an elaborate and seemingly rigorous system of requirements and trials, called beatification and canonization, to try to determine who is blessed and who has ascended to heaven and is therefore recognized as a saint. This corresponds to nothing extant in any of the Indic traditions. In the first place there is no central authority to undertake such a process in Hinduism, Buddhism, or Jainism. Secondly, there is a wide array of final goals in the Indic traditions and very few of them resemble the Christian notion of "going to heaven." Many of the final goals of various Hindu sub-traditions fall under the rubric of *mukti*, emancipation or liberation. But *mukti* is a mysterious, elusive concept that no one is able to explain satisfactorily. It is mostly defined in terms of what it is not. The most fundamental and concise characterization of *mukti* is that it is the permanent cessation of misery.[4] But what it is in positive terms is never clearly said.

If one takes the idea of the saint in its most generic form, as one who is sanctified or made sacred, then perhaps the most comparable idea in

[4]Actually, it is "the cessation of misery that is not simultaneous with a prior absence of more misery (*duhkha-prag-abhava*)," but who needs such detail?

Indic religion in general, and in Chaitanya Vaishnavism in particular, is that of the *siddha*, the accomplished or perfected being. The word *siddha* comes as one of a group of related terms that fit together into a system that characterizes the whole of religious cultivation in India. The *siddha* is the one who has reached the goal (*sadhya*) of religious practice or cultivation (*sadhana*). Before reaching success (*siddhi*), the successful one (*siddha*) is called a practitioner (*sadhaka*). Thus we have the triad: the goal (*sadhya*), the striver after that goal (*sadhaka*), and the means to achieve the goal (*sadhana*). Once the goal is achieved, the striver becomes recognized as a *siddha* who has gained success (*siddhi*). What constitutes success varies in the different Indic traditions, but in Chaitanya Vaishnavism one is considered successful if one has developed attraction or love for Krishna (*jata-krishna-rati*). The appearance of love for Krishna is something that need not wait until after death. It can appear while a practitioner is alive and thus the word *siddha* may be applied to someone while still living.

How does one recognize a *siddha*, then? And along with this who is it that recognizes someone to be a *siddha*? In the Chaitanya tradition there is no central authority like the Pope in Roman Catholicism who can initiate and oversee the process of canonization. Yet, there are a number of Chaitanya Vaishnavas who have somehow been recognized as *siddhas*. Most of those who have been so recognized are no longer alive, but sometimes living *siddhas* are heard of. There are, indeed, some alive today who have reputations of being *siddha*. Though there is no Pope in the Chaitanya community, there are prominent members of the community, the *mahanta* (abbot) of the renunciant community at Radhakund, elder members of respected families of Goswamis in Vraja and Bengal, other respected leaders of sects or branches and gurus who are considered authorities on the tradition, whose pronouncements on such matters are taken seriously. Thus, though there is no central authority in the tradition, there is something like a distributed authority that is shared at any given time by various respected members of the Chaitanya community at large.[5] Stories about particular practitioners

[5]This distributive structure parallels in many ways the structure of the institution of the guru, or the initiating teacher, in Chaitanya Vaishnavism. The guru has both a distributed (*vyasti*) aspect in form of various individual *bhaktas* who act as or incarnate the guru and a collective (*samashti*) aspect regarded as a direct expansion or form of Krishna who exists, according to Shri Jiva Goswami (*Bhakti-sandarbha*, para 286), on one's left side at Krishna's throne in the supernal abode.

circulate among some of the distributed authorities who might come to recognize in them the qualities of a *siddha* and if enough of them recognize a particular person as a *siddha* then the rest of the community will follow. Karunamayi Das's efforts in producing this account of the life of his guru-deva,[6] Shri Krishna Das Baba, would seem, therefore, to be not only an effort to introduce his guru to those who have never before heard of him but also an effort to collect together and regularize the various stories about his teacher and to provide them with a vehicle for circulation among the distributed authorities so that they might come to regard Krishna Das Baba as a *siddha* (if they do not already). *Siddhas* are generally known by their stories and through their stories they provide models of behavior, practice, and teaching for aspiring but less developed members of the community. In addition, they inspire the hope in those aspirants that one day they too will meet with success (*siddhi*).

What traits are used to recognize a *siddha* in the Chaitanya tradition, then? One often hears the presence of the eight *sattvika* conditions mentioned above offered as one of those traits. The *sattvika* are external signs of the inner experience of sacred rapture (*bhakti-rasa*). Those signs, as important as they are, however, can be faked and as Shri Rupa points out occasionally appear in people who have not developed the attraction for Krishna upon which they depend. Moreover, the *sattvika* were originally understood in Sanskrit dramaturgy as some of the tools of actors meant to impart realism to the actor's portrayal of various roles. Good actors are able to turn them on and off at will. Thus, as important as the *sattvika* may be in the popular imagination, they need to be joined with and supported by other traits.

Rupa Goswami discusses the *siddha* when he talks about the *bhaktas* or devotees of Krishna in the context of his discussion of *vibhavas*), or the excitants, one of the conditions for the arousal of sacred rapture (*bhakti-rasa*). Since the *siddha* is a type of devotee, they share the qualities of the devotee with all the other types. Here is what Rupa says about Krishna's *bhakta*:

tadbhava-bhavitasvaantah krishnabhakta itiritah
ye satya-vakya ity adya hriman ity antima gunah

[6]Guru-deva is a compound word combining guru, the teacher or master, and *deva*, god. It might be translated, therefore, as "teacher-god." In Chaitanya Vaishnavism, the teacher, especially the initiating teacher (*diksha-guru*) is regarded as a descent (*avatar*) or form of Krishna. We shall see this in more detail later.

proktah krishne 'sya bhakteshu te vijneya manishibhih
te sadhakash cha siddhash cha dvividhah parikirtitah[7]

Those whose hearts are infused with fondness [*bhava* or *rati*] for him [Krishna] are called Krishna's *bhaktas*. The qualities beginning with truthfulness and ending with modesty that are said to exist in Krishna are understood by the thoughtful to also be found in his *bhaktas*. They are of two kinds: the practitioners and the accomplished.

A *bhakta* of Krishna is one whose heart is infused with or perfumed by fondness for or delight in Krishna. Earlier Rupa has given a list of sixty-four qualities that are found in Krishna.[8] Here he says that a subset of those, beginning with speaking the truth (number 8) and ending with modesty (number 36), are also found in his *bhaktas*. The *bhaktas* are then divided into two groups: the practitioners, who are still in the process of cultivating their fondness for Krishna, and the accomplished ones, who have already have it fully developed.

For reference, here is what Rupa says about the practitioner:

utpannaratayah samyan-nairvighnyam anupagatah
krishna-sakshatkritau yogyah sadhakah parikirtitah[9]

Those whose delight [in Krishna] has arisen, who have not yet overcome all obstacles, who are worthy of seeing Krishna are widely known as practitioners.

A *sadhaka* or practitioner, then, is a *bhakta* who already has love for Krishna but who has not yet overcome all of the obstacles on the path. His *sadhana* or practice is aimed at trying to overcome those obstacles. Already, though, Rupa deems such a practitioner worthy of meeting Krishna. The implication, of course, is that the practitioner has not yet had the fortune of meeting Krishna directly. Rupa cites a verse from the Bhagavata that characterizes in his opinion the situation of such a practitioner:

ishvare tad-adhineshu balisheshu dvishatsu cha
prema-maitri-kripopekshaa yah karoti sa madhyamah[10]

[7] Rupa Goswami, *Bhakti-rasamrita-sindhu*, 2.1.273-5.
[8] ibid., 2.1.23-217.
[9] ibid., 2.1.276.
[10] ibid., 2.1.277 and *Bhagavata*, 11.2.46.

> One who extends to the Lord love, to the those depending on the Lord friendship, to the ignorant compassion, to enemies patience is the middlemost.

Finally, Rupa takes up the *siddha bhakta*:

> *avijnatakhila-kleshah sada krishnashrita-kriyah*
> *siddhah syuh santata-prema-saukhyasvada-parayanah*
> *sampraapta-siddhayah siddha nitya-siddhash cha te dvidhaa*[11]
>
> They are *siddhas* who know nothing of affliction, whose acts are always dependent on Krishna, and who are always intent on relishing the joys of their love [for Krishna]. There are two kinds of *siddhas*: those who have attained their accomplishment and those who are eternally accomplished.

The *siddha* is one who has overcome all kinds of *klesha* or affliction. While *klesha* can mean afflictions or pains in general, it may also refer to the five specific *kleshas* of the Yoga system. Since there seems to be an intended parallelism between the path of *bhakti* and the path of yoga in Rupa's characterization, the *kleshas* of yoga were probably intended here. They are: ignorance, egotism, desire, aversion, and tenacity, the persistence of material existence. These may be the obstacles referred to in the case of the practitioner. Aside from overcoming the afflictions, all of a *siddha's* actions rest on or are dependent on or are done for the pleasure of Krishna. Finally, the *siddha* is constantly engaged in tasting the happiness of loving Krishna.

There are two types of *siddha*: those who have gained their success and those who eternally have it. Those who have gained their success have done so in two ways, says Rupa. They have gained it by practice or by the grace of either Krishna or his *bhakta*. Rupa's few examples come from the rarefied air of various scriptural texts and thus seem more literary or even mythic than filled with the warmth and blush of life. Nevertheless, he creates the scriptural model that will be internalized and brought to life by many members of the later tradition. More will be said later about the specially nuanced relationship between sacred text and religious life. Suffice it to say here that Rupa's characterizations are vague and open-ended enough to leave room for the inclusion in them of

[11]ibid., 2.1.280-1.

a wide variety of lived experiences. Since Rupa's time many stories have been collected about those who are believed to have reached success, and those stories give particular and recognizable faces and contexts to the idea of the *siddha*. Thus, in addition to Rupa's more theoretical and literary characterizations, important as they are for providing the underlying structure of the *siddha*, it seems both necessary and useful to look at some of the specific stories told about those the tradition has recognized as accomplished. From such a sampling of stories we will be able, perhaps, to isolate some of their common traits and thus arrive at a set of criteria for determining whom the tradition is likely to recognize as "perfected."

One of the best sources for stories about the lives and experiences of Chaitanyite *siddhas* is Haridas Das's collection of biographies published in his Bengali work called *Shri Shri Gaudiya Vaishnav Jivan* (Biographies of Gaudiya Vaishnavas).[12] The first section of the second volume of Haridas Das's book bears the identification in brackets *Siddha-gana* (The Siddhas), and so it seems that he understood those placed in that section to be *siddhas*. Those in the second section, which he does not identify in any way, though regarded as exemplary or famous Vaishnavas, were not necessarily thought of as *siddha*.

Glancing quickly through the collection, several brief but interesting and rather surprising examples present themselves. There is the life of Krishna Das Baba of Ranabari (in Vraja), for instance.[13] He was born as Krishna Prasad Chattopadhyay in Mahammadpur in the district of Jashohar (now in Bangla Desh).[14] Haridas Das does not give his birth

---

[12]Haridas Das, *Shri Shri Gaudiya Vaishnav Jivan, Dvitiya Khanda, Pratham o Dvitiya Paryay*. (Navadvip: Haribol Kutir, 3rd ed., Gaurabda 489 [1975 C.E.]) Other good sources are the books of Dr. O.B.L. Kapoor such as *The Saints of Bengal*, *The Saints of Vraja*, and *Experiences in Bhakti*. Dr. Kapoor does not discuss in any of those books, however, the meaning and application of the word "saint" in the Chaitanya tradition. He appears to use it loosely for any respected or prominent Chaitanya Vaishnava, not in the more technical sense of *siddha* to which I wish to narrow it here.

[13]This is not, of course, the same Krishna Das whose life and teachings are presented here. Krishna Das, "servant of Krishna," is a very common name in the Chaitanya Vaishnava tradition. To distinguish Krishna Das Baba, the guru of Karunamayi Das and the subject of this book, from other Krishna Dases, he is referred to here as Madrasi Krishna Das Baba. As mentioned before, this means the Krishna Das Baba who was originally from South India.

[14]Though this is an example of a *siddha* who was also a *brahmin*, it is not the case that most *siddhas* are *brahmin*. In fact, it is probably true that there are more non-*brahmin* *siddhas* than there are *brahman siddhas*. A number of *siddhas* were women, though there

date, but he was probably born in the last decade of the 18th century. His father, Gokulachandra Chattopadhyay, was a priest of the sacred image, Shri Harekrishna Ray. It is said that Krishna Prasad was even as a child was absorbed in the service of the image. When arrangements were being made for his marriage, he stole away in the night and ran off to Vrindavan.[15] For a while he served the image Shri Madanmohan and then moved to Ranabari. Ranabari was in the midst of a dense jungle. Baba built himself a cottage and engaged in private worship (*bhajan*). He practiced *madhukari* (begging for alms food) at a nearby village and ate what he needed, giving the rest to the cows. He always had extra food because the residents of the village were very insistent that he had to visit everyone's house. If he didn't appear they would have been upset.

Since Krishna Das Baba left home at an early age and went directly to Vrindavan, he did not have a chance to see any of the other holy places of India. After nearly fifty years in Vrindavan the desire to visit the four abodes (on the four sides of India) arose in his heart. In a dream Shri Radha appeared to him and said: "You have come to me here in Vrindavan. Do not leave this holy place and go anywhere else. Stay here and do your private worship; by that you will achieve every success. There is no need for you to visit other places of pilgrimage." But Krishna Das Baba thought that Radha's dream instructions were produced by his own imagination. Therefore he took off on his journey to the other holy places.

When Krishna Das Baba arrived in Dvaraka, Krishna's capitol city on the west coast of India, he had himself branded (as was the practice in that holy place). When the Vaishnavas of the four communities go to Dvaraka they have themselves branded. This is not, however, in agreement with what is considered proper behavior by the *raganuga* (passion-pursuing) Vaishnavas of Vrindavan, even though it is a recognized practice in the *Hari-bhakti-vilasa* (The Delight of Bhakti to Hari), the authoritative ritual text of the Chaitanya tradition. Babaji disregarded the unwritten, accepted behavior of Vraja and accepted the view of the *Hari-bhakti-vilasa*. From that moment on he became distracted and lost his desire to visit the holy places. The night of the day that he returned to Vraja Shri Radha appeared again to Babaji in a dream

---

are many more stories about men than there are about women.

[15]Haridas Das (p. 19) attributes this account of the life of Krishna Das Baba of Ranabari to the journal *Shri Shri Vishnupriya-gauranga* (vol. 7, no. 8, p. 321).

and said: "You were branded in Dvaraka and have become thereby a follower of Satyabhama [one of Krishna's chief queens in Dvaraka]. Therefore, you are not fit to live in Vraja any more. Go to Dvaraka." This time though he did not think his dream was the product of his imagination. Becoming confused he went to other *siddha babas* of Vraja and asked them. They, too, agreed with the order of Shri Radha. In answer to his question of whether there was any remedy for the situation he was told: "Any other instruction beyond the direct order of Priyaji [Radha] is beyond the mind and intellect."

Losing all hope, Babaji returned to Ranabari and gave up eating and drinking altogether. His heart began to burn from the pain of the result of what he had done and from intense feelings of separation from Radha. The story is that Baba spent three months in this way and after that the inner fire [of separation] became an external one. In three days his body burned gradually from his feet to his head and became ashes. It is said that on that third day the *siddha baba* Jagannath Das Babaji was in Ranabari in a little cottage not far from where Krishna Das Baba was. Towards the end of the night he called his helper Bihari Das and asked him to look in at the hut of Krishna Das Baba and see what was happening there. Bihari Das checked into it and discovered that the Baba (Krishna Das Baba) of Ranabari's body was burning. Since the hut was locked from within he was not able to discover any more of the details of what was happening. He went back to Jagannath Das Baba and told him what he knew. Jagannath Das Baba shouted: "Alas! The fire of separation! The fire of separation!" Jagannath Das Baba asked Bihari Das to carry him to Krishna Das's hut.[16] When they got there he had Bihari break down the door and they entered the hut. They saw that the fire had advanced almost up to his throat and that it did not appear to be moving any higher. Jagannath Das Baba asked Bihari to go find some cotton. Bihari went out into a nearby field in the darkness and by merely feeling around found some cotton there and brought it back to Jagannath Das Baba. Baba twisted the cotton and made three wicks which he draped over the head of Krishna Das Baba. They immediately burst into flame and thus the rest of his body was burned to ashes. Haridas Das remarks that Krishna Das Baba's tomb is still present there and that it is shaped in the same way he was sitting when his body was burned to ashes. The local people believe that whatever one prays for

[16]Jagannath Das Baba was crippled and unable therefore to walk on his own. Bihari Das carried him wherever he went.

at the tomb of Krishna Das Baba one will receive. Moreover, the local residents observe a yearly day of fasting and then a feast in honor of the Baba.[17]

The account of the life of Siddha Krishna Das Baba of Ranabari contains most of the elements that make up the Chaitanya community's expectations for a *siddha*. He was precocious in his youth; that is, he showed early signs of being deeply devoted to Krishna. Sometimes this is indicated by unusual happenings occurring at the time of the future *siddha*'s birth or early childhood. He demonstrated detachment from the world by running off before his marriage could be arranged. In this account there is no mention of who his guru was, but often a future *siddha* receives initiation and/or instruction from another *siddha*. Perhaps the role that *siddha* Jagannath Das Baba played in the final act of Krishna Das Baba's life can be regarded as fulfilling that function. The *siddha* has dreams or visions of Radha and Krishna in which he or she is instructed or advised. There are miracles associated with the life of a *siddha*. In this case, the miraculous burning of the body of Krishna Das Baba provides that element. Finally, the tomb or *samadhi*, as it is called, of a *siddha* is regarded as having special sacredness or power. Though the *sattvikas* are not mentioned, it is likely that they were involved in the Baba's life especially in his feelings of separation from Radha and Krishna at the end. It would seem that Krishna Das Baba of Ranabari made a mistake by having himself branded when he visited Dvaraka. He definitely did not act in a way approved by the Chaitanya community of his time. Still, one might say that his response to his mistake, being overcome and eventually undone by intense his feelings of loss and separation from Radha, was highly approved by the community. In that sense, the community would regard Krishna Das Baba's life as bearing an important lesson for neophyte and less developed members of the community. Thus, the *siddha*'s life is celebrated as an example of someone who has reached success and as a source of instruction for others on how they might also become successful.

Not all of the accounts of *siddhas* contain all of these elements. Haridas's account of yet another Krishna Das Baba, for instance, this one of Navadvip, mentions neither miracles nor *sattvikas*. He was born in 1225 *Bangabda* (1819 C.E.) near Phultala Bazar into the Barui family

[17]Haridas Das, *Shri Shri Gaudiya Vaishnava Jivana, Dvitiya Khanda*, pp. 19-22, summarized.

of the Navashakha community.[18] His given name was Keshava. From his childhood he had a natural fondness for the Vaishnava faith. When he was thirty years old he went to Navadvip and was initiated by Siddha Chaitanya Das Baba. Though he made it known to his guru that he wanted to take the vows of renunciation, when his guru heard that Keshava had a wife at home he ordered him to return to his home. Following his guru's order he returned home and remained there for ten years until his wife passed away. Then in 1265 (1859 C.E.) after wandering on foot to many holy places he arrived at Shrikshetra (Jagannath Puri) where he took renunciation from Shri Dinahina Das Baba and was given the name Krishna Das Baba. After engaging in religious practices for fourteen years in Shrikshetra, he went to Vrindavan where he lived for twenty-four years doing private worship (*bhajan*) and staying at Bhramara Ghat, Lotanakunja, and finally at Totaram Das Babaji's *ashram*. Then he returned to Bengal. There he was sent by the order of his guru to live and practice at Shrikhandha where he stayed for seven years and then returned to Navadvip. He passed away in 1326 (1920 C.E.) while repeating the names of Gaura (Chaitanya). People particularly admired him for his intense detachment, magnanimity, fearlessness, straightforward speech, and so forth.[19]

Although the narrative makes no reference to miracles, visions, *sattvikas* and so forth, this does not mean that those were not part of the narratives told about him, only that the sources used by Haridas Das did not mention them. There is, however, the hint of his early inclination towards Vaishnavism, his detachment from worldly life, and his connection with a guru who was recognized as a *siddha*. His main qualities seem to have been his obedience to the orders of his guru and the respect with which others viewed him. Nevertheless, Krishna Das Baba of Navadvip has been widely accepted as a *siddha*. Thus, there appears to be no rigidly set group of parameters required in the stories about the *siddhas*.

How then does Karunamayi Das go about his presentation of the life and teachings of Krishna Das Baba of Radhakund in his hagiography? Karunamayi Das appeals to many of the features of the life of a *siddha* noted in the biography of Krishna Das of Ranabari. There is the auspicious sign at the time of Krishna Das Baba's birth (a trum-

[18]This is a community made up of an alliance of nine Hindu sub-groups: spice dealers, garland-makers, weavers, etc.

[19]Haridas Das, pp. 23-24.

peting elephant). There is the connection with another accepted *siddha* (Sakhicharan Das Baba, Krishna Das's guru) whom Krishna Das followed obediently. There are miraculous occurrences like the sudden return to health of Karunamayi's father-in-law and so forth. But mostly Karunamayi chose another tact that is very interesting from the point of view of the history of religions. He presents his guru as a veritable walking, talking embodiment of the sacred texts of the Chaitanya tradition. Krishna Das Baba becomes in Karunamayi's account a sacred text incarnate, someone who has imbibed and memorized the fundamental and essential texts of the tradition to such a degree that he has become in some sense a walking text himself. Everything he said is supported by the tradition's texts, everything he thought is supported by those texts, and everything he did is supported by those texts.

The tendency to try to "live the texts" is something that Chaitanya Vaishnavism shares with many other highly literate religious traditions of the world. The well-known scholar of religion, Gavin Flood, wrote recently in an issue of the *Journal of the American Academy of Religion*:

> The text pervades religious practices, and the appropriation and internalization of the text is fundamental to religions. Indeed, we might say that within scriptural traditions, religion can be understood as a form of reading or mode of textual reception (Davies and Flood forthcoming). This mode of reception is distinctive of a genre of textual material, and we might claim that religions are forms of human belief and practice that occur when people in communities inhabit their texts in a particular way. Fundamental to the forms of life we call religions is a text that is set aside by a community as having special status in coming from a transcendent source and in providing a blueprint for how people should live their lives (it provides prohibitions, injunctions, and stories to live by). The sacred text has a "voice" from the past that is complex in its formation — perhaps being the totality of authorial voices that have composed it — and enlivened by the present communities who set the text aside, breathe life into it through their reading or reception, and enact it.[20]

[20]Flood, "Reflections on Tradition and Inquiry in the Study of Religions," *Journal of the American Academy of Religion*, vol. 74, no. 1 (March 2006), p. 53.

Karunamayi Das represents Krishna Das Baba as breathing life into and enacting the sacred texts of the tradition. In so doing, he suggests that Krishna Das Baba, as an embodiment of those sacred texts, deserves recognition among the *siddhas* of the Chaitanya tradition. Perhaps this is the most important way of understanding who in a tradition is a *siddha* or a saint. Those other elements: auspicious signs at birth, connections with other *siddhas*, miracles, dreams, and so forth are just signposts pointing us in the direction of this central achievement in the lives of those who follow a religious tradition, their success in breathing life into and becoming walking embodiments of the most trusted and valued texts of their traditions.

The last points raises the question: "what are the most trusted texts of the Chaitanya tradition?" Karunamayi Das gives us a sense of his and his guru's answer. The texts of the Chaitanya tradition are numerous and diverse. Not all of them point to the core beliefs and practices of the community as it exists today. Remember Krishna Das Baba of Ranabari. His branding in Dvaraka is mentioned and approved in the community's authoritative work on ritual practice, the *Hari-bhakti-vilasa*. Yet, that practice, though textually supported, is no longer an accepted part of the practices of the living community. Karunamayi Das has done a superb job of collecting together the major texts "providing a blueprint for how people should live their lives" in modern Chaitanya Vaishnavism, at least as it is being practiced among the renunciants at places like Radhakund. In this way, Karunamayi Das has not only introduced us to his beloved guru, Shri Krishna Das Baba of Radhakund, he has also given us, through his meditation on and recollection of of the teachings of his guru, an excellent, textual introduction to Chaitanya Vaishnavism.

Others might disagree with Karunamayi Das on what the most important sacred texts of the Chaitanya tradition are. Karunamayi's position is that the core beliefs and practices of the Chaitanya tradition center around private worship or *bhajan*. That for him and many others is the beating heart or the life force of Chaitanya Vaishnavism. Others might claim that the core is preaching (*prachar*) or worship of the sacred images in temples (*puja*). But Karunamayi Das is only following the directives of his guru. Whatever one's guru instructs, that is the disciple's *dharma*, duty, law, foundation, road to success. This is the what the Chaitanya tradition and many other Indic religious traditions believe. There is no reason to fault Karanamayi Das because someone else's guru has instructed his disciples differently. Preaching is the *dharma* for the followers of other gurus; Karanumayi's *dharma* is private worship. Both are justified.

There is an interesting example of following the guru exemplified in the story of yet another *siddha* named Krishnaprasad Das Baba. Again I am following the account given in Haridas Das's book. Krishnaprasad Das Baba received renunciation initiation from *siddha* Nityananda Das Baba of Madanmohan Thor in Vrindavan. After that he asked his guru with folded hands: "What shall I do? Please instruct me." Nityananda Das Baba replied: "Well, you are a fool. Therefore, studying scripture, analyzing books, the conclusions of the study of *rasa* are beyond your abilities. Therefore, you should serve some great *bhakta*." Hearing the words of his guru he asked with deep humility: "Master, order me. Where and in whose service will I become fulfilled?" The *siddha* baba replied: "Go! Go serve Gulluji Maharaj. If you serve him your every purpose will be achieved." Gulluji Maharaj was the father of Shri Radhacharan Goswami. Among the priests of Shri Radharaman at that time he was known to be deeply engaged in the cultivation of *bhakti*, free of fault-finding, and large-hearted. Krishnaprasad went and fell at his feet and from that day on he was not only Gulluji Maharaj's servant, he served all in his household from the Maharaj's children to his servants, even his animals and birds. He was then not even able to touch his chanting beads. While waiting he used to be able to remember the holy names only about ten times. At every moment some one of the children would be on his lap. Cleaning up their stool and urine, and so forth, all sorts of such chores were his regular practice and the highest reaches of *bhakti* began to appear in him. One after another, twenty years passed and he served the great *bhakta* in that way. When Gulluji entered eternal sport [passed away], Krishnaprasad Das Baba also departed from that house like a freed bird, and at the request of many people he stayed for two or three years at the Gopal Temple near the Rasghera in front of the Radharaman Temple, supporting himself by begging for alms (*madhukari*). Everyone used to call him Gudhri Baba [Quilt Father] because he used to put the corner of a torn, worn-out quilt under his left arm and drag the rest along behind him. The purpose was to erase his footprints from the dust of the road behind him so that someone could not take that dust and put it on their heads. Later he stayed near Govindakund in Govardhan and after that he lived at Kamya-van. His rule was that when he saw a Vaishnava he would lay himself down in full prostration on the ground and remain that way until after the other Vaishnava had raised himself up from his prostration.[21]

Not only does this story nicely illustrate the importance of following the instructions of one's guru, it also broadens the point made earlier about how the followers of a tradition become embodiments of the texts of that tradition. Krishnaprasad Das Baba become a *siddha* by serving a great Vaishnava. He never cracked a book nor did he apparently have much time even to repeat the holy names, so busy was he serving that Vaishnava. Therefore, one must not think that one needs to be "literate" in order to breathe life into or embody the texts of a tradition. Krishnaprasad Das Baba became in his own way a living embodiment of sacred text by merely following the instructions of his guru. Moreover, he in his turn became a sacred text. How do we know he became a living text? Haven't I just repeated a version of the living text that was made out of his life. His life became a new text for later Chaitanya Vaishnavas, teaching them that success is possible even if one is unable to read or study the texts, or understand or teach the philosophy and theology of the tradition, or even chant the holy names or do any other form of practice except serve a great Vaishnava and the members and animals of his family. So, too, has Karunamayi not only portrayed his guru Krishna Das Baba as a walking embodiment of the accepted sacred texts of the tradition, he has transformed the life of his guru into a new, living, sacred text of Chaitanya Vaishnavism. This is after all the primary meaning of hagiography ("sacred text").

It is impossible to tell if Karunamayi Das will succeed in convincing the distributive authorities of the living Chaitanya community of the *siddha*-hood of his guru. In a way, though, this hardly matters. Krishna Das Baba was what he was and whether he is recognized by the "keepers" of the tradition or not hardly matters to him or to anyone who knew him. Instead, we should recognize that Karunamayi Das has already succeeded in several of the more weighty ways suggested above. He has collected together a fine group of texts presenting an important understanding of the essential beliefs and practices of Chaitanya Vaishnavism. He has presented those texts in the course of his recollection of or meditation on the life of his guru, often placing them in the context of some recalled incident or moment of instruction. Finally, he has turned the life of his guru into a new text that portrays another way, Shri Krishna Das Baba's way, in which the sacred has entered the world

[21] Haridas Das, ibid., 24-26.

and transformed it, adding more richness to the already rich, literary world of Chaitanya Vaishnavism.

Editorial Approach

Karunamayi Das wrote this work in English. He has had it posted on his web-site (www.madrasibaba.org) for years now. What then did I do as the editor of the work except dot some "i"-s and cross some "t"-s? When Karunamayi Das asked me to edit the book a little over two years ago, that is probably what he had in mind. I have, however, become more deeply involved in the text and taken a more active approach than perhaps he wanted me to. It has certainly taken me a great deal longer to do my work than he wanted. I must thank him for his incredible patience with me and beg his pardon for taking so long. The work I did on the book can be roughly placed into two categories: 1) making the work more accessible to a wider audience, and 2) insuring the accuracy of the texts cited in the work and of their translations.

In order to make the book more accessible to English readers in the West, I have taken a number of liberties with Karunamayi's original version. The first set of liberties was with his use of language. Karunamayi is not a native speaker of English. Although his spoken English is good, his first language was French and he now lives part of the year in Italy (Turino) and part of the year in northern India (Radhakund, District of Mathura, U.P.). Over his many years of visiting and living in India, he has picked up a number of Indian-Englishisms and words borrowed from Indian languages, mostly from Bengali, which though quaint and charming in themselves are not immediately meaningful to ordinary western speakers of English. Thus, I have tried in the first place not only to fix the grammar of Karunamayi's language but also to find alternate expressions for some of the more peculiar forms of Indian English.

Most of what I have done can be described as attempting to broaden the target audience of the book. I am not sure who Karunamayi Das originally envisioned as the book's target audience, but based on the work itself it seemed to have been a rather small, circumscribed audience, one that was already very familiar with Chaitanya Vaishnava beliefs. practices, and terminology and one that was either very familiar with or in the habit of using many of the Indian-Englishisms he employed. I have replaced his assumption of a pre-existing knowledge about Chaitanya Vaishnavism in the target audience with an assumption of an absence or near absence of such knowledge. I have therefore in addition to fixing the grammar replaced all non-English words in the text with suitable English expressions and either removed them altogether or placed them in parentheses. There are a few Indic words that have become part of the English language, like yoga, pandit, karma or guru, that I have left. In addition, some words really have no good English equivalents and I been forced to leave them in the text. For those words, which are relatively few in number, I have added entries to the glossary at the end of the book. An example of such a word is *bhakti*, which some translate as devotion but which means on the one hand more and on the other less than devotion. Rather than mistranslate it, I have decided to leave it and treat it like the technical term it is in Chaitanya Vaishnavism.

There is another quality in Karunamayi's language that I felt needed alteration. His long immersion in Indic culture has affected the way he speaks and writes. A well-known Indian writer-poet, Ramchandra Sharma, once pointed out, during an interview with my wife, a fundamental difference between western literature and the literatures of India. He called his idea Sharma's Stabilization Theory. The literatures of India, he said, like its foods, are highly rich and spiced with ornamentation and exaggerated sentiments and actions. On the other hand, western literature is far less ornate, a plainer fare that aims more at filling the belly than at making the mouth water and bringing about an explosion of the taste-buds. Both types of literature are satisfying and highly appreciated by their respective audiences, but sometimes it is harder for one audience to appreciate the literature of the other audience. Ramchandra suggested that when the literature of India is translated into a western language, it has to be toned down and some of the spicing needs to be removed, much the way Indian cooks put in fewer chilis when they know their eaters are westerners. Karunamayi's original text was indeed highly spiced, filled with emotional effusiveness, high praises, enthusiastic declamations and hyperbolic proclamations. Some of the effects of this bombastic style of writing can be seen in the plethora of “Shri-s” and ”lotus-feet” the text was strewn with. While this effusive and overwrought style looks right at home in Indic languages like Bengali, in English it appears gaudy, melodramatic, and even in some places a bit grotesque. Of course, Karunamayi is not to blame for this. He is writing as a *bhakta* would in Bengali or Hindi, expressing the strong feelings of his heart, his wonder at and admiration for his guru and his guru's blessings upon him, the great value and power he sees in the practices and beliefs of the Chaitanya tradition, and so forth. Unfortunately, in English this comes across as overstated, self-indulgent, and perhaps even insincere. Therefore, I have felt the need to heed Ramchandra's advice and tone the book down somewhat, not out of any wish to disrespect Karunamayi, his gurus, and his sense of the divine, but out of a desire to insure that his message gets through to an intelligent but not very patient English audience.

Compounding the translation problem somewhat is the fact that Karunamayi Das is also a song-writer/poet who has a feel for rhythm, rhyme, and repetition. While this has definitely contributed much to the charm of his text, in places it becomes too much to hold the attention of modern western readers. The text, when it moves along the border between prose and poetry, moves too slowly and is too repetitive, the same phrase being repeated half a dozen times in one paragraph in an almost ritualistic fashion. Parts of Karunamayi's original texts remind one of some of the ancient Buddhist texts in the Pali canon, and of numerous other ancient, orally transmitted texts, where phrases and lists are repeated over and over again as a technique that insured their being remembered. In our society such techniques are largely unnecessary, out of place, and even somewhat bothersome. Most modern readers want to read a book quickly, get the essential points of its meaning, and move on to the next book or activity. Right or wrong, this is the way of modern life in the information age.

Speaking of information, there is a great deal of information in this book. In its original form, it had a very long second chapter. The second chapter was the chapter in which Karunamayi Das presented the teachings of his master. He has used no system of organization to do this as far as I can tell. Rather than try to impose an order onto that second chapter and move things this way and that, I have instead opted to divide it into brief labeled sections, each corresponding to a particular instruction and its supporting texts. That way, a reader can survey the table of contents, see all of the topics listed there, and turn to one that is of particular interest at the moment. In addition, I divided that one chapter into four smaller chapters, leaving the sections in their original order. That should make it easier for one to move profitably through the material, chapter by chapter and section by section if one wishes.

My second task as an editor, insuring the accuracy of the texts cited and of their translations, was a daunting one. Karunamayi has quoted many verses from Sanskrit and Bengali works and he has supplied the translations of those verses from various other sources. I have been successful at finding and correcting or confirming all but one or two of the sources he cites. The sources are all represented in the text in transliteration along with translation and citation reference. I have decided not to follow the standard rules for the transliteration of Sanskrit in this book. Instead, I have adopted a simpler way of representing the original languages that can be followed and pronounced, more or less correctly, by any English reader. No knowledge of diacritics is necessary. Palatal and cerebral "s" (ś and ṣ) are both written "sh." No distinction is made between the various forms of "n," "t," or "d" and "c" is written "ch." The long a short versions of the vowels are not noticed and vocalic "r" (ṛ) is written "ri." *Visarga* (ḥ) is written simply "h" and *anusvara* (ṃ) "m." Those who know Sanskrit will know what is what and those who don't need not bother with it.

Since the Sanskrit or Bengali originals of the sources are presented in the text, I decided it necessary to separate out the commentary from the translation of the verses. In Karunamayi's original, the translations were rather loose and inexact, mixing in commentary with translation. I have placed the commentarial additions embedded in the "translations" of the verse in square brackets ([ ]). That way readers will be able to tell what a verse literally says and what has been added by way of commentary by the Chaitanyite commentators. Western scholarship demands that text and commentary be carefully set apart, with additions annotated in ways which may seem awkward and unnecessary to practitioners. This does not imply in any way that the Chaitanyite commentators misrepresent the meaning of the verses. The verses are often difficult and obscure and therefore demand some kind of commentary. A particular verse might have many lines of commentarial elaboration. Distinguishing between the two, translation and commentary, both illumines how some followers of Chaitanya read a particular text and leaves room for other lines of commentarial illumination.

Finally, a bibliography containing some of the books used and cited in the work. Wherever possible English translations of works originally in other languages are given. Also, a glossary is provided at the end of the book in which some of the important terms that occur in the book are discussed at greater length.

Author's Preface

Auspicious Invocations

ajnana-timirandhasya jnananjana-shalakaya
chakshurunmilitam yena tasmai shrigurave namah

I offer my humble obeisance to my initiation-giving teacher (guru), who has opened my eyes by treating them with the balm of divine knowledge, dispelling in this way the darkness of my ignorance.

vande 'ham shri-guroh shri-yuta-pada-
kamalam shri-gurun vaishnavamsh cha
shri-rupam sagrajatam sahagana-
raghunathanvitam tam sajivam
sadvaitam savadhutam parijana-
sahitam shri-krishna-chaitanya-devam
shri-radha-krishnapadan sahagana-
lalita-shri-vishakhanvitamsh cha

I praise the lotus-like feet of my initiating guru; and I praise my other gurus,[22] the Vaishnavas,[23] of Shri Rupa Goswami and his elder brother Sanatan Goswami, as well as Raghunath Bhatta, Raghunath Das and Shri Jiva Goswami. I praise Shri Krishna Chaitanya-deva with Shri Nityananda and Shri

[22]The instructing, hearing, holy name, and path-showing gurus (*shiksha*, *shravana*, *hari-nama*, and *vartma-pradarshaka*). These are the four varieties of of guru or spiritual teacher recognized in the Chaitanya tradition. Sometimes one guru plays the roles of all of them, but often the various roles are played by different teachers.

[23]Devotees or *bhaktas* of Vishnu-Krishna.

Advaita as well as Shri Radha and Krishna with their companions, headed by Lalita and Vishakha.

acharyam mam vijaniyan navamanyeta karhichit
na martya-buddhyasuyeta sarva-devamayo guruh[24]

[Shri Krishna told his friend Uddhava:] "You should recognize the *acharya*[25] as me. Never disrespect or be displeased with him, thinking that he is just an ordinary man. The guru is an aggregate of all the gods."

yadyapi amar guru chaitanyer das
tathapi janiye tinho tanhar prakash[26]

Although my guru is a servant of Shri Krishna Chaitanya [the Supreme Person himself], yet I know him to be the Lord's very manifestation.

guru krishna-rupa han shastrer pramane
guru-rupe krishna-kripa karen bhakta gane[27]

The guru is a form of Krishna; that is proven by the scriptures. Krishna bestows his grace upon his devotees in the form of the guru.

tatprasado hi sva-sva-nana-pratikara-dustyajyanartha-hanau parama-bhagavat-prasada-siddhau cha mulam[28]

The pleasing of the guru is the root cause of the elimination of all harmful habits, which are difficult to give up by other means, and of obtaining God's grace.

tatha pitha-pujayam bhagavad-dhame shri-guru-paduka-pujanam evam sangacchate yatha ya eva bhagavan atra vyashti-rupataya bhaktavataratvena shri-guru-rupo vartate, sa eva tatra samashti-rupataya sva-vama-pradeshe sakshad-avataratvenapi tad rupo vartate iti[29]

---

[24]*Bhagavata Purana*, 11.17.27.
[25]The guru who teaches by personal example.
[26]Krishna Das Kaviraj, *Chaitanya-charitamrita*, Adi 1.44.
[27]ibid., Adi 1.45.
[28]Jiva Goswami, *Bhakti-sandarbha*, para. 237.
[29]Ibid., para. 286

The worship of the throne (*pitha*) in the Lord's abode goes along with the worship of the guru's shoes. The Supreme Person descends [into this material world] in the distributive form (*vyashti-rupa*) of the guru as a devotee [experienced in his service]. He also exists there [at the Lord's throne in the Lord's abode] in the collective form (*samashti-rupa*) of the guru, as the Lord's direct descent (*sakshad-avatar*), on his left side.

sat-karma nipuno vipro mantra-tantra-visharadah
avaishnavo gurur na syat vaishnava-shvapacho guruh[30]

A *brahmin* who is expert in the pious rites, as well as in the *mantra* and *tantra*, but who is not a Vaishnava [devotee of Vishnu-Krishna] should not be one's guru, while someone born in a family of dog-eaters who is a Vaishnava should be one's guru.

anarpita-charim chirat karunayavatirna-kalau
samarpayitum unnatojjvala-rasam sva-bhakti-shriyam
harih purata-sundara-dyuti-kadamba-sandipitah
sada hridaya-kandare sphuratu vah shachi-nandanah[31]

May Lord Hari, whose form shines with beautiful and golden light, who has compassionately descended in this Age of Kali as the Son of Shachi [Shri Chaitanya Mahaprabhu], in order to bestow [on all] the treasure of *bhakti* to himself which culminates in an elevated, splendid flavour (*rasa*)[32] not given for a long time [since his last appearance in the previous day of Brahma], always be visible in the cave of your hearts.

After requesting my eternal guru-deva, 108[33] Shri-Shrimad Krishna Das Madrasi Babaji Maharaj, to allow me to write something on his life

[30] *Padma Purana*, ?

[31] Rupa Goswami, *Vidagdha-madhava*, 1.1.

[32] That is, it culminates in a particular kind of *rasa*-experience or experience of sacred rapture as a result of cultivating passion-pursuing (*raganuga*) *bhakti* in the identity of a *manjari* of Shri Radha.

[33] One hundred and eight, here, stands for one hundred and eight "Shris" which are affixed to the names of persons one wishes to show the highest respect to. Naturally, Karunamayi Das wishes to show that sort of respect to his guru. [Ed.]

and receiving his most compassionate permission, I questioned him in great detail and thus gathered the information for the book. May I always have increasing devotion for my Shri guru-deva so that Shri Hari will be satisfied with me and grant me his personal companionship, as is promised in a verse from a text called the *Vamana-kalpa* (The Ordinances of Vamana):

> *yo mantrah sa guruh sakshat yo guruh sa harih svayam*
> *gurur yasya bhavet tushtas tasya tushto harih svayam*[34]
>
> [Brahma said:] The initiation *mantra* is identical with the guru and the guru is identical with Shri Hari himself. [There is no substantial difference between them.] Whoever the guru is pleased with Shri Hari himself is also pleased with.

And in the *Padma Purana*:

> *bhaktir yatha harau me 'sti tadvan-nishtha gurau yadi*
> *mamasti tena satyena svam darshayatu me harih*[35]
>
> If I have devotion to my guru like that to Shri Hari, then by that truth may Shri Hari show himself to me.

And in the *Bhakti-sandarbha*:

> *harau rushte gurus trata gurau rushte na kashchana*
> *tasmat sarva-prayatnena gurum eva prasadayet*[36]
>
> If Hari is displeased with someone the guru can still save him, but if the guru is angry with someone, nobody can save him. Therefore with all effort one must please one's guru.
>
> *sutan hitveti pativrata patyur iva guroh sevayam pravrittah shishyah shravana-kirtanadiny api bhogan tad-utthana-premanandan api grihan tad-uchita-vivikta-sthalam api naivapekshate. sri-guru-sevayaiva sukhena sarva-sadhya-siddhyartham ity upadesha-vyanjitah ... guru-sevaya sarva-vedena sarvadhikasyoktatvat.*[37]

[34] *Vamana-kalpa*, cited in the *Bhakti-sandarbha*, para. 237.
[35] *Padma Purana*. Cited in the *Hari-bhakti-vilasa*, 4.358.
[36] *Bhakti-sandarbha*, 238 and in the *Hari-bhakti-vilasa*, 4.360.
[37] Vishvanath Chakravarti's *Sarartha-darshini* commentary on *Bhagavata*, 4.28.34.

When a chaste wife is absorbed in the service of her husband, she does not care even for her sons. Similarly, a disciple who is deeply absorbed in the service of his guru knows that by such service alone he can easily attain success in *bhakti* and consequently does not depend on hearing, chanting, and so forth [of the names, forms, qualities and sports of Shri Radha and Krishna]. Just as a chaste wife does not covet any sensual pleasure and home comfort, so a disciple, who is completely absorbed in the service of his guru, does not long for the bliss derived from such hearing and chanting, nor for a suitable place for practicing *bhakti* to the Lord. This is what this verse [*Bhagavata*, 4.28.34] teaches us. Service to the guru is declared the highest of all in all the Vedas.

nri-deham adyam sulabham sudurlabham
plavam sukalpam guru-karnadharam
mayanukulena nabhasvateritam puman
bhavabdhim na taret sa atmaha[38]

[Shri Krishna told Uddhava:] Anyone who is fortunate enough to attain a human body, which is like an exceptionally fit ship, piloted by an expert captain, the guru, propelled by the favorable breezes of my blessings, and which is rarely attained and useful, but who fails to cross the ocean of repeated birth and death, is undoubtedly a killer of his own soul.

[38] *Bhagavata*, 11.20.17.

Expression of Gratitude

Let me offer my humble obeisance and express my most deeply felt eternal gratitude to Pandit Shri Ananta Das Babaji Maharaj, my instructing guru, the present *mahanta* (abbot) of Shri Radhakund in whom my guru-deva found immense and intense spiritual pleasure, while hearing his discourses on the sweet sports (*madhurya-lila*) of Shri Radha and Krishna in Vraja, and who revealed to me the details of the story of how the famous notes on the *Shri Vilapa-kusumanjali* were received from my guru-deva.[39]

na kahile hay mor kritaghnata dosh;
dambha kori boli shrota na kariho rosh
toma sabar charan dhuli karinu vandan[40]

If I did not say this I would be guilty of ingratitude. May my audience not be angry with me, calling me arrogant. I praise the dust of the lotus feet of all of you.

jagai madhai hoite mui se papishtha;
purisher kita haite mui se laghishtha
mora nama shune yei tara punya kshay
mora nama lay yei tar papa hay[41]

I am more sinful than Jagai and Madhai and I am lower than a worm in stool. Anyone who hears my name loses his virtuous merit and anyone who utters my name commits a sin.

---

[39] See Section Five of Chapter Two, "Baba's Treasure," for this story.
[40] *Chaitanya-charitamrita*, Antya 20.91-2.
[41] ibid., Adi 5.205-206.

Radhakund

After reading in Shri Rupa Goswami's *Upadeshamrita* (The Ambrosia of Instruction)[42] about the greatness of Shri Radhakund[43] because it is not different from Shri Radhika herself and thus is the paramount place to practice the *raganuga* (passion-pursuing) cultivation of the feelings of *manjaris* of Radha, my heart brought me there first in November, 1978.

---

[42]Rupa Goswami, *Upadeshamrita*, 9:

> *vaikunthajjanito vara madhuripuri tatrapi rasotsavad*
> *vrindaranyam udara-pani-ramanat tatrapi govardhanah*
> *radhakundam ihapi gokulapateh premamritaplavanat*
> *kuryad asya virajato giritate sevam viveki na kah*
>
> Greater than Vaikuntha is Mathura; greater than that is Vrindavan, where the Rasa-festival (Circle Dance) took place; greater than that even is Govardhan, which was beautified by the charming hand of Giridhari (Krishna holding the mountain aloft); but greatest of all is Radhakund which is inundated by ambrosial love of the Lord of Gokula (Krishna). What discerning person will not serve this Radhakund, which is situated at the base of Govardhan?

[43]The pond of Shri Radha.

I already had been staying in Vraja for two months, appreciating the spiritual sweetness of that holy place and its people's lovely devotion to Shri Radha and Krishna. But as soon as I stepped into the outskirts of the village surrounding Shri Radhakund I felt that the concentrated essential part of Vraja was present here. That is to say, I felt that the living heart of Vraja and of the most perfectly sweet form of the Supreme Person, Shri Krishna, was really present there exactly as asserted in India's scriptures. In the ancient scripture the *Padma Purana*, for instance, it is said:

> *yatha radha priya vishnos tasyah kundam priyam tatha*
> *sarva-gopishu saivaika vishnor atyanta-vallabha*[44]
>
> Just as Shri Radha is dear to Vishnu [Krishna], so is her pond, Radhakund, [dear to him]. Of all the cowherd women she alone is extremely dear to Vishnu.

The whole place seemed inundated by a special type of incredibly fresh love flowing constantly through the atmosphere and permeating everyone and everything contained in it. What struck me at once was the special devotional attitudes of its inhabitants, which disclosed their being specially sheltered by Shri Radha! In fact, as I entered the village everyone fervently uttered `Jai Shri Radhe! Jai Shri Radhe!,' more than anywhere else in Vraja. As I walked forward, the sweet beating of this supreme, original heart of highest spiritual love sounded closer and closer, finally revealing itself as the most simple, charming pond surrounded on its four sides by stairs leading down into its waters and by a few shade trees. I felt I had arrived at the most important and sacred reality of the greatest of all spiritual paradises on earth, the pond of Shri Radha. I felt like I had finally reached my spiritual home and I was moved by deep emotions. It was then that I saw for the first time 108 Shri-Shrimad Krishna Das Babaji Maharaj, who was to become my eternal spiritual father --- my initiating guru --- nine years later.

As I had come with the intention of staying one week, Baba let me stay in his meditation hut (*bhajan kutir*) situated in front of Shri Radharaman Mandir (Temple). Then I left and returned after a couple of weeks to stay one more week before traveling to Bombay. That week

[44] *Padma Purana*, cited in Rupa Goswami, *Ujjvala-nilamani*, 4.5.

turned into five months because I became so ill with malaria and hepatitis that I was unable to travel anymore. Having survived that period, I left India for Europe. A few years later, I returned to India once more and went again to Shri Radhakund, this time for just a few hours out of which I spent only half an hour at Shri Radharaman Mandir. That was the First of November, 1984, the day after Indira Gandhi's assassination and Baba was just getting the news from his radio.

In May, 1985 I started corresponding with Krishna Das Babaji regularly from Europe (and that continued until his passing away in 1998), and in September, 1987, I was back by his side in the hope of having his holy association (*sat-sanga*) and engaging in his service, which he granted me out of his compassionate divine love. On the Fifth of November of the same year he blessed me by giving me the initiation *mantras*, the guru lineage, the perfected lineage and later the eleven details of my eternal identity as a *manjari* and his guru's *Gaura-govinda-lila-smarana-gutika-sutra* (Aphorisms on the Medthod of Remembering the Sports of Shri Gaur and Govinda), an abridged manual for remembering Shri Gaur and Govinda's supernatural sports. I continued to serve him until March, 1988, and then returned to Europe. I was back again in October, 1988, and resumed my service to him until March, 1989. During this period Baba's hipbone fractured spontaneously due to osteoporosis and I remained with him in a private room at the hospital for nearly two months. Then, from 1991 to 1998, I came regularly every year (except in 1993) with my wife Karunamayi Dasi, for five to six weeks each trip, to serve him and have his holy association. In December, 1992, Baba had me make twenty-four hours of video film of him translating Shri Mahanamabrata Brahmacari's Bengali version of Rupa Goswami's *Uddhava-sandesh* (Instructions to Uddhava) into English, and in March, 1994, he did the same for eighteen hours on one part of Pandit Shri Ananta Das Babaji's edition of Shri Narottam Das Thakura's *Shri Prema-bhakti-chandrika* (Moonlight on the Devotion of Love) and *Prarthana* (Prayers). Those videos are still with me and have been transferred into mpeg format. They can be viewed for those who are interested from my website (www.madrasibaba.org)

Let me thank Advaita Das for his great and precious assistance in the preliminary editing of this book and Nitai Das for its final editing and printing. Let me also thank all those fortunate souls who rendered varied kinds of loving service to my guru-deva, in particular Shri Harimohan Das Babaji, Padma Ma, Govinda Ma, Govinda Charan Ghorai and his relatives (Radha Dasi, Vishakha Dasi, Dulal Ghorai and his wife, etc.), Anup Das, Shiva Das, Hari Das, Vasudeva Das, the rest of my guru-brothers and sisters who nursed him selflessly when he was lame and bedridden.

Special thanks to my wife Karunamayi Dasi for bearing, for a considerable period of time during Shri Gurudeva's life, practically all the expenses of his service. After Gurudeva's demise, she made possible a huge *viraha-utsav*, "farewell celebration," for him and the construction of his tomb. This structure (*samadhi*) also incorporated the tomb of Shrila Sakhicharan Das Babaji Maharaja and is part of the Shri Gurukripa Bhavan. It is located at Gauradham Colony of Radhakund in the disctrict of Mathura, Uttar Pradesh, India. It was also mainly due to the financial support of my wife and her parents that a free festival, including *kirtans*, a series of lectures given by Pandit Shri Ananta Das Babaji Maharaja, and a feast for everyone has been regularly held at this place every year to celebrate the disappearance day of our Shri Gurudeva.

Special thanks go to my guru-brother Govinda Ghorai, his wife, my guru-sister, Radha Dasi, and their daughter Vishakha, for faithfully conducting the daily ritual worship at our Guru-maharaja's *samādhi* shrine since its installation in 2001. Special thanks also go to Harimohan Das Babaji for his important assistance in helping to organize our Guru-maharaja's tirobhava festival every year.

May this narration delight the hearts of those who love my gurudeva, who knew him directly or indirectly, as well as those who are yet to know him. This is all I hope for and in this way my heart will rejoice.

Chapter 1

The Life and Times of Shri Krishna Das Baba

In the town of Calicut (Kerala), on Friday the 21st of February, 1919,[1] while the Svati asterism[2] was predominant, my guru-deva Shri Krishna Das Babaji took his birth in a house situated on the northern side of a big pond. On its southern side there was a temple with images of Krishna and Shiva, and on that particular day some kind of religious festival was going on. Around 3 P.M., a mahout brought an elephant to be washed at the bathing place reserved for the animals. After a while, the elephant became so joyful that it went out of control, left the bathing place and went to frolic in the waters right in front of the birth house, all the while trumpeting with its trunk. It did not come back to its normal state until 6:15 P.M. when the delivery was over and its keeper was again able to gain control over it. This event was appreciated by the baby's parents as an auspicious omen in favor of their newly born son. During the name-giving ceremony the baby was named Kalpathi Naganath Raja Gopal Krishnan. He naturally was given the name of his father: Kalpathi Naganath Raja Vaidya, but without the Vaidya, which when connected with `Raja' means 'priest of the king.' His father and grandfather indeed had worked in that capacity while living in Palghat.

[1]In the native lunar calendar of India this day is known as Phalguna Krishna Sashthi, the sixth day of the dark lunar fortnight of the month of Phalguna (February-March).

[2]The fifteenth of the twenty-seven lunar asterisms according to Hindu astrology. *Svati* means Arcturus and forms both the 13th and 15th lunar asterisms.

Since he was the second son, the family tradition was for him to take the first name of his maternal grandfather also, which was Gopal, and because his mother would not dare pronounce her father's first name out of respect for him, they named him Krishnan for her convenience in addressing him.

Krishnan was his mother's last child. Before him, she gave birth to an uncommonly handsome and fine-limbed baby with arms reaching down to his knees. That boy lived for just twenty-six days. People said that he was a great, spiritually advanced person (*maha-purusha*) who came to finish the last of his remaining *karma*, thus blessing his family and the others about him. Since his mother still carried the breast milk meant for that older brother, Krishnan drank it and later he declared he got the unique privilege of drinking the great soul's lip-nectar (*adharam-rita*). Just before the birth of that brother and after the births, first of a daughter, and a few years later, in 1910, of a son, his mother unfortunately had a miscarriage. Krishnan's mother was a native of Travenku and her character was so meek and humble that she would never quarrel with anyone. When there were religious feasts she would cook for hundreds of people. Krishnan's father worked privately as a vendor for the court. Every morning he would go to his rented office, which was situated at the seashore, and porters would bring him from the court the forms to be sold. An astrologer visited the family annually, and he once foretold that they would all have to leave Kerala because of Krishnan and that he would pass away at a holy place of pilgrimage.

At home, Krishnan's father read daily from *Bhagavata Purana* and *Mahabharata* to his family members. Once during one such reading, a snake came into the house and left without harming anyone. Their house was located under a huge coconut tree and a bamboo-net was strung above the tiled roof, protecting it from any falling coconuts. In those days the cost of living was very low. One could purchase 1,000 coconuts for the equivalent of 15 to 20 Indian rupees. Only wholesome food was available in the market, and refined aliments like white rice and white sugar were nowhere to be found.

When Krishnan was five years of age, his parents celebrated his head-shaving ceremony (*munda-samskara*) according to the South Indian style, characterized by leaving uncut a thick and long tuft of hair (*shikha*) running backwards from the crown of the head. Belonging to the *brahmin* caste, the family privately worshiped a *shalagram shila*[3] and had a strong attachment to Lord Krishna and his divine sports. At the age of nine Krishnan was invested with the sacred thread according to Vedic rituals.

Once, Krishnan's parents were frantic because they could not find him anywhere and they were afraid that he may have drowned in the pond. Finally, after a long search, they joyfully found him sleeping peacefully in a sari strung like a hammock inside their house.

Necessity forced the family to leave Calicut and wander from town to town for a while. They first reached Cochin, where they lived for a while at the house of Krishnan's sister who was married to her cousin (the son of her father's elder sister).[4] Next, they lived at Bangalore and then went to Madurai, where they stayed for one year. During this period Krishnan's father performed a rite called *mantra purashcharana* in the Minakshi temple there. That is to say, he took a vow to chant daily a certain number of repetitions of a *mantra*, a Sanskrit prayer-formula, on beads in order to achieve a particular spiritual goal. He used to arrive at the temple early in the morning, complete his chanting on an empty stomach by midday, and then break his fast.

Leaving Madurai for Pune, where they remained for a month and half, the family finally arrived in Bombay. Krishnan was sent to the Antonio da Silva Christian school. The schoolmaster named Dikula, a native of Goa, kindly volunteered to help him, after school hours, fill in the gaps in Krishnan's education that had developed because of the family's moving from place to place.

One day a next-door neighbor, who was an artist-painter, gave Krishnan the English book *Lord Gauranga*[5] by the Gaudiya[6] Vaishnava savant Shri Shishir Kumar Ghose, founder and editor of the *Amrit Bazar Patrika*, one of the major newspapers of Calcutta. After that, the family changed its residence to Matunga, which was the south-Indian neighborhood of Bombay. Once the Gaudiya Math[7] mission organized a religious festival

---

[3]A *shalagram shila* is a type of black stone with fossil markings in it that is identified as a form of Vishnu and that is found in the Himalayan river called the Gandaki.

[4]Marrying one's first cousin is a practice common among South Indian *brahmin* families. [Ed.]

[5]Gauranga is another name for Shri Chaitanya (1486-1533 C.E.). It means "golden-limbed" and refers to the golden complexion that Shri Chaitanya had.

[6]Gaudiya means relating to Gauda, an old name for the part of India now called Bengal. It thus is equivalent to the adjective Bengali.

[7]The Gaudiya Math, or monastery, is an institution founded in Bengal in 1918 by

in that vicinity and Krishnan together with his relatives attended. On that occasion a German Gaudiya Vaishnava ascetic named Sadananda Das Swami was eloquently lecturing on Lord Gauranga, the dual incarnation of Shri Radha and Krishna. Krishnan was spontaneously attracted by the subject and moved closer to the lecturer to give him some relief from the scorching heat of the sun by fanning him. He remained impressed by the extraordinary character of Lord Gauranga and thought to himself that there is something really special about him. When he returned home he noticed that the book given to him by his former neighbor was about the same Lord Gauranga and he started to read it with eagerness. One morning, while traveling by train to his place of work (he was working as a salesman in a multi-millionaire's jewelry shop), he forgot to get off the train at his stop because of being carried away by reading the book, and he had to return to his stop on the opposite train. Since the book referred to a second volume, he asked the Bengalis working with him where he could get it. One of them directed him to a nearby temple of the Gaudiya Math where he was redirected to someone else in possession of a copy of the book. That person agreed to lend it to him. Once Krishnan's brother, Hari, found him crying profusely while reading it in his room and was surprised. He asked him why he was crying, but Krishnan was so moved he was unable to say a word. So Krishnan's brother took the book from his hands and leafed through it to see what is was about. Then he too began to read it and he also was deeply impressed by the story of Lord Gauranga.

One Sunday Hari, Krishnan's brother, had a meeting with someone for a job-interview in a nearby temple of Maha Lakshmi and he took this opportunity to bring his relatives with him. Nitai Das Brahmachari, who had informed Krishnan where to borrow the second volume of *Lord Gauranga*, happened to be there also and Krishnan introduced his brother to him. Soon after this meeting, the two brothers started to visit the Gaudiya Math daily after work, getting acquainted with the fundamental principles of Gaudiya Vaishnavism. On Sundays their family members also accompanied them.

During World War II, in 1940, Krishnan married. As the situation started to become dangerous in Bombay due to frequent bombings by the Japanese Air Force, Krishnan's family, except for him and his brother, moved to Trichur. There, his wife gave birth to his son,

---

Bhaktisiddhanta Saraswati to spread the teachings and practices of the religious movement founded by Shri Chaitanya.

Mukunda, but unfortunately it was also there that Krishnan's father got gangrene from a cut on his toe and passed away, leaving Krishnan's mother overwhelmed with grief. During that period Krishnan's brother traveled to Shri Mayapura and stayed there for fifteen days. Krishnan stayed at home alone, carrying on the daily worship of the family *shalagram shila* who occupied a nice altar together with pictures of Shri Radha and Krishna, one of which was a print of a painting by Raja Ravi Varma. When the threat of war subsided, Krishnan's family came back to Bombay.

Krishnan's brother had been introduced to the practice of *japa*[8] of the Hare Krishna *maha-mantra* by Puri Das Maharaj, then the head of the Gaudiya Math. That took place on the day after Gaura Purnima, the birthday of Lord Gauranga, 1942, at the Gaudiya Math's Calcutta temple. Hari was also given the name Hari Das, the servant of Hari or Vishnu. When he returned he asked Krishnan to meet with Puri Das Maharaj, who had left Calcutta for Mathura. Krishnan met him there at the Gaudiya Math's temple, which was situated just in front of Sati Burj at Vishram Ghat and was similarly introduced to the practice of *japa* of the Hare Krishna *maha-mantra* and given the name Krishna Das (servant of Krishna). [9]

After visiting Shri Vrindavan, Shri Govardhan, Shri Radhakund and other places in region of Vraja, Krishna Das left for Calcutta, from where he traveled to Shri Mayapur and toured the 'Navadvipas,' the town of nine islands where Shri Chaitanya was born. Unfortunately, he came down with malaria there. After returning to Calcutta he proceeded to Gaya where he saw the most important holy sites. He continued his pilgrimage through Benares where he went to the temple of Vishvanath and to the temple of Bindu Madhava, and then to Allahabad, where he stayed for one month and recovered from malaria. He then went back to Mathura, where he remained for a short while before returning to Bombay.

In 1943, Krishna Das traveled with his baby son and Hari Das to Delhi, where they were invited to attend a series of lectures on Shri

---

[8] *Japa* is the remembering, whispering, or audible repetition of a *mantra* while counting the number of repetitions on a string of beads. See the glossary.

[9] In consideration of the fact that Krishna Das and Hari Das were born in a brahmin family and had already undergone the sacred thread ceremony in their childhood, Puri Das Maharaja never gave them the brahminical initiation commonly given to others in the Gaudiya Math.

Jiva Goswami's *Bhakti-sandarbha* given by Puri Das Maharaj. It went on for five or six hours daily for nearly a month and a half and then continued in Mathura for another twenty days. The series of lectures, however, had originally started in Shri Mayapur at the rate of three classes daily for a period of four and a half months. As a great Vaishnava and an accomplished Sanskrit scholar, Puri Das Maharaj was lecturing with profound theological sensitivity, finding it almost impossible to check his deep religious emotions, to the point of often completely drenching his chest with tears. At the concluding session he announced that he was relinquishing all of his followers to the existing, authentic Gaudiya Vaishnava spiritual lineages, whichever they chose to affiliate themselves with. He then left the order of renunciation (*sannyasa*) and got married, later having a daughter and a son and dedicating the rest of his life to editing and publishing in Bengali script some sixty-two volumes of the works of the Vrindavan Goswamis and their followers. The books were meant for free distribution to the leading scholars of India.

When Krishna Das and Hari Das returned to Bombay, the latter was transferred by his company (Metro-Goldwyn-Mayer) to New Delhi, where he assumed the post of assistant manager. He used to spend his weekends together with his wife and son in Mathura. In 1944, Krishna Das resigned from his job and also left Bombay. He arrived in Mathura with his mother, wife, and son, on Saturday, the 9th of April. He was then engaged in receiving visiting pilgrims related to the Gaudiya Math at the train station and guiding them to the different holy sites of Mathura. Later, with the help of Hari Das he started working for the Metro-Goldwyn-Mayer cinema in Agra. At first he lived alone in a rented room situated just in front of the cinema, but after he found a bigger residence, his mother, wife, and son came from Mathura to live with him there. Since his new residence was far from his place of work, he commuted to it by bicycle.

Hari Das's superiors wanted to promote Hari Das to the post of manager of the company, but instead of accepting the promotion he handed in his resignation, choosing instead to dedicate his life entirely to religious pursuits. He then moved with his family to Mathura, where he assisted Puri Das as his secretary and private cook. In 1945, when his wife passed away due to tuberculosis, leaving alone him with their small son Narayan, Hari Das married the last of her three younger sisters.

In 1946, Krishna Das's wife also passed away due to round-worm in Agra's public hospital. The brother of a man whose wife died in the next bed transported the two corpses with his truck to the Yamuna, where the widowers consecrated them after reciting prayers. Having been informed of the loss, Krishna Das's maternal uncle came to Mathura to take Krishna Das's son Mukunda back with him to Kerala and raise him there. However, his sister, Krishna Das's mother, was so disconsolate that they decided instead to leave him in her care. In 1948, she too passed away in Mathura, and 6-year old Mukunda was brought to Bombay by his father, where his maternal uncle took charge of him and returned with him to Kerala.[10] Krishna Das then returned to stay with Puri Das and assist him in his work. When Puri Das moved his residence to Vrindavan, Krishna Das followed him and started living in Radharaman Ghera, the residences buildings connected with the Radharaman temple, as a neighbor of Vishvambhar and Krishna Chaitanya Goswamis. This gave him a chance to attend daily the seven *arti* ceremonies[11] of Shri Radharaman, the name of the sacred image in the temple. Puri Das lived near the Radharaman temple for a while and then moved to a room in Purushottam Goswami's residence in Bankicha. During this period, Krishna Das and his dear friend Binay Babu traveled together to visit different sacred sites in India, like Kedarnath, Badrinath, and so forth.

In 1951, Puri Das decided to build a house at Ambika Kalna and entrusted the task to Hari Das and Krishna Das. They went to the place by train, bought a plot of land near Gauri Das Pandit's Gaur-Nitai temple, and broke ground for the construction. Hari Das returned to Vrindavan after a few months, but Krishna Das remained, continuing to supervise the work. During that period he used to bike almost everyday to Navadvip and back, and at Ambika Kalna he regularly went and meditated at the tomb (*samadhi*) of the saint Shri Bhagavan Das Babaji. Because he read the *Chaitanya-bhagavata* and *Chaitanya-charitamrita* everyday at Gauri Das Pandit's Gaur-Nitai temple with a few listeners attending, and

[10]After his completing his education, Baba's son, Mukunda, settled in Kolkata (Calcutta) where he married and had two sons. His wife was a great Vaishnavi, very fond of reciting Jayadev's *Gita-govinda* (Song of Govinda) daily, her voice choked up with spiritual emotions and her eyes filled with tears. Mukunda went to Radhakund in 1980 and stayed for a whole year before returning to Kolkata. During that time Baba introduced him to Shri Kishorikishorananda Baba (Tinkadi Goswami). He eventually received initiation from Shri Kishorikishorananda Baba. I have never met him and have only heard these things from Baba. Whether he is still alive or not I do not know. We have not received any more news from him since 1998, the year when Guru-deva passed away.

[11]*Arti* or *aratika* ceremony is a welcoming ceremony in which lights are waved in front of the sacred images in a temple. Other articles like flowers, water, incense, and so forth are also offered to the images then.

because he resided in Bengal for such a long time, he naturally became familiar with the Bengali language. On one occasion he had the privilege of conducting the worship of the images of Gaur and Nitai for two days, substituting for their regular priest.

Once, being deeply inspired by Gaur and Nitai, he composed the following lines of Bengali as a reminder of a pattern for him always to follow:

> *gaurer amar sob bhalo ar boro. ami ek-matra manda ar choto. ami shata doshe doshi, sahasra doshe doshi, lakho doshe doshi, koti doshe doshi. eto gune guni ami sob somoy sakaler dosh-ta-i dekhi, kintu amake sakaler gun-ta-ke khujte beraibe. tabe ta'hole se-o ei adhamer madhye ye gun dekhite pabe. ekatra ubhoy bose ki korile bhalo hoy. ei sob somoy cinta kora jay.*[12]
>
> The whole world belongs to my Gaura, the Supreme Person himself (*svayam bhagavan*) and everyone is very good and very great. I am the only one who is very bad and insignificant. I have a hundred faults, a thousand faults, a million faults, ten million faults. Because of these shortcomings, I always try to find faults in others [although in reality I possess them myself in a concentrated way]. Rather, I should always try to find the good qualities in others. If I adopt such behavior, maybe they will discover some good qualities in me, too [though I don't have any]. In this way we may then find a place to sit down together and converse about what it would be good to do. One should always think like this.

Three years later, in 1954, Krishna Das was back in Vrindavan. Then, in 1957, he moved to Barsana, where he lived at different places

[12] *gaurer* - of Gaura; *amar* - my; *sob* - all; *bhalo* - good; *ar* - and; *boro* - great(er); *ami* - I; *ek-matra* - only; *manda* - inferior; *ar* - and; *choto* - small; *ami* - I; *shata* - hundred; *dosher* - of the fault; *doshi* - a person who has faults; *sahasra* - thousand; *dosher* - of the fault; *doshi* - a person who has faults; *lakho* - a hundred thousand; *dosher* - of the fault; *doshi* - a person who has faults; *koti* - ten million; *dosher* - of the fault; *doshi* - a person who has faults; *eto* - so many; *gune* - in the qualities; *guni* - a person who has qualities;*ami* - I; *sab* - all; *somoy* - the time; *sakaler* - of everyone; *dosha-ta-i* - faults; *dekhi* - I see; *kintu* - but; *amake* - unto me; *sakaler* - of everyone; *gun-ta-ke* - unto the qualities; *khujte* - seeking; *beraibe* - will go out; *tabe* - then; *ta'hole* - if that is so/ in that case; *se-o* - even he; *ei* - this; *adhamer* - of this fallen soul; *madhye* - within; *ye* - whatever; *gun* - quality; *dekhite pabe* - he/she will see; *ekatra* - together; *ubhoy* - both; *bose* - sitting; *ki* - what; korile - if doing; *bhalo* - good; *hoy* - is; *sab samoy* - all the time; *cinta* - thinking; *kora jay* - is done.

until 1959. There he got a chance to associate with and render service to the famous saint Shrila Shachinandan Das Babaji. Once, when the saint was sweeping up and down the main steps connecting the Larli Lal or Shriji ka Mandir (the main temple) to the village, Krishna Das stayed behind him until he finished, ushering out of the way the crowds of onlookers who had come out to see the saint. In this way he kept the saint from being hampered in his service. In the meantime Puri Das passed away in Vrindavan, four days after Gaura Purnima in 1958, and his corpse was brought to Radhakund where he was given a tomb (*samadhi*). Krishna Das lived at the tomb, located in the vicinity of the local cremation ground, in the company of a Vaishnava named Sudarshan Das, for nearly four months. During this time he copied Shri Vishvanath Chakravarti's book *Shri Prema-samputa* (Jewel Box of Love) by hand. On Gaura Purnima, 1959, the saint Shri Sakhicharan Das Babaji, who belonged to the disciplic lineage of Shrila Lokanath Goswami,[13] blessed him with *mantra* initiation (*diksha*):

> *sa vai satkarmanam sakshaddvijater iha sambhavah*
> *adyo'nga yatrashraminam yathaham jnanado guruh*[14]
>
> [Shri Krishna said:] "Friend, the father from whom one gets one's body is the first guru in this world. Next comes the guru who invests the members of the three higher social classes [*brahmins*, *kshatriyas*, and *vaishyas*] with the sacred thread and teaches them their rites and duties; he is worthy of devotion like myself. Superior to these two types of guru is the guru [a pure Vaishnava] who imparts [by Vishnu-mantra initiation] knowledge of the self [Supreme and infinitesimal] to faithful men of all classes [including *shudras* and barbarians and who helps them to meet God]. Such a guru is identical with me."

On Guru Purnima[15] of the same year Shri Sakhicharan Das Babaji gave him initiation into the life of a *babaji* or renunciant, at which point he

[13]Lokanath Goswami was one of the first close companions of Lord Gauranga and the first to be dispatched to the region of Vraja by the Lord, along with Shrila Bhugarbha Goswami, to rediscover the lost holy sites in the ancient homeland of Krishna. Lokanath Goswami's disciple was Shri Narottam Das Thakur, the famous writer of Bengali songs and verses.

[14]*Bhagavata Purana*, 10.80.32.

[15]A holiday in honor of one's guru, observed on a full moon day.

gave up wearing his sacred thread. From then on Krishna Das became known as Krishna Das Babaji. He was sometimes called Madrasi Baba because he was from South India.

Hari Das received initiation and renunciation from Shri Ananta Das Babaji, a paternal cousin of Puri Das and disciple of the saint Shri Manohar Das Babaji of Shri Govindakund (Govardhan), who belonged to the disciplic lineage of Shri Advaitacharya. Hari Das was renamed Haripada Das Babaji.

After his initiation Shri Krishna Das Babaji started to chant three hundred thousand names of Hari[16] each day. He began to live at Gantholi, near the town of Govardhan, coming everyday to Radhakund to visit his guru. He also began to copy by hand various books necessary for the remembering (*smarana*) form of his private worship (*bhajan*). In 1962, he moved to Radhakund and took a vow not to leave the place for one full year. After having resided at ten different places around Radhakund until 1963, he settled at the Shri Radharaman temple, on the request of his guru, with the purpose of assisting the invalid monk, Shri Vrajabhushan Das Babaji, also known as 'Delhi Baba,' until he breathed his last. Besides lending assistance to Delhi Baba, he was also available to serve in various ways other *babajis* in need who resided at Radhakund. He also took care of the worship (*puja*) of 'Delhi Baba's' images (a stone from Govardhan and letters in Devanagari of the Hare Krishna *maha-mantra* engraved in silver plates) for some time. His brother Haripada Das Babaji lived in Tala-van except during the rainy season when he used to reside at Radhakund, Mukharai, or in Vrindavan. Shri Krishna Das Babaji often walked or biked over to visit him, returning the same day.

One day in 1965, while Baba was returning to Radhakund from Tosh through some fields he fell near the village of Basoti on account of slippery ground and fractured the neck of his left thigh bone. He remained lying on the muddy ground from 7 A.M. to 2 P.M., when finally a passing farmer noticed him. Later, it took five men to put him on a cot, after spending a half an hour in several attempts, and to carry him to a house at Basoti. While carrying him they lovingly tried to comfort him by singing in chorus "*ram nam satya hai*"[17] and telling him jok-

[16]This was accomplished by the repetition the Hare Krishna *maha-mantra*, counting 192 times around a Vaishnava "rosary" of 108 beads.

[17]"The name of Ram is true." It is a slogan traditionally chanted in India during a funeral-procession when a body is carried to the burning grounds.

ingly that they were carrying him to the burial ground. A disciple of Radhakrishna Das Babaji, the *mahanta* (abbot) of Shrila Raghunath Das Goswami's Gaddi (chair) at Radhakund, happened to be there in the house and gave him some assistance. The next evening he was transported back to the Radharaman temple at Radhakund by horse cart, and the following day he was taken to Vrindavan where his dear friend Binay Babu accompanied him to the Ramakrishna Mission Hospital. Binay Babu kindly stayed with him for the next fifteen days to lend him assistance. Three months later, as his guru urgently called for him, Baba left the hospital for Radhakund and with great difficulty arrived at his guru's bedside. Shrila Sakhicharan Das Babaji was very pleased by his presence and lovingly told him that his blessings were upon him in his worship. The following day, on the morning of June 30, 1965, the day preceding the Ratha-yatra festival,[18] Shrila Sakhicharan Das Babaji passed away, joining Shri Gauranga and Shri Radha and Krishna's manifest divine love play in some other place in the universe.[19]

In 1973, Shri Krishna Das Babaji started doing a circumambulation with full-length prostrations (in his case 1128 and later 1200 at each spot) of Shri Radhakund and Shri Shyamakund, reciting a verse from the *Radha-rasa-sudha-nidhi* (Ocean of Nectar of the Rasa of Radha) before performing each prostration. He thus memorized many of that poem's verses. On February 15, 1980, he was present at the passing of Delhi Baba, who departed while listening to Krishna Das Baba repeat the holy name `Radha' and then uttering it himself in full awareness.

My first encounter with Baba occurred in November of 1978 and by his kindness I was able to remain for five months with him at Radhakund. He lived there for 39 years in all, from the time he received *mantra* initiation and information on the accomplished identities of his predecessors in the lineage, called the *siddha-pranali*, from Shri Sakhicharan Das Baba in 1959 until his departure from the world in 1998.

The characteristic of Baba's I recall most from that period was his attitude of service which was expressed by a constant eagerness to render any type of service, in particular toward the residents of Radhakund,

---

[18]The festival of the cart performed in Jagannath Puri every year in the summer. [Ed.]

[19]Chaitanya Vaisnavas believe that when a saint or perfected practitioner dies he or she is transported to some place in the universe where Krishna is currently carrying on his sports. This is called "manifest" sports (*prakata-lila*) because it is happening in the material universe. After playing a role in those sport in one's eternal identity the saint enters into the "unmanifest" sports (*aprakata-lila*), which take place in the non-material, eternal abode of Krishna. [Ed.]

but also toward anyone else he met. He was *chestotkuntha* --- always eager to serve just for the sake of serving. Of course, there are many people endowed with such a spirit of disinterested service in so many different fields, but Baba's spirit of service was prompted by an uncommon, loving force which did not seem to belong to this world. Although it was evident to me then that his entire being was floating in a magical, bliss-giving divine love, I was not yet ready at that time to accept him as a guide. I was entrapped, sentimentally, intellectually, mentally and physically, in the strong grip of numerous erroneous beliefs about the nature of Chaitanya Vaishnavism (and Vaishnavism in general), especially concerning its practice and the system of disciplic succession. Unfortunately, at that time I refused to recognize two correlative points: (1) the importance of the uninterrupted succession of masters and disciples and the way *bhakti* is transmitted through that system, and (2) the idea that the internal practices of Chaitanya Vaishnavism called remembering the divine sports (*lila-smarana*) and the imaginative participation in those sports as a servant (*manasa-seva*) applied not only to the liberated level (the soul's state of spiritual emancipation), but also to the conditioned state of being before that. Although aware of my misconceptions, Baba still gave me shelter, located a place for me to stay, fed me, and even nursed me during a period of sickness.

I remember that once during that time we stood on the road just near the Shri Radharaman temple and though I was harshly opposing him in some matter, a strong outburst of his spiritual emotions struck my inner being. At that moment, much to my surprise, I spontaneously told myself: "he is my guru." This thought rejoiced my heart, but just for a moment, because my invasive, stubborn reason refused to accept it. Despite such a handicap, a loving relationship developed between us and I was always very happy to be in his company. He was like the good father and I was like the bad son, but we were still linked to each other by bonds of affection. By his grace, Shri Radhakund and all the different, lovely places surrounding it always remained deeply impressed in my heart, even after I had left it.

In 1983, Baba gave shelter and granted full initiation to a twenty-three year old Croatian man, who excelled in his service to Baba. Day and night he stood ready to engage in Baba's personal service. Baba responded by calling him 'Mukunda,' after his own son. Unfortunately, only six weeks later, the man passed away after contracting malaria, on the day before Shri Krishna Janmashtami (the birthday of Krishna).

He died while offering obeisance at the feet of Baba at 1 P.M., when Radha and Krishna engage in their daily water-sports in Radhakund. Baba declared that the man must have attained Shri Radha and Krishna's eternal sports and was now waiting there for him to come and join him.[20]

In 1984 and 1985 Baba was put in charge of the distribution of the offerings of sweets (*balya-bhoga*) given to the audience at Shri Ananta Das Babaji's lectures.

In April, 1985, Baba's brother Shri Haripada Das Babaji passed away in Tala-van. In May, 1985 Baba had his own English guide book for Radhakund printed through Vidyapati Das of Singapore. In 1987, Shri Nitai Das (one of Shri Haripada Das Babaji's disciples) invited Baba to come to visit his home in Lunde (Northern Sweden), sending him a round trip airline ticket. Consequently, Baba left the Indian subcontinent on July 15 for his first and only trip abroad. He returned on September 17 of the same year.

Nine years after I first met Baba, in 1987, I came back to Radhakund motivated by an eager desire to render service to Baba and learn something more about how to cultivate the spiritual identity of a *manjari* of Shri Radha.[21] The month of Kartik (October-November) was in full swing and hundreds of pilgrims had arrived from Bengal to celebrate it. The main program was to listen to the three daily reading-lectures of Pandit Shri Ananta Das Baba. Krishna Das Baba always recorded those lectures and translated them for us in the evening. It was very hot as is usual during that time of year and most of the men in the audience including myself had removed their shirts. After a few days, during one of the readings I noticed that I was the only one wearing a *brahmin*'s thread[22] among all those swanlike, saintly *bhaktas* and this made

---

[20]When I came to know of his demise I was deeply moved. I had met him in Zagreb a few months before his departure for India and he told me while bidding me farewell: "You will not see me again in this life. I am now going to Vraja-mandal and will not return." I responded to him: "What are you saying? Of course we shall meet each other again." He gravely replied: "No! I know that when I reach there I shall not come back and shall leave my body this year." It is noteworthy that he arrived in Delhi with only a one-way air ticket and had his name changed officially into `Vrindavan.'

[21]See the discussion of the *manjari* identity in the glossary.

[22]Certain modern Chaitanya Vaishnava groups believe in giving the *brahma-gayatri* and the sacred thread to initiates at the time of their initiations. In Hindu social custom the sacred thread and the *brahma-gayatri* are given to male members of the top three classes of the Hindu caste system as an initiation into the study of the Vedas and the performance of Vedic rites. Mainstream Chaitanya Vaishnavism disagrees with this practice and only

me feel rather embarrassed. Over the following days my uneasiness increased to such an extent that my reason dictated that I should take off that *brahmin*'s thread. I thought to myself: "After all, I wasn't born in a brahmin family. Why should I wear its insignia?"

One morning, after having attended the reading, I stopped in front of the Shri Bankebihariji temple, bowed down to Shri Radhakund, sprinkled the usual three drops of water in my mouth, and then deposited my *brahmin*'s thread as an offering to Shri Radhakund. After that I felt the heavy load of my false pride, symbolized by that thread, lifted from my shoulders. The power of Shri Radhakund, Baba, and the assembled Vaishnavas had exorcized an infernal "spirit" from me. The next day Baba conveyed to me Pandit Ananta Das Baba's congratulations for my act. Since I used to sit near him during his lecture, he noticed that the "false *brahmin*'s pride" had disappeared from my chest.

I did not have any intention of receiving *mantra* initiation from Baba, because I still mistakenly thought of myself as already initiated by another guru. Nevertheless, I felt like surrendering to him, serving him closely, and learning from him the things related to the *manjari* practice. Though I did not tell him anything of my intentions, somehow he understood them, and one day to my surprise and great satisfaction, he asked me to help him by accompanying him to the toilet during the night and by drawing water from the well for his wash afterwards. To my even greater satisfaction he told me that I could sleep on the floor in his room.

Although I had come so close to Baba then, I felt somehow disconnected from him. Despite our mutual affection and the compatibility of our characters, I sensed that something was missing, something necessary for there to be a real, complete relationship with him. Although his two disciples were not as intimate with him as I, I noticed the presence of a very special, supernaturally personal link between them and Baba, which I did not have and which intrigued me.

At one point, feeling more and more the presence of this inexplicable gulf between us, I asked Baba if he would give me a new string of beads on which to chant the holy names after first blessing it by chanting

---

gives the tradition's Vaishnava *mantras* during the initiation process. It is believed that initiation into Vaishnavism moves one beyond those mundane forms of self-identification, intimately connected with status in the social hierarchy, to a whole new order of being. The author at the time of his meeting with and acceptance as a disciple by Krishna Das Baba belonged to one of those groups. [Ed.]

on it himself. His reply was a categorical no. He pointed out that I already had received the holy names from another guru and that it was not necessary that he should also give them to me. Although I insisted, Baba would not change his mind, leaving me speechless and in complete despair.

Few days later, Pandit Ananta Das Babaji was about to start his usual reading in the Shri Radharaman temple. Before sitting down in the audience, I hung my bead bag on a clothes line above my head, after completing the round I was chanting. When the reading was over, I stood up to take my bead bag, but to my great surprise it was empty; my beads had disappeared. Puzzled, I searched everywhere in the courtyard, but without success. I immediately excluded the possibility that someone from the assembly had taken them, because, firstly, I refused to believe that a devotee would be interested in stealing the beads of another devotee and, secondly, I had been sitting right under the bag. If someone had taken them I would have noticed. Rather than upsetting me, however, this incident kind of pleased me, because now I had a good reason to ask Baba for a new string of beads.

I told Baba what had happened and said: "You see Baba! Now you should give me a new string of beads and bless it by chanting on it. Otherwise, how can I continue reciting the holy names?" In this way Baba gave me a new string of beads. His mercy did not stop there, however. Some time later, during a morning circumambulation of Shri Radhakund, he stopped and told me, with tears of spiritual joy in the eyes: "I was looking for a name for you and the name *karunya-ghana-vigraha* came to my mind. It is a name of Shri Radha which means that she is the embodiment of concentrated compassion. She is so full of grace! In his *Shri-radhastottara-shata-nama-stotra* (Hymn of One Hundred and Eight Names of Shri Radha), Shri Raghunath Das Goswami has named Shri Radha *karuna-vidravad-deha* or one whose body melts out of compassion. So, henceforth you shall have the name Karunya-ghana-vigraha Das." Due to the length of this name, Baba later changed it to Karunamayi Das which basically means the same thing.

Baba's grace did not stop there, however, and towards the end of Niyama-seva,[23] he announced to my great surprise that if I consented he would give me *mantra* initiation. I was moved, although I still thought of myself as the disciple of another who was both my path-showing guru

[23]A month-long set of austerities observed during the month of Kartik (October-November).

and my holy name guru. I still mistakenly believed him to be my *mantra* initiation guru. My opposition to the idea was only fleeting, however, because after seeing Baba so enthusiastic to give me initiation, I agreed, not wanting to hurt his feelings by refusing. So at a moment chosen as auspicious, the morning of the 5th of November, Baba gave me the Krishna initiation-*mantra* together with the other initiation-*mantras*. He also explained to me their different meanings and how to conduct worship of Shri Mahaprabhu (Shri Krishna Chaitanya, Lord Gauranga) and Shri Radha and Krishna. He also revealed to me the names of his line of gurus going back to Shri Narottam Das Thakur,[24] together with their spiritual identities, both in the world of Shri Gaur and in the world of Shri Radha and Krishna. I was then officially and spiritually affiliated with that great lineage.

I have to confess that only after initiation by Baba did I begin to understand that proper initiation into an authentic line of initiation-mantra transmission was not just a formality. It is God's created system, widely prevalent in India, through which *bhakti* as cultivation or practice makes her appearance in one who is a candidate for divine love (*prema-bhakti*).

Later Baba's grace extended to the point of revealing to me the details of my own eternal accomplished nature (*siddha-svarupa*) as a *manjari*, revealing to me the eleven essential details of that identity.[25] He also taught me his guru's manual for the practice of remembering the divine sport of Shri Gaur and Govinda and the nature of my own eternal service to them in that accomplished identity. The next step is to advance through the different stages of this practice and ultimately to pass beyond this mundane world by being blessed with the divine love characteristic of a *manjari* of Shri Radha.

When I acted as Baba's servant, we used to visit different saints together, saints from whom Baba wanted me to receive blessings by bowing down to them in full devotional surrender. A few times we visited the saint Shrila Manohar Das Babaji of Manasa Ganga (at the town of Govardhan), who was said to be at that time about 130 years old. The

---

[24]Shri Narottam Das Thakur was a great *bhakta* of the 16th century who wrote many songs in Bengali and helped spread the writings of the Goswamis of Vrindavan in Bengal.

[25]The eleven details of the accomplished identity are: name, form, age, type of dress, relationship, group, permission, service, highest goal, protected servant, and residence. These are given in the text of Shri Gopala-guru Goswami (16th century) called the *Shri-gaura-govindarchana-smarana-paddhati*.

saint was always lying on his bed, perfectly absorbed in contemplation of and service in Shri Gaur and Govinda's sports. Baba said that this saint had been living in Vraja for nearly ninety years, out of which he had spent fifty years acting as a priest for the Shri Gaur and Nitai and other images in the temple on the immediate right side of Shri Sanatan Goswami's meditation hut at Chakleshvara Mahadeva. We also went to see Shri Govinda Gopala Goswami, the middle son of the illustrious Shri Ananda Gopala Goswami, at his house at Pattharpura in Vrindavan. Once Baba took me to Kamya-van, where we visited the image of Vrinda Devi. We also went outside the town to an isolated and abandoned old house overgrown and invaded by grass and vines. Baba revealed to me that it was there that the famous 19th century saint Shrila Jayakrishna Das Babaji did his private worship and that it was very important for him to have been able to come and see the place again. After staying overnight at the temple run by a son of Damodar Das, the Bengali vegetable and fruit-seller at Shri Radhakund, and after buying two earthen cooking pots, we went back to the Shri Radharaman temple the next day.

No matter where Baba spent the night, his morning private worship, accompanied with his usual loud chanting (*kirtan*) of prayers, went on undisturbed. This always made me feel spiritually protected and empowered to continue my own humble service to him and in my leisure time, my own private worship of their Lordships. I felt like a dependent baby who received his sole nourishment from his mother. His words were always full of a love that showered my whole being and dissipated whatever doubts arose in me. His company was so delectable that it was never enough to be with him, and when it happened that fate separated us even for a short period, my heart instinctively yearned for the lost pleasure of his association.

In 1988, Baba took me and a few of his other disciples to spend three days and nights at Barsana during the Holi festival. On another occasion we went with him to the hilltop of Barsana where Ram Baba, a local saint, sang the whole of the *Shri Radha-rasa-sudha-nidhi* for us, accompanying himself with a harmonium. In the same year we were also invited to the memorial festival of a holy man held at a Gaudiya Vaishnava temple with uninterrupted *kirtan* of the holy name. The temple was located near the Pucchari ka Lotha temple at the base of Mount Govardhan and we had an opportunity to meet the saint Shri Kishori Das Babaji of Kalidaha in Vrindavan. When in Vrindavan Baba always had a special interest in visiting the sacred image Shri Radharaman, taking into consideration that, together with Shri Vrinda Devi of Kamyavan and Shri Radhadamodar of Vrindavan, they were the only images installed by the six Goswamis still present in Vraja. A few times we also visited Tala-van where Baba's brother engaged in his private worship, Suryakund, Nandagram, Yavat, Sanket and Ranabari where we attended the annual festival held by the Vrajavasis of the village on the disappearance anniversary of the 19th century saint Shri Krishna Das Babaji.

On December 30, 1988, after climbing on the roof-terrace of the Shri Radharaman temple, Baba tripped and due to his osteoporosis fractured the neck of his right thighbone. He was then carried down the narrow spiraling staircase with great difficulty and driven by car to the Ramakrishna Mission Hospital in Vrindavan.

Before agreeing to the surgical operation that he was to undergo, he sent me to Delhi to see Swami Nathan, a naturopathic doctor of the Lakshman Sharma School, and ask his advice. In June, July and August of 1985, Swami Nathan had hospitalized Baba as a `free of charge holy man (*sadhu*)' at the Naturopathic Clinic in the South Indian town of Puddukottai for the rheumatic disorders of the finger joints of his left hand and of his knee joints. Baba improved so much that when he returned to Shri Radhakund he could fully close his hand and almost crouch down to his heels, things he could only half do previously. Thus, Baba trusted him because of his competence and because there were bonds of friendship between them. Baba also recognized Swami Nathan as a saint, although his conception of God was apparently impersonal, and Baba's conception of deity was that of Supreme Person in his sweet, human-like aspect.[26]

When I related to Swami Nathan what had happened to Baba he became deeply troubled. After receiving his instructions for Baba's care, I returned that same day to the Ramakrishna Mission Hospital. The injury was grave and since Baba refused to take any pain-killers, he depended on my massage for some relief. He was practically always

---

[26]Bhagavan, or the Supreme Person, is the basic spiritual reality behind the *brahmajyoti*, the light of Brahman, which is said to be his bodily effulgence and which is realized by those who pursue spiritual knowledge (the *jnanis*). He is also the basis of the Supreme Self (*paramatman*), also known as Vishnu, an expansion of the Supreme Person who oversees the material worlds and who is realized by the practitioners of yoga (the *yogis*). The Supreme Person is also the source of innumerable other forms abiding in the spiritual world who are realized by their respective votaries.

awake. During the night he used to wake me up every couple of hours, asking me to massage his leg. We remained there in that condition for twelve days and after making arrangements with the prime physician of the Methodist Hospital at Mathura for Baba to be transferred there and to be operated on there, I hired a taxi and we went to the Mathura hospital. In the new hospital the accommodations were much better, except for the food, which I had to bring in from outside. In the previous hospital the cook was a Gaudiya Vaishnava known to Baba, so we were fortunate to get cooked food offered to Shri Radha and Krishna as their grace (*prasad*). Baba mainly used to eat raw fruits and salads, however, which I procured for him from the market. All the nurses who were from Baba's native state of Kerala were surprised and impressed to have among them someone who was `one of their own' and who was so uncommonly kind-hearted and accommodating, despite his precarious physical condition. Although he had almost forgotten his mother-tongue, he still spoke with them in Malayalam and they were pleased.

Baba was operated on the day after his arrival. Since the superior crown of his thigh bone was broken and detached, it had to be fixed in place with a pin. The intervention was supposed to last only an hour, but it instead it took almost three hours. While the operation was under way, Govinda Das and I, out of concern for Baba, went to propitiate the guardian and protector of the holy land (*dhama*), Lord Shiva, in the nearby Gokarna Mahadeva temple. Some time after we returned one of the surgeons came out of the operating arena and announced to our great relief that the operation had been successful. When Baba was transferred to the emergency room he was still under the effect of the anesthesia and although still unconscious he was repeating in a spiritual absorption: "Radhe Go!....Radhe Go!" to the astonishment of the anxious nurses. When Baba started calling out someone's name and muttering indistinctly some other words which they could not understand, the nurses asked Govinda Das to enter. He returned to take me in and when I came into Baba's presence, with his eyes still closed, he was softly repeating: "Radhe Go! Karunya! I can't swallow! Give me some water!" I started to give him a little water, letting him take only small sips. After a few days Baba was moved back to his private room where I too stayed to continue giving him assistance.

One month later, Baba returned by ambulance to the Shri Radharaman temple at Shri Radhakund. Since his leg did not recover properly, he remained bedridden for the rest of his life, his only alternative being sitting up uncomfortably during spiritual discourses, his bath, and his meals. Baba took this trial as Shri Radha's grace. He said that already in 1965 the superior crown of his left leg had been broken, creating for him great difficulty in walking afterwards. Now, exactly the same thing had happened with his right leg and thus he was unable to walk any longer. He saw and felt it as Shri Radha's blissful arrangement for him to remain at Shri Radhakund for the rest of his life and to allow him to leave his body there. He also told me that Shri Radha was making him suffer all the remainder of his bad karma in one fell swoop and that it was a terrible ordeal for him and also for me. A few years later he told me in a confidence that if he was able to tolerate this awkward invalidity, it was only because the Lord was personally present in him, otherwise it would have been impossible for him to do it.

In 1991, the owner of the Radharaman temple evicted Baba's images from their room. That prompted Baba to say that if the owner was chasing his images out he was chasing him out also. Baba consequently moved to a house at Gopi Kuwa near Shyamakund, until he returned to Radharaman temple on January 6, 1992. While at Gopi Kuwa, Govinda Dasi had a dream in which she saw Shri Radha circumambulating Baba to give him protection just as Krishna protected Maharaja Parikshit in the womb of his mother.

In 1995 Baba blessed the community of Western Vaishnavas, disciples and non-disciples alike, by spreading the powerful teachings on the nature of the guru of Shri Shukadeva Goswami of Calcutta and of Pandit Shri Ananta Das Babaji of Shri Radhakund. He sent their respective booklets on the subject to be translated into English, thus dispelling all doubts about the principle of the guru, boosting and even saving the spiritual and devotional lives of many.

On the First of June, 1996, Baba became so sick that he was unable to talk until the 15th of June. His sickness went on for nearly two months and became so critical that he was close to passing away. However, just before the 16th of July, Shri Radha appeared to him and told him to wait a little longer. On November 30, 1996, at 4:30 P.M., Padma Ma, Baba's cook and *pujari*,[27] passed away.

In November, 1997, after my wife and I booked our tickets for India, my father-in-law ended up in a desperate condition due to bone-marrow

[27] A *pujari* is a person who has the responsibility of performing the ritual worship of a sacred image or images. [Ed.]

cancer. Already a few times this terrible disease had perforated the bones of his arm and shoulder, but this time the x-rays showed that the bones of the pelvis were cracking. He was suffering unbearable pain and he became paralyzed. My mother-in-law was desperate as the doctor told her that there was no cure and that he would pass away soon. Hence, I immediately phoned Shri Radhakund to inform Baba of the situation and to tell him that we could not come to visit him as planned. The next day in the evening, my father-in-law suddenly got up from bed and went out of his hospital room for a walk. The nurses immediately brought him back to his bed. The following day early in the morning he got up again, unchecked by anyone, and wandered about freely throughout the hospital's corridors in a kind of trance for nearly two hours. His attending physician was flabbergasted and sent him back home the next day, saying that it was a miracle. After this incident my father- and mother-in-law became faithful and started to chant the holy names of Radha and Krishna and to sprinkle a few drops of Radhakund water on their heads daily, on Baba's recommendation. Since then, by Baba's grace, my father-in-law's health has been good. Later, my father-in-law revealed to me privately, that while wandering in trance in the corridors of the hospital, he saw himself dressed in a very elegant and costly feminine attire, strolling in a green country side with orchards, flowers. He said that he was feeling at home, thinking it to be his native place.

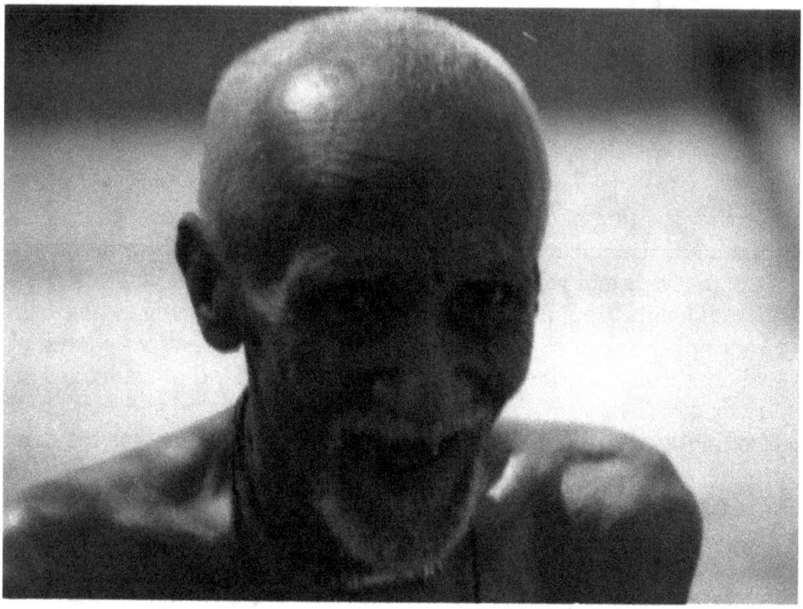

In December, 1998, Baba's own physical condition again became very bad and it deteriorated day after day. He was no longer able to talk or write and his body became cold. During the last fifteen days of his life he stopped eating, accepting only a little of the foot wash of the sacred images (*charanamrita*). On the 20th of December, he told Govinda Das that the days up to his disappearance were now numbered and three days later everyone was astonished to hear him ecstatically lecturing in English on topics relating to Shri Radha and Krishna for the whole day and night. The following three days and nights he chanted the Hare Krishna *maha-mantra* continuously while counting it on his fingers, without getting any sleep. On Sunday the 27th Govinda Das came at 7 P.M. and at his request placed a little Shri Radhakund water in his mouth. Baba then requested Govinda Dasi Ma to bring Harimohan Das Babaji who, feeling that Baba was going to leave, immediately came and started to chant `Radhe Radhe' and `Hare Krishna' before him. Baba repeated `Radhe Radhe' in full consciousness until his last breath, as he had always wished to do, and passed away at 7:15 P.M., thus joining Shri Gaur and Govinda's manifest sports in loyal adherence to Shri

Radha as one of her beloved *manjaris*.

1.1 The Holy Land

Questioned by the sage Narada on the truth about Vrindavan, that consists of twelve forests, Shri Krishna answered:

> *idam vrindavanam ramyam mama dhamaiva kevalam*
> *atra ye pashavah pakshi-mrigah kita-naramarah*
> *ye vasanti mamadhishne mrita yanti mamalayam*[28]
>
> Narada! This Vrindavan is most charming and is my only abode. All the animals, birds, deers, trees, insects, humans and gods who reside here attain my abode after leaving their bodies.

Moreover, Shrila Raghunath Das Goswami has glorified even more the uncommon excellence of leaving one's body on the bank of Shri Radhakund:

> *vrajotpanna-kshirashana-vasana-patradibhir aham*
> *padarthair nirvahya-vyavahritim adambham saniyamah*
> *vasamisha-kunde giri-kula-vare chaiva samaye*
> *marishye tu preshthe sarasi khalu jivadi-puratah*[29]
>
> Free from pride I will reside only at Radhakund and at the base of Govardhan, drinking milk from Vraja, using food, clothes, plates, and other articles from Vraja. In time, I will leave my body at the best of ponds in the presence of Shri Jiva Goswami and the others.
>
> *pura premodrekaih pratipada-navananda-madhuraih*
> *krita-shri-gandharvacyuta-charana-varyarchana-balat*
> *nikamam svaminyah priyatara-saras-tira-bhuvane*
> *vasanti sphita ye ta iha mama jivatava ime*[30]

---

[28] *Brihad-gautamiya Tantra.*

[29] Shri Raghunath Das Goswami, *Sva-niyama-dashaka*, 9.

[30] Shri Raghunath Das Goswami, *Vraja-vilasa-stava*, 101.

Because of having worshiped the beautiful lotus feet of Shri Gandharva (Radha) and Achyuta (Krishna) with the ever-fresh sweetness of pure spiritual love in their previous lives, some great souls, rich in love, are able to live on the bank of Swamini's (Radha's) dear-most pond (Shri Radhakund). These great devotees are my life and soul!

shri-vrinda-vipinam suramyam api tach-chriman sa govardhanah
sa rasa-sthalikapy alam rasamayi kim tavad anya-sthalam
yasyapy amsha-lavena narhati manak-samyam mukundasya tat
pranebhyo 'py adhika-priyeva dayitam tat-kundam evashraye[31]

The delightful forest of Vrindavan, the beautiful hill Govardhan and the nectar-filled place of the Rasa dance [the Circle Dance], not to mention other places, are not equal to even a tiny part of Shri Radhakund. I take shelter of that divine pond, which is dearer to Mukunda than his own life breath.

[31] ibid., 53.

Chapter 2

Teachings and Practices (I)

2.1 Baba's Favorite Recitations

Baba's specialty was his strikingly beautiful fixation on Shri Radha in the pure, sweet feeling of a *manjari*. His favorite book was Shri Raghunath Das Goswami's *Vilapa-kusumanjali* (Handful of Flower-like Laments), which he completely memorized and loudly recited daily during his early morning prayers. He also recited from memory the *Radhashtottara-shata-nama Stotra* (The Hymn of One Hundred and Eight Names of Radha) by the same author, the first fifty verses of Shri Prabodhananda Saraswati's *Radha-rasa-sudha-nidhi* (Ocean of the Nectar of Radha's Rapture) and many other verses from other books. He started in this way:

Jaya Guru-dev Shri Guru-dev!
Jaya Guru-dev Shri Guru-dev!
Jaya Guru-dev Shri Guru-dev!
Jaya Guru-dev Shri Guru-dev!

Nitai Gaura Sitanath, Nitai Gaura Sitanath!
Nitai Gaura Sitanath, Nitai Gaura Sitanath!
Nitai Gaura Sitanath, Nitai Gaura Sitanath!
Nitai Gaura Sitanath, Nitai Gaura Sitanath!

Gaura Gaura Gaura Gaura
Gaura Gaura Gaura Gaura he!
Gaura Gaura Gaura Gaura
Gaura Gaura Gaura Gaura raksha mam [Keep me safe]!
Gaura Gaura Gaura Gaura
Gaura Gaura Gaura Gaura pahi mam [Protect me]!

Radha Krishna Radha Krishna!
Radha Krishna Radha Krishna!
Radha Krishna Radha Krishna!
Radha Krishna Radha!

He also recited many times two verses from Shri Raghunath Das Goswami's *Stavavali* (Garland of Praises):

radheti nama nava-sundara-sidhu-mugdham
krishneti nama madhuradbhuta-gadha-dugdham
sarva-kshanam surabhi-raga-himena ramyam
kritva tad eva piba me rasane kshudharte[1]

Thirsty tongue! The name "Radha" is delicious, fresh, enchanting nectar and the name "Krishna is wonderfully sweet condensed milk. Making them even more delightful with the ice of fragrant, passionate love and drink them at every moment!

and

bhajami radham aravinda-netram
smarami radham madhura-smitasyam
vadami radham karunabharardram
tato mamanyasti gatir na kapi[2]

I worship lotus-eyed Radha. I remember Radha with a sweet smile on her face. I speak of Radha, who melts with compassion. I have no other shelter than her.

Then he continued with the remaining texts mentioned above. He used to say that even if we do not understand the meaning of these

[1] Raghunath Das Goswami, *Abhista-sucana*, 10.
[2] Raghunath Das Goswami, *Vishakhananda-da-stotra*, 131.

verses we should recite them with love, humility and faith, and they will reveal themselves to us in such a beautiful way that we will be struck with wonder. The reason for that is that those verses have been written by eternally perfected companions of the Lord and are thus endowed with an astonishing power. In this regard, he told the story of a South Indian Vaishnava Brahmin who, following his teacher's order, daily recited the eighteen chapters of the *Bhagavad-gita* at the Ranga-kshetra temple in South India, although his pronunciation was imperfect and he did not understand the meanings of the verses.[3] Baba told me once that although such a practice unfailingly yields the result of visions of Shri Radha and Krishna and ultimately leads to their personal appearances, no one teaches this in a straightforward way, despite the fact that Shri Krishna Das Kaviraj Goswami cleverly did so in the above story in his *Chaitanya-charitamrita*.

2.2 Shishir Kumar Ghose

Baba added that in order to get such a result, the mercy of a great-souled teacher was an absolute necessity. In this regard he narrated the story of the Vaishnava saint Shri Shishir Kumar Ghose, who at the request of his brother began to read the *Prema-bhakti-chandrika* (Moonlight of the Bhakti of Love) and the *Prarthana* (Prayers) of Shri Narottam Das Thakur and lamented because he had none of the signs of divine love for God that were promised in the book. Heeding his brother's advice to find an authentic great being as his teacher, he eagerly looked everywhere and finally found such a one in Hugli from the lineage of Shri Narottam Das who blessed him with initiation (*diksha*). As a result, he became successful not only in reading the *Prema-bhakti-chandrika* and the *Prarthana* and other scriptures (*shastras*) but also, out of divine ecstasy, in writing wonderful books explaining them. Specifically, in his last years Baba stressed the importance of those two books, saying that they were wonderful syntheses of all the books of the Six Goswamis of Vrindavan and that he wanted to hold those books on his chest when he passed away. In 1984, he himself translated them into English and later, on his request, Advaita Das translated them with Pandit Ananta Das Babaji Maharaj's commentaries. Baba thought it so important that

[3] See *Chaitanya-charitamrita*, 2.9.93-107.

he sent his own personal copies of the books to Advaita Das, in order to urge him to translate them, although other devotees told him that Advaita Das already had copies of the books.

During one of his readings of the *Shri Prema-bhakti-chandrika* Baba said: "By reading this book you are sure to get divine love for Shri Radha and Krishna, but you must read it with eagerness!"

2.3 *Bhajan*

Baba was always lovingly concerned for the spiritual well-being of those close to him who were assisting him in his invalid condition. He knew very well that without doing private worship (*bhajan*), even residing in the holy region of Vraja would not satisfy anyone. Once when he saw them absorbed in merry-making he exclaimed sadly: "If they don`t want to worship then let them not worship, but they will not be happy and will just suffer."

> *vrindavane kim athava nija-mandire va*
> *karagrihe kim athava kanakasane va*
> *aindram bhaje kim athava narakam bhajami*
> *shri-krishna-sevanam rite na sukham kadapi.*
>
> Whether I am in Vrindavan or in my home, in prison or on a golden throne, in heaven or in hell, I never have happiness without serving Shri Krishna.[4]

2.4 Dust of Vrindavan

Once Baba sent us to Gian-Gudri in Vrindavan to his friend Vinay Babu in order to get from him the new almanac. He also asked us to bring from that place a small bag of dust for him. He remarked that it was there that Uddhava Mahashay's prideful knowledge of Shri Krishna's majestic divinity (*aishvarya-jnana*) was crushed into powder by the dust of Shri Radha's feet. Baba's intention was to pass away lying on the ground with this dust sprinkled on him. Often Baba exalted the dust of Shri Radha`s feet, ecstatically reciting the following verse of Shri Prabodhananda Saraswati.

[4] Krishna Das Kaviraj, *Chaitanya-charitamrita*, ?

yo brahma-rudra-shuka-narada-bhishma-mukhyair
alakshito na sahasa purushasya tasya
sadyo vashikarana-churnam ananta-shaktim
tam radhika-charana-renum anusmarami.[5]

I constantly remember the dust of Shri Radha's feet which possesses unlimited power, able to subdue immediately the Supreme Being, Shri Krishna, who is not so easily seen even by great *bhaktas* like Brahma, Shiva, Shuka-deva, Narada and Bhishma.

2.5 Baba's Treasure

Baba had in his possession an incomparably valuable treasure: the elaborate notes taken by a *shruti-dhara*, a person who can remember and recite a text after a single hearing, named Shri Nivaran Babu. The notes were of a famous series of lectures on Shri Raghunath Das Goswami's *Vilapa-kusumanjali* (Handful of Flower-like Laments) given by the saint Shri Ananda Gopal Goswami (1897-1961 C.E.). Shri Nivaran Babu, who was a disciple of Shri Ananda Gopal Goswami, repeated what he had heard to a Bengali Goswami, who wrote it down in Bengali.[6]

In the early 1970s Pandit Shri Ananta Das Baba had begun to give lectures in Radhakund's Govindaji temple and the Vaishnavas wanted to hear the *Vilapa-kusumanjali* from him. Baba told Panditji that a Goswami in Vrindavan had the notes of Ananda Gopal Goswami's lectures on the same text that a *shruti-dhara* had recorded. That *shruti-dhara* had passed away, but now the notes were in the hands of the Goswami. Panditji went to Vrindavan and told the Goswami that he was serving the Vaishnavas at Radhakund with lectures and that hence he wanted to have the notes in his possession. The Goswami refused to give him the notes, afraid that word would get out, but he said that since Panditji came from Radhakund and was a Vaishnava, he could look at them. Panditji said: "I don't have the memory of the previous age when all could be learned from a single hearing or reading." Still, he read them but could not remember all of them. When he returned to Radhakund

[5] Shri Prabodhananda Saraswati, *Radha-rasa-sudha-nidhi*, 4.

[6] Baba reported that the text was later shown to and approved by Shri Ananda Gopal Goswami himself.

Baba asked him what had happened and Panditji said: "He will not give me the notes." Baba laughed and said: "You see, I have them with me. If you like I can read them to you. They are written in the Malayalam script."

How did Krishna Das Baba get a copy of the notes? The story goes like this. One day the same Goswami in Vrindavan left the notes outside and by chance a monkey carried them off and dropped them at the place where Krishna Das Baba's brother Haripada Das Baba resided. Haripada Das could read Bengali. The Goswami searched everywhere for the notes and eventually heard that a monkey had carried them away and dropped them at Haripada Das' place. He came to Haripada Dasji and said: "Look, please return the notebook to me. It is very dear to me. I don't loan them to anyone." Haripada Dasji replied: "If you think about it, properly speaking this notebook is now mine. I did not steal it. Why after all did the monkey bring the notebook to me? If you consider it duly, the notebook is now mine." There was nothing the Goswami could do. But Haripada Das ultimately agreed to return the notebook to him after making a copy of it. The Goswami objected: "Why should you copy it? It will be spread all over the place." Haripada Das replied: "No problem. I will copy it into the Malayalam script, a script that Bengali Vaishnavas cannot read." The Goswami said: "Good. If you copy it in the Malayalam script, I will let you copy it but not if you copy it in Bengali." So he let Krishna Das and Haripada Das copy it in the Malayalam script. Though the script is Malayalam, the language of the notes is Bengali, so there was no problem for Shri Ananta Das Baba to understand them when Krishna Das Baba read them to him. Panditji was giving readings at that time in Govindaji temple from 2:30 to 3:30 P.M. Then he would take a little rest and at 4 P.M. he would come to Krishna Das Baba and write down what he dictated. The final page of the notebook had been torn out by the monkey but was somehow reconstructed.

Baba himself said of the incident: "Our Mahant (Shri Ananta Das Babaji) heard that these notes were at Shri Vrindavan, but could not get them. So, with a broken heart he returned here to Shri Radhakund, where this humble servant informed him that the same notes were already here. When they were given to him there was a marked change in his readings and lectures. After that, he wrote commentaries first on the *Radha-rasa-sudha-nidhi* (Ocean of the Nectar of Radha's Rapture) and then on the *Vilapa-kusumanjali*, the *Stavavali* (Series of Hymns) and the *Stavamala* (Garland of Hymns)." Baba later also recorded the original notes on tape to help Advaita Das with his English translation of the *Vilapa-kusumanjali*.

Baba often praised Shrila Ananda Gopal Goswami, reminding us of his particular divine ability, during his lectures on the *Vilapa-kusumanjali*, to elevate his audience to the level of cultivating passionate *bhakti* in the identity of a *manjari*. Because of his special divine power even the disciples of the illustrious Prana Gopal Goswami used to come to hear his lectures. Once during a tape recording of Baba reading the notes from Shri Ananda Gopal Goswami's lectures on *Vilapa-kusumanjali*, he exclaimed with ecstatic eagerness and humility: "Mahaprabhu is so kind! So kind! He gave me the chance to stay at his place (Gauda-mandala-bhumi, "the land of the circle of Gauda," now known as Bengal) and after allowing me to visit many of its places, he sent me here to Shri Radhakund! Therefore, all of you please bless me so that I may always be able to read these notes on the *Vilapa-kusumanjali*, may always be able to think of them during the remainder of my life and may be able to leave my body in such a state of consciousness!" It was not uncommon during his readings for Baba to burst into tears of joy, asking for similar blessings from the members of his audience.

On another occasion when he was reading the *Vilapa-kusumanjali*, Baba remarked that even when one is envisioning oneself as a practitioner in Shri Mahaprabhu's sport, the feeling of being a *manjari* is the most important thing and is always present in one's mind with greater or lesser intensity. During complete absorption in it one completely loses one's awareness of being a practitioner in the world of Navadvip and is only absorbed in one's identity as a *manjari* in the world of Vraja.

Baba loved to read the scriptures about devotion to the Lord with commentaries on them translated or written in English. He said that it was very significant for him, because his first spiritually ecstatic experience with Mahaprabhu occurred while reading Shri Shishir Kumar Ghose's English book *Lord Gauranga*.

2.6 His Room

Baba had his small room carpeted and hung with framed paintings and pictures, the works of different artists: one of a shaven-headed Shri Mahaprabhu with begging bowl, one of his guru, Shri Sakhicharan Das

Babaji Maharaj and one of Padma Ma by Govindachandra Das. There were also paintings of Radha and Krishna, one of Makhan Chora Krishna Gopal (Krishna as a young cowherd boy stealing butter) by Asim Das, one of Shri Krishna mounting an elephant composed acrobatically by Shri Radha (whose body formed the trunk) and her eight principal girl-friends painted by Radhika Dasi, and another painting of Shri Sakhicharan Das Babaji Maharaj by Nicolas. There was also a painting of Shri Radha protecting Shri Raghunath Das Goswami from the scorching heat of the sun with her own veil, sketched by Govindachandra Das and painted by Bhaktisiddhanta Das and two framed vermilion typographies on white cloth by Charles: a huge one of Shri Mahaprabhu's bodily imprint preserved in a stone slab at the Alalanath temple in Orissa where he stretched out in full length, causing the stone to melt and leaving the impression of his body, and a small one of the footprints of the image of Shri Radha at Barsana's Larli Lal temple, also an impression made through the melting of the rock. Besides all these pictures he also had framed pictures of Shri Lokanath Goswami's sacred image named Shri Radhavinod, Shri Gopal Bhatta Goswami's image named Shri Radharaman and a few framed prints of Sital's paintings. He also kept Charles' hand-carved wooden images of Jagannath, Baladev and Subhadra on a wooden altar. Baba was most fond of all those representations.

2.7 Hope

Baba often taught us to hope against hope, even looking beyond death, for the attainment of success in achieving *prema-bhakti* or divine love in our private worship by saying: "If not in this life, it will be in the next one."

Baba's style of private worship was in fidelity with the process described in the *Gaur-govinda-lila-smarana Gutika* (Manual on the Process of Remembering the Sports of Gaur and Govinda) of Siddha Krishna Das Baba (18th century C.E.) of Govardhan. He said that to nourish this type of worship three books were essential for us: the *Govinda-lilamrita* (Immortal Sports of Govinda), the *Vilapa-kusumanjali* (Handful of Flower-like Laments) and the *Radha-rasa-sudha-nidhi* (Ocean of the Nectar of Radha's Rapture).

2.8 Cowherd Women of Vraja (*Gopis*)

Baba had a completely spiritual conception of the cowherd women of Vraja. One morning we were sitting, waiting for our turn at the Syndicate Bank of Radhakund. I saw a magazine lying on the table, with a photo of Indian ladies dressed in beautiful saris and fully decorated with make up and jeweled ornaments on its cover. I pointed it out to Baba, trying to sublimate this mundane picture into a spiritual one of the cowherd women (*gopis*) of Vraja, but Baba stopped me at once, rebuking me severely with loving anger and gravity. He said that the ladies of this material world were absolutely no comparison to the cowherd women of Vraja.

2.9 Love-in-separation (*Vipralamba*)

Baba often remarked that feelings of separation from Shri Radha and Krishna were more important for us than feelings of union with them and that Shriman Mahaprabhu and his companions taught the power of love-in-separation and gave us perfect examples of it as well. For instance, in the *Chaitanya-charitamrita* it is said:

> *ayi dina-dayardra natha he*
> *mathura-natha kadavalokyase*
> *hridayam tvad-aloka-kataram*
> *dayita bhramyati kim karomy aham*[7]
>
> [Shripada Madhavendra Puri exclaimed with his last breath]: "You who melt with compassion for the wretched! Lord! Lord of Mathura! When will I see you? My heart, aching for want of seeing you, is spinning around! Beloved! What shall I do?"
>
> *ei to shloke krishna-prema koilo upadesha*
> *krishner virahe bhakter bhava-vishesha*
>
> By this verse, [Shri Madhavendra Puri] taught mankind the nature of love of Krishna. In separation from Krishna the *bhakta* cherishes special feelings.

[7] Krishna Das Kaviraj, *Chaitanya-charitamrita*, 3.8.34-35.

2.10 Humility

Shri Krishna Das Baba's humility and tolerance were so perfect that he always considered himself fallen and even accepted mistreatment, slander, insults and disservices without protesting. Baba taught humility by telling the following story: "Once there was a guru who was approached for initiation by two boys. One boy was of a low caste and the guru said: "Never forget where you came from!" The other boy was a *brahmin* and the guru said: "Now you, you must completely forget where you came from!"

Once, when I informed Baba about the misdeeds of one *bhakta* who had previously acted as a guru, Baba gratefully replied that this devotee was his *acharya-guru* (one who teaches by example) because he has taught him by his own example the things that should not be done.

2.11 Offenses to Vaishnavas

Regarding offenses to a devotee of Vishnu and its seriously negative consequences, Baba often reminded us of the famous example of Durvasa Muni who offended Maharaj Ambarisha[8] and could only get relief from the disastrous effects by begging the pardon of the Maharaj. The Maharaj naturally forgave him. Also related to this subject are the following words of Sati-devi (Lord Shiva`s consort) which should be taken seriously:

nashcharyam etad yad asatsu sarvada
mahad-vininda kunapatma-vadishu
sershyam mahapurusha-pada-pamshubhir
nirasta-tejahshu tad eva shobhanam[9]

It is not at all strange that among evil persons, who think the corpse to be the self, there is always malicious blasphemy of the saintly. [Though the saintly tolerate their blasphemy,] the power of those persons is vanquished by the dust of the feet of those great souls. It is proper [that such evil persons reap the effects of their blasphemy].

---

[8] The story is found in the *Bhagavata Purana*, 9.4-5.

[9] *Bhagavata*, 4.4.13.

The *Chaitanya-bhagavata* gives the following warning:

> *shulapani-sama yadi bhakta-ninda kare*
> *bhagavata-pramana tathapi shighra mare*
> *sarva-maha-prayashchitta ye krishner nam*
> *vaishnavaparadhe sei name laya pran*[10]
>
> Though one may be as powerful as Shiva who holds a trident, if he blasphemes a Vaishnava, as the *Bhagavata* is our evidence, he is quickly destroyed. Although chanting Krishna`s name is the greatest of all atonements, that same name takes one's life when someone blasphemes a Vaishnava.

and in the *Bhakti-rasamrita-sindhu* (Ocean of the Nectar of Devotion) we find that:

> *bhavo 'py abhavam ayati krishna-presthaparadhatah*
> *abhasatam ca shanakair nyuna-jatiyatam api*[11]
>
> If a devotee who has been blessed with *bhava* [that is, *krishna-rati*, the budding stage of divine love], commits an offense to a dear companion of Krishna that *bhava* vanishes altogether [if the offense is serious] or [when the offense is moderately serious] it turns into a semblance [of *bhava*] or [when the offense is small] it gradually becomes a *bhava* of an inferior type [for example, friendship or parental *rati* can turn into the less intimate *rati* of a servant].

To make it clear that no type of Vaishnava should be blasphemed, Shri Vishvanath Chakravarti has written in his *Madhurya-kadambini* (Rain Cloud of Sweetness):

> *na ca "kripalur akrita-drohas titikshuh sarva-dehinam ity adi-sampurna-dharmaka eva santas tesham eva ninda aparadha ity vacyam. "sarvacara-vivarjitah shatha-dhiyo vratya jagad-vancha-kah" iti tatprakarana-vartina vacanena tadrisha-dushcharitam api bhagavantam bhajatam kaimuttika-nyayena sacchabda-vachya-tvena suchitatvat.*[12]

[10] Vrindavan Das, *Chaitanya-bhagavata.*, 2.13.386, 388.
[11] Rupa Goswami, *Bhakti-rasamrita-sindhu*, 1.3.54.
[12] Shri Vishvanath Chakravarti, *Madhurya-kadambini*, 3.2.

The *Bhagavata* (11.11.29) says that persons who are compassionate, not envious and tolerant towards all embodied beings are saintly since they strictly follow *dharma* [the Vaishnava religion]. However, one should not think from such statements that only by blaspheming them is an offense committed because in the *Padma Purana* it is stated: "Even a person who lacks all proper behavior, who is wicked, fallen and deceitful is liberated if he takes shelter of the lotus feet of Govinda." In this verse, by the application of the maxim of "how much more so" (*kaimutika-nyaya*), even ill-behaved persons who worship the Lord are also recognized as saintly.

2.12 The Residents of Vraja (*Vraja-vasis*)

Worried that I might view the residents of Vraja (Vraja-vasis) as ordinary persons and this terrestrial Vraja as part of the material creation, Baba constantly kept guardianship over me and was always greatly concerned when I associated with them too closely. In this regard Shri Prabodhananda Saraswati has given the following instructive recommendations:

svananda-sach-chid-ghana-rupata matir
yavan na vrindavana-vasi-jantusu
tavat pravisto 'pi na tatra vindate
tato 'paradhat padavim paratparam[13]

You may enter the land of Vrindavan but as long as you do not always consider all the creatures who live there as having eternal forms of concentrated bliss, being, and consciousness, you will never attain the highest goal of life [divine love].

yadaiva sach-chid-rasa-rupa-buddhir
vrindavanashtha-sthira-jangamesu
syan nirvyalikam purusas tadaiva
chakasti radha-priya-sevi-rupah[14]

[13] Prabodhananda Saraswati, *Shri Vrindavana-mahimamrita*, 17.83.
[14] ibid., 17.84.

> When an offenseless person begins to consider all the moving and non-moving creatures of Vrindavan as endowed with eternal forms full of being, consciousness, and delight, that person's eternal accomplished form of a cowherd girl who is a dear friend and servant of Shri Radha, appears.

> *parasva-steyaika-vyasanam api nityam paravadhu-*
> *prasaktam visvesam ahaha bahudha himsakam api*
> *duracharam lobhady-upahatam api bhratar arunam*
> *divandhas tam vrindavana-gata-janam navaganayeh*[15]

> Brother [my mind]! A resident of Vrindavan may be attached to another man's wife or only be interested in stealing someone else's property. Sadly, he may commit many acts of violence on everyone and he may be misbehaved and overwhelmed by greed and the rest. Still, you should not in any way disrespect him [considering him to be an ordinary sinner]. If you do so, you are like an owl who cannot appreciate the rays of the rising sun.

> *sad-yogindra-sudrisya-sandra-rasadanandaika-san-murtayah*
> *sarve 'py adbhuta-sanmahimni madhure vrindavane sangatah*
> *ye krura api papino na cha satam sambhasya-drisyash cha ye*
> *sarvan vastutaya nirikshya parama-svaradhya-buddhir mama*[16]

> Although the saintly are not to see or speak with cruel and sinful persons, when I see such persons gathered in the astonishing, glorious, sweet, eternal Vrindavan I think of them as most honorable, as veritable kings of the mystics with handsome, eternal forms of intense bliss and delight.

One time Baba was moved to tears while recalling how his brother Shri Haripada Das Babaji went into raptures over some Vraja-vasi votaries of Shri Ram whom they venerated as Narayan (God). Their customary practice was to worship first Shri Sita and Ram and then show the offered items with affection to their Giriraj Shilas (stones from Mount Govardhan) which were placed on the Tulasi (Sacred Basil) pedestals

[15] ibid., 17.47.
[16] Prabodhananda Saraswati, *Radha-rasa-sudha-nidhi*, 265.

in their courtyards. Having noticed their way of doing this, Shri Haripada Das Babaji started to wonder why, being Vraja-vasis, they were not offering *puja* (ritual worship) to Shri Radha and Krishna, who are the supreme male and female persons. Instead, they only gave them items offered already to Shri Sita and Rama? It did not take a long time for him to discover that these Vraja-vasis, though showing an inherent loving attachment to Shri Radha and Krishna and their sports, did not consider them to be God. For them God was Shri Rama and Krishna was just their local heroic celebrity whom they loved with all their hearts. Although Baba quoted them numerous proofs from *Bhagavata Purana* demonstrating that Krishna was God, they replied to him that the same book mentioned very clearly that the Vraja-vasis worshiped Krishna as their dear master, friend, son and lover but never as God. So they too, as heirs of that tradition, were following their ancestors by doing the same thing.

The encounter with the local Vraja-vasis' deeply rooted, natural inclination to loving Shri Radha and Krishna in the tradition of the Vraja-vasis of old thrilled Shri Haripada Das Babaji, and, when he realized their elevated status in *bhakti*, he began to weep uncontrollably.

vraja-loker bhave pai tanhara charan
tanre ishvara kori nahi jane vraja-jan
keho tanre putra-jnane udukhale bandhe
keho tanre sakha-jnane jini chore kandhe
vrajendranandana tanre jane vraja-jan
aishvarya-jnana nahi nija sambandha-manan
vraja-loker bhave yei koraye bhajan
sei jana pai vraje vrajendranandan[17]

By the feelings of the Vraja-vasi one attains Shri Krishna's lotus feet. The people of Vraja do not think of him as God. Some, thinking him their son, bind him to a grinding mortar. Others, beating him in games, climb on his shoulders, considering him a friend. The people of Vraja consider him to be the son of the leader of Vraja. They have no awareness of his divine opulence. They consider him related to themselves. Anyone who worships Krishna according to the

[17]Krishna Das Kaviraj, *Chaitanya-charitamrita*, 2.9.118-121.

feelings of the Vraja-vasis will attain Krishna, the son of the leader of Vraja, in Vraja.[18]

raga-bhaktye vraje svayam bhagavan pay
vaidhi-bhaktye parshada-dehe vaikunthe yay[19]

By the path of passionate *bhakti*, [following that of the inhabitants of Vraja, who do not consider Krishna to be the Supreme Person and who love him instead in various intimate relationships,] one attains the Supreme Person himself in Vraja [as the son of its communal leader, Nanda]. However, by rule-driven *bhakti* one [who thus considers him to be the Supreme Person and who worships him accordingly] will go to Vaikuntha taking a body as one of his companions.

tatra vidhi-margena radha-krishnayor bhajane maha-vaikuntha-stha-goloke khalv avivikta-svakiya-parakiya-bhavam aishvarya-jnanam prapnoti. madhura-bhava-lobhitve sati vidhi-margena bhajane dvarakayam shri-radha-satyabhamayor aikyat satya-bhama-parikaratvena svakiya-bhavam aishvarya-jnana-mishra-madhurya-jnanam prapnoti. raga-margena bhajane vrajabhumau shri-radha-parikaratvena parakiya-bhavam shuddha-madhurya-jnanam prapnoti[20]

If one worships Shri Radha and Krishna through the path of rules and injunctions (*vaidhi-bhakti*) one attains awareness of their divine opulence, in which there is no distinction between extramarital and marital conceits, in the Goloka region that is situated in the majestic Vaikuntha. If one longs for an amorous relationship with Krishna but follows only the path of rules and injunctions (*vaidhi-bhakti*), one will attain awareness of sweetness mixed with knowledge of divine opulence invested with feelings of marital love as a companion of Satyabhama in Dvaraka, since Shri Radha and Satyabhama are identical. If one only worships on the

[18]See also Cc., 3.7.23: *aishvarya-jnane nahi pay vraje vrajendranandan.*
[19]ibid., 2.24.61.
[20]Vishvanath Chakravartin, *Raga-vartma-chandrika* (Moonlight on the Path of Passion), 2.6.

path of passion in the form of amorous desire (*kamarupa-raganuga-bhakti*), then one attains awareness of pure sweetness invested with feelings of extramarital love as a companion of Shri Radha in Vraja-bhumi.

2.13 The *Manjari* Identity

Regarding the *manjari*'s permanent feeling of love (*sthayi-bhava*) pursued in the practice of passionate *bhakti* by those wishing to cultivate the identity of a *manjari*, Baba very clearly taught us that in no case do *manjaris* have sexual relations with Krishna since this trait is what distinguishes them from the other girlfriends (*sakhi*) of Radha. Such staunch loyalty to Shri Radha, devoid of rivalry with her, enables them to render the most intimate kinds of service to Shri Radha and Krishna, get unique favors from their mistress, and taste the highest spiritual bliss. Those things are inaccessible to any other kind of girlfriend.

siddhasya lakshanam yat syat sadhanam sadhakasya tat[21]

The characteristics of an accomplished (*siddha*) devotee become the practices of a devotee in training (*sadhaka*).

sanchari syat samano na va krishna-ratyah suhrid-ratih
adhika pushyamana ced bhavollasa itiryate[22]

When the girlfriends' love for Radha is equal to or less than their love for Krishna, their love is counted as a transient feeling [*sanchari-bhava*] of their permanent emotion, which is love for Krishna (*krishna-rati*). But if their love for Radha is greater than their love for Krishna and it is nourished, it is "love that delights in their [Radha and Krishna's] feelings [*tad-tad-bhavollasa-rati*]."

tambularpana-pada-mardana-payo-danabhisaradibhir
vrindaranya-maheshvarim priyataya yas toshayanti priyah

[21]Sanatan Goswami, comm. on his *Brihad-bhagavatamrita*, 2.3.167.
[22]Rupa Goswami, *Bhakti-rasamrita-sindhu*, 2.5.18.

prana-preshtha-sakhi-kulad api kilasankocita bhumikah
keli-bhumishu rupa-manjari-mukhas ta dasikah samshraye[23]

I seek shelter in Shri Radhika's *manjari* servants headed by Rupa Manjari. They serve the Divine Couple by offering them betel leaves, massaging their feet, offering them water and making possible their secret meetings. Because these servants are even more dear to Vrindavan's great queen, Shri Radha, than her other girlfriends, like Lalita and Vishakha, who are dearer to her than her very life, they are not at all shy or embarrassed before the lovers in their meeting places.

sva-mukhan man-mukhe devi kada tambula-charvitam
snehat sarva-disho vikshya samaye tvam pradasyasi[24]

O splendid girl! When will you affectionately give me, from your own mouth, your chewed betel nut, looking around in all directions [to be sure that no one unintended notices]?

ananya-shri-radha-pada-kamala-dasyaika-rasadhir
hareh sange rangam svapana-samaye napi dadhati
balat krishna-kurpasaka-bhidi kim apy acharati kapy
udashrur meveti pralapati mamatma cha hasati[25]

The *manjaris*' minds are filled with the sole pleasure of serving the lotus-like feet of Shri Radha and they do not even dream of making love with Hari [not to speak of actually doing it]. When Krishna tugs [jokingly] at someone's blouse she tearfully cries out: "No, no!" Shri Radha watches the fun and laughs.

tvaya yad upabhujyate murajid-anga-sange sukham
tad eva bahu janati svayam avaptitah shuddha-dhih
maya krita-vilobhana 'py adhika-chaturi-charyaya
kadapi mani-manjari na kurute 'bhisara-spriham[26]

---

[23] Raghunath Das Goswami, *Vraja-vilasa-stava*, 38.
[24] Raghunath Das Goswami, *Vilapa-kusumanjali*, 93.
[25] Prabodhananda Saraswati, *Vrindavana-mahimamrita*, 16.94.
[26] Rupa Goswami, *Ujjvala-nilamani*, 8.89.

[One of Radha's girlfriends tells her:] Radha! Mani-manjari finds more happiness in your meetings with Krishna than in her own! How pure her mind is! Although I cleverly tried to tempt her in so many ways to go to meet Krishna [for love-making] she did not do it, since she never desires such a thing.

bakaripu-parirambhasvada-vancha-viraktim
vratam iva sakhi kartri svali-saukhyaika-trishna
phalam alabhata kasturyadir alih sakhinam
harivana-vararajye sinchate tam yad adya[27]

Friends like Kasturi-manjari and others, who seem to have made a religious vow of giving up the desire to enjoy the embraces of the Enemy of Baka [Krishna], desiring only the pleasure of their friend [Radha in her meetings with Krishna and who arrange for those], have obtained the result of that vow in this great forest kingdom of Hari [Vrindavan], since now they sprinkle [anoint] her!

yadyapi sakhyo hi sva-sva-yutheshvarinam shri-radhadinam eva shri-krishnanga-sanga-sukhena sukhinyah na tu svasam, tad api tah samanyato dvidha bhavati prema-saundarya-vaidagdhyadinam adhikyena shri-krishnasyati-lobhaniya-gatryas tesham nyunatvena tasyanati-lobhaniya-gatryash cha. tatra purvah shri-krishna-sukhanurodhat tata eva sva-yutheshvarinam apy agrahadhikyach cha kadachit shri-krishnanga-sanga-sprihavatyo 'pi bhavanti, tash cha lalitadyah parama-preshtha-sakhyadayah. uttaras tu tad dvayabhavat kadapi krishnanga-sanga-sprihavatyo na bhavanti, tash ca kasturyadayo nitya-sakhyah[28]

Although the girlfriends are satisfied with the pleasures their leaders, like Shri Radha and others, have in intimate contact with Shri Krishna's body and do not desire such pleasures with him for themselves, still we can generally distinguish two varieties among them. The first girlfriends have bodies that are attractive to Shri Krishna because of their greater

[27] Jiva Goswami`s *Madhava-mahotsava*, 7.131.

[28] Vishvanath Chakravarti, *Ananda-chandrika* on Rupa Goswami's *Ujjvala-nilamani*, 2.15.

love for him, greater beauty, greater cleverness, and so forth. The second girlfriends have bodies that are less attractive to him than the first girlfriends. The first girlfriends, because of being requested by Krishna and because of greater eagerness on the parts of their leaders, desire intimate physical contact with Krishna. They are Lalita and the other dearest girlfriends. The second girlfriends, because of not having those two encouragements, do not desire intimate physical contact with Krishna. They are the eternal girlfriends (*nitya-sakhi*) or the *manjaris* like Kasturi and others.

ye yatha mam prapadyante tams tathaiva bhajamy aham
mama vartmanuvartante manushyah partha sarvashah[29]

Partha! I reciprocate the worship of my devotees in the very way they surrender unto me. Human beings follow my path in all respects.

2.14 Sakhicharan Das Baba and his Bead-bag

While talking about the glorious accomplishments in private worship of his initiation and renunciation guru, Shri Sakhicharan Das Babaji Maharaj, Baba mentioned that on the rare occasions when his guru-deva put his bead-bag aside, his reciting and counting of the Hare Krishna *maha-mantra* on the beads continued automatically and anyone present could clearly hear the beads moving by themselves in the bag. At another time he said that when Shri Radha once came to Sakhicharan Das Babaji she gave him the service of preparing *kheer*, a sweet pudding made of milk, rice, and sugar. Baba also said that Sakhicharan Das Baba was very fond of verse seventy-five of the *Radha-rasa-sudha-nidhi*, which he always used to repeat.

gaurange mradima smite madhurima netranchale draghima
vakshoje garima tathaiva tanima madhye gatau mandima
shronyam cha prathima bhruvoh kutilima bimbadhare shonima
shri-radhe hridi te rasena jadima dhyane 'stu me gocharah[30]

[29] *Bhagavad-gita*, 4.11.
[30] Prabodhananda Saraswati, *Radha-rasa-sudha-nidhi*, 75.

> Shri Radha! May the softness of your golden body, the sweetness of your smile, the wideness of your eyes, the heaviness of your breasts, the slimness of your waist, the slowness of your gait, the broadness of your hips, the crookedness of your eyebrows, the redness of your cherry-lips and the stillness of your heart saturated with *rasa*, be present in my meditation.

Baba remarked also that in the last years of his earthly life a quarter of a liter of milk boiled with some tapioca was Sakhicharan Das Baba's only daily meal.

2.15 Chanting the Holy Names

I once asked Baba about counting the holy names while repeating them. He ecstatically narrated the following story from *Chaitanya-bhagavata*:

> Once Mahaprabhu announced to his devotees that he would only accept invitations to eat from those who were *lakh-patis*.[31] Many of those devotees told the Lord: "We are sorry, but we do not have so much money. Therefore, we cannot invite you. Why are we thus deprived of your mercy?" To this Mahaprabhu replied with a smile: "No, no, my dears. By *lakh-pati* I mean someone who daily chants one *lakh* of the holy names of Krishna.[32]

In this way Mahaprabhu taught the devotees that they must daily chant one *lakh* of the holy names of Krishna if not more.

> *trinad api sunichena taror api sahisnuna*
> *amanina manadena kirtaniyah sada harih*[33]

---

[31] In Bengali someone who has a *lakh* (100,000) of rupees is called a *lakh-pati*.

[32] A *lakh* of the holy names is sixty-four rounds on the 108-bead, Vaishnava string of beads. This story is found in the *Chaitanya-bhagavata* of Vrindavan Das at 3.9.117 and following.

[33] Shri Chaitanya, *Shikshashtaka*, 3.

> One should always chant the holy names of Hari [Krishna] in a state of great humility, feeling oneself more insignificant than a blade of grass, being more tolerant than a tree, never expecting any honor from anyone and always honoring every living entity.

Baba also recommended performing loud, congregational chanting (*sankirtan*) of the Hare Krishna *maha-mantra* as it was Mahaprabhu's wish, practically demonstrated in the company of his companions and expressed in his *Shikshastaka* (Eight Verses of Instruction) verse number one :

> *ceto-darpana-marjanam bhava-maha-davagni-nirvapanam*
> *sreyah-kairava-chandrika-vitaranam vidya-vadhu-jivanam*
> *anandambudhi-vardhanam pratipadam purnamritasvadanam*
> *sarvatma-snapanam param vijayate sri-krishna-sankirtanam*[34]

> Supreme victory to the congregational chanting of Shri Krishna's names, which cleanses the mirror of the mind, extinguishes the forest fire of material existence, spreads moonlight on the white lotus of spiritual happiness, is the very life of bride-like spiritual knowledge, increases the ocean of spiritual bliss, enables one to taste full spiritual ambrosia at every step, and showers the entire self!

Baba mainly counted his *mantras* during *mantra-smarana* (remembering or meditating on *mantras*) and during his chanting of the holy names (*hari-nama-japa*) on a garland of big *tulsi* beads that had belonged to one of the companions of Mahaprabhu. It was given to him by Shri Radhagovinda Das Babaji of Vrindavan's Harabari. Sometimes he used to touch our heads with those beads to bless us.

2.16 The Names of Radha

During the last years of his life, Baba chanted 192 or more rounds of the Hare Krishna Mahamantra on his beads each day. He added two more *mantras* which were very dear to him because they had been been

[34]ibid., 1.

used by two holy men towards whom he was very affectionate, and he chanted them everyday. One of them was taken from a *Chaitanya-charitamrita* verse and Puridas sung it every day: *Shri Krishna-chaitanya Shachisuta Gaura Gunadham*, "The golden-skinned son of Mother Shachi, Shri Krishna Chaitanya, is the repository of all virtues." The other one had in it the name *Radha* which Baba considered the highest of holy sounds. Shri Radha and her names were everything to him, even more than Krishna and his names, and often he expressed that to us by reciting the following verses:

> *vraja-chandrendriya-grama-vishrama-vidhushalika*
> *krishna-sarvendriyonmadi-radhety-akshara-yugmaka*[35]
>
> [Although Krishna, like the cooling moon, gives pleasure to all the inhabitants of Vraja, Radha is] the moonlight that provides a resting place for his senses. The two syllables "Ra-dha" drive all of Krishna's senses mad.
>
> *yaj-japah sakrid eva gokulapater akarshakas tat-kshanad*
> *yatra premavatam samasta-purushartheshu sphuret tucchata*
> *yan-namankita-mantra-japana-parah pritya svayam madhavah*
> *shri-krishno 'pi tad-adbhutam sphuratu me radheti varna-dvayam*[36]
>
> May the two strikingly wonderful syllables `Ra-dha' appear to me! They immediately attract the Lord of Gokula [Krishna] when they are pronounced even once; they reveal the insignificance of all human pursuits [other than *bhakti* and *prema*] for those who have love; and they are included in the *mantra* repeated with great love by Lord Madhava [Vishnu] and even by Shri Krishna himself.
>
> *kalindi-tata-kunja-mandira-gato yogindravad yat-pada-*
> *jyotir-dhyana-parah sada japati yam premashru-purno harih*
> *kenapy adbhutam ullasad-rati-rasanandena sammohitah*
> *sa radheti sada hridi sphuratu me vidya-para dvy-akshara*[37]

---

[35]Shri Raghunath Das Goswami, *Radhikashtottara-shata-nama Stotra* (Hymna of One Hundred and Eight Names of Radhika), verse 45.

[36]Prabodhananda Saraswati, *Radha-rasa-sudha-nidhi*, 95.

[37]ibid., 96.

May the two syllables of Radha's name, the highest wisdom, forever appear in my heart. Hari himself constantly repeats those two wondrous syllables as he sits like a great *yogi* in a bower cottage on the bank of the Kalindi [Yamuna], meditating on the light from her lotus-like feet, his eyes filled with tears of love, entranced by the indescribable bliss of the flavor of increasing erotic passion.

devanam atha bhakta-mukta-suhridam atyanta-duram cha yat-
premananda-rasam maha-sukhakaram choccharitam prematah
premnakarnayate japaty atha muda gayaty athalisv ayam
jalpaty ashrumukho haris tad amritam radheti me jivanam[38]

That which is far beyond the reach of gods, devotees, liberated souls, and even Krishna's own friends and that which when uttered out of love is the very essence of the love's bliss and causes great happiness, this Hari himself listens to and repeats with love, sings among the girlfriends with joy, and murmurs with tears on his cheeks. That ambrosial "Radha" is my very life.

radha-namaiva karyam hy anudina-militam sadhanadhisa-kotis
tyajya nirajya radha-pada-kamala-sudham satpumarthagra-kotih
radha-padabja-lila-bhuvi jayati sada 'manda-mandara-kotih
shri-radha-kinkarinam luthati charanayor adbhuta-siddhi-kotih[39]

If everyday one can repeat the name of Radha, millions of the finest spiritual practices can be given up [except for the various forms of *bhakti* practice] and millions of the highest aims of human life, which adore the nectar of Shri Radha's lotus feet, can also be dispensed with. That is so because millions of wish-fulfilling trees flourish in Radha's playground [Vraja] decorated by her lotus-like footprints, and millions of wonderful, mystical perfections roll about at the feet of Radha's servants [but those servants care nothing for them].

anullikhyanantan api sad-aparadhan madhu-patir
maha-premavistas tava parama-deyam vimrishyati

[38]ibid., 97.
[39]ibid., 144.

tavaikam sri-radhe grinata iha namamrita-rasam
mahimnah kah simam sprishatu tava dasyaika-manasam[40]

Shri Radha! Madhupati [Krishna] does not take note of innumerable offenses committed to the saintly by someone who has enjoyed even once the sweetness of repeating your delicious name. Rather, overwhelmed with great love, he considers bestowing your highest gift [your personal service] on such a person. Who can touch the limit of the greatness of those whose minds always dwell on your service?

And Narottam Das Thakur has this to say:

jaya jaya radha-nam, vrindavana yara dham
krishna-sukha-vilaser nidhi
heno radha-guna-gan, na shunilo mora kan
vanchita korilo more vidhi[41]

Glory, glory to Radha's name,
that dwells forever in Vrindavan,
treasure chest of Krishna's blissful sports.
Due to my terrible misfortune,
I have not heard of Radha's many good traits.

Despite the superiority of Radha and her name over Krishna and his name, Baba still recommended the chanting of both. The following verse of Narottam Das Thakur was often on his lips:

krishna nam gane bhai, radhika-charan pai
radha-nam gane krishna-chandro
sankshepe kohinu kotha, ghuchao manera vyatha
duhkamay anyo kotha dhanda[42]

Brothers! [and sisters, too!]
By singing Krishna's name
Radhika's lotus feet you gain;

---

[40]ibid., 155.

[41]Narottam Das, *Prema-bhakti-chandrika*, Song 9, p. 444. Niradprasad Nath, *Narottam Das o Tanhar Racanabali*, (Kalikata: Kalikata Vishvabidyalay, 1975.

[42]ibid., Song 9, p. 444.

and by singing Radha's name
Krishna-chandra you will tame.
Now I've told you this in brief,
from mental torment gain relief.
Other topics bring misery and despair.

2.17 Radha

As a traditional follower of Shrila Rupa Goswami (i.e, a *rupanugi*) Baba worshiped both Radha and Krishna, but felt more love and preference for Radha. He used to say that in this particular, exclusive devotion the main target is not Krishna but Radha and that it is only because he is her beloved that we also worship and serve Krishna. We do not have to try to achieve him; he will automatically come to us, attracted by our loyalty to Radha. As a general survey of this type of devotional orientation the following verses were very dear to Baba:

padabjayos tava vina vara-dasyam eva
nanyat kadapi samaye kila devi yache
sakhyaya te mama namo 'stu namo 'stu nityam
dasyaya te mama raso 'stu raso 'stu satyam[43]

Splendid girl [Radha]! I never ask for anything from you but blessed service to your lotus feet. I bow down again and again with respect to being your friend. Truthfully, though, may my pleasure always derive from being your servant [*manjari*].

tavaivasmi tavaivasmi na jivami tvaya vina
iti vijnaya devi tvam naya mam charanantikam[44]

I am yours; I am yours! I cannot live without you! Splendid girl [Radha]! Please recognize this and bring me near your lotus feet.

ashabharair amrita-sindhumayaih kathanchit
kalo mayatigamitah kila sampratam hi

[43] Raghunath Das Goswami, *Vilapa-kusumanjali*, 16.
[44] ibid., 96.

tvam chet kripam mayi vidhasyasi naiva kim me
pranair vrajena cha varoru bakarinapi[45]

Radha with the shapely thighs! Burdened with longing for the ocean of ambrosia, I have somehow managed to pass my time here [at Radhakund]. Now, if you do not give me some grace, what is the use of my life, of living in Vraja and even of Krishna for me?

radhika-charan-renu, bhushana koriya tanu,
anayase pabe giridhari
radhika-charanashraya, ye kore se mahashaya
tare mui jai bolihari[46]

One who decorates his body with the dust of Radhika's feet will easily attain Giridhari [Krishna]. One who seeks shelter at Radhika's lotus feet is a great soul [of very fine spiritual taste and intelligence]. Such a one I repeatedly praise.

radha-dasyam apasya yah prayatate govinda-sangasaya
so 'yam purna-sudha-rucheh paricayam rakam vina kankshati
kim cha syamarati-pravaha-lahari-bijam na ye tam vidus
te prapyapi mahamritambudhim aho bindum param prapnuyuh[47]

Anyone who gives up Shri Radha's service out of a desire to gain Govinda's personal company is like somebody who expects to find the full moon on a night other than a full-moon night, and anyone who does not know that Radha is the seed of the ocean of love for Shyam [Krishna] is like someone who, though reaching a great ocean of ambrosia, obtains only a drop of it.

anadrityodgitam api muniganair vainika-mukhaih
pravinam gandharvam api cha nigamais tat-priyatamam
ya ekam govindam bhajati kapati dambhikataya
tad-abhyarne sirne ksanam api na yami vratam idam[48]

[45]ibid., 102.
[46]Narottam Das, *Prema-bhakti-chandrika*, Song 9, p. 444.
[47]Prabodhananda Saraswati, *Radha-rasa-sudha-nidhi*, 80.
[48]Raghunath Das Goswami, *Sva-niyama-dashaka*, 6.

I vow not to approach even for a moment that contaminated place where a fraudulent hypocrite out of arrogance worships Govinda alone without worshiping his most expert and dear Gandharva [Radha], of whom the Vedas and great sages like the Player of the *Vina* [Narada] loudly sing praises.

anaradhya radha-padambhoja-renum
anashritya vrindatavim tat-padankam
asambhasya tad-bhava-gambhira-chittan
kutah syamasindho rasasyavagahah[49]

How can one possibly enter the Shyama-ocean of ambrosial flavor (*rasa*) without worshiping the dust of Shri Radha`s lotus feet, without taking shelter of Vrindavan where her footprints are found, and without conversing with those devotees whose hearts are filled with deep, loving feelings for her?

2.18 To Radha for Love

Once, when Baba and I were accompanying a French devotee to the Radhakund bus stand, he asked Baba if he would pray to Shri Radha so She would bless him with success in acquiring lots of money when he returned to his country. In this way he said he would also donate some part of the money to him (Baba). Baba replied that since Shri Radhika was "Prema-Lakshmi" (the Goddess of Love) and not "Maha-Lakshmi" (the Goddess of Wealth), he could only ask Her for loving *bhakti* on his behalf, but not for any money.

[49]Raghunath Das Goswami, *Sva-sankalpa-rakasha Stotra*, 1.

Chapter 3

Teachings and Practices (II)

3.1 The Sampradayas (Communities)

After putting the twelve traditional Vaishnava marks on his body with clay from Shri Radhakund, Baba also inscribed in Malayalam script on his forehead the name of Shri Radha, using a thin wooden stick. The particular clay design on his nose was a *tulasi* leaf, the distinctive sign of the lineage of Shri Narottam Das, the only disciple of Shri Lokanath Goswami, to which he belonged. He instructed his disciples to wear only two lines of *tulasi* beads around their necks and for their forehead and nose markings to model themselves upon the Vaishnavas from Manipur who mostly belong to this lineage and who are expert in drawing the markings on themselves.

In the *Hari-bhakti-vilasa* it is said:

> *sampradayika-mudradi-bhushitam tam kritanjalim*[1]
>
> [The guru should offer him, the disciple,] adorned with the sectarian [*sampradayika*] markings, his hollowed palms joined tegether in reverence, [to Krishna].

Shrila Sanatan Goswami comments on this verse as follows:

[1] Gopal Bhatta Goswami, *Hari-bhakti-vilasa*, 2.129.

sampradayikam guru-parampara-siddham, mudra tilaka-maladi[2]

> *Sampradayika* means received through the guru succession and *mudra* refers to markings [*tilaka*], strings of beads, and so forth.

Baba's guru lineage, through which the Krishna initiation *mantra* was received in an uninterrupted way from mouth to ear, was started by the Supreme Person, Shri Krishna himself.[3]

Several close companions of Shriman Mahaprabhu were also Shri Radha's eternal *manjaris* in the world of Vraja. Being empowered and ordered by him personally, they pragmatically established their own Shri Krishna initiation lineages and for the first time in this day of Brahma (viz. in 4,320,000,000 years), as far as the history of Vaishnavism is concerned, they established the practice of passion-pursuing *bhakti* in the identity of a *manjari* as described in the *Padma Purana Patala khanda*, Chapter 83. They did this by inaugurating the mystical transmission [in addition to the transmission of the initiation *mantra*] called the *siddha-pranali* (succession of the accomplished devotees). The *siddha-pranali* consists in part of the reception from the guru of eleven characteristics of one's eternal *manjari* body in the world of Vraja. With this secret information one can begin the esoteric practice of passion-pursuing *bhakti* in the identity of a *manjari*. Some of Chaitanya's close companions also wrote books focusing on this type of religious cultivation meant to help one improve one's skill in reaching the goal of attaining divine love for Radha and Krishna as a *manjari*.

Thus Shriman Mahaprabhu unveiled through his personal companions, a unique way of promulgating Hari-nama Sankirtan, the loud singing of the names of Radha and Krishna, which is the religious dispensation prescribed in the Puranas for the Age of Kali, this present age of violent rivalry and pretense. This practice leads to full God- and self-realization in this present age. He did this by starting his own unprecedented, charismatic lineage of teachings in devotion known as the

---

[2] Shri Sanatan Goswami, *Dig-darshini*, 2.129.

[3] This is the Chaitanyite belief. In real terms, though, most modern members of the Chaitanya tradition trace their guru successions back to Chaitanya or one of his close companions. There are four "living" lineages in the modern tradition. Those are the lineages coming from Nityananda Prabhu, Advaitacharya, Gadadhar Pandit, and from Lokanath Goswami (aka. Narottam Das' lineage). [Ed.]

Nimananda Community (*sampradaya*). Shri Narahari Chakravarti wrote in his *Bhakti-ratnakara*:

> *prabhur adbhuta bhakti ke pare bujhite*
> *nimananda sampraday chalilo prabhu haite*[4]
>
> Who can understand the Lord's [Shriman Mahaprabhu's] amazing devotion? The Nimananda Sampradaya came from him.[5]

Baba's own lineage, whose members have eternal identities as *manjaris*, starts with the spiritual identity of Lokanath Goswami.

> *smartavya satatam sadbhih sviya guru-parampara*
> *sidhyaty ekantita naisam siddhihetur yaya vina*[6]
>
> One's own lineage of initiating gurus, through which the single-pointed *bhakti* is accomplished, is to be constantly remembered by the saintly. There is no other cause of success [in bhakti].

3.2 Color of Clothes

Regarding the proper color for the Vaishnava dress to be worn by him and his disciples (regardless of their professional and civil status) both on the material body and on the internally envisioned body of a young *brahmin* follower of Mahaprabhu, Baba followed the current, unanimous, traditional Chaitanya Vaishnava practice:

> *shukla-vasa bhaven nityam raktam chaiva vivarjayet*[7]
>
> Always wear white and avoid red cloth.

---

[4]Shri Narahari Chakravarti, *Bhakti-ratnakara*, 5.2164.

[5]Nimananda, the bliss of Nima, community is a reference to one of Chaitanya's early names, Nimai, given to him by his mother Shachi to protect him from envious gods and men. *Nim* is a type of tree that produces bitter leaves which Shachi hoped would repel any unwanted attention her son might attract. [Ed.]

[6]Hariram Vyas Goswami, *Nava-ratna*, 4.

[7]*Hari-bhakti-vilasa*, 4.152.

> *raktam nilam adhautam cha parakyam malinam patam paridhaya*[8]
>
> Wearing red, blue, unwashed garments, the garments of another, or soiled woven cloth [and then touching or performing rites for Hari brings sin].

Also, in Dhyanachandra Goswami's *Gaura-govindarchana-paddhati* (Method of Worshiping Gaura and Govinda) it is said: "[The disciple's internally envisioned body as a young male, *brahmin* follower of Mahaprabhu should be attired in] clean, white, new garments."[9] And: "[the disciple should meditate on his guru's accomplished body ...] attired in shining, white garments".[10] Then again: "[the guru's accomplished body ...] is eternal, of golden complexion, and attired in white clothes."[11]

3.3 The Guru

When I was helping Baba at night by guiding him through the darkness to the latrine and drawing water from the well for his wash afterwards, a few times he became ecstatically absorbed in remembrance of Shri Narottam Das Thakur's similar service to Shri Lokanath Goswami. He narrated the whole story with sobs in his voice. He also pointed out that Narottam had rendered such service to Lokanath Goswami incognito for an entire year and for another year in Lokanath's knowledge after that before receiving initiation from him.

Regarding the imperative in the Chaitanya Vaishnava tradition of accepting only one initiating guru with his preceding succession of gurus (the *guru-pranali*) along with details of their accomplished bodies in Radha and Krishna's eternal sport (the *siddha-pranali*), Baba was uncompromising. He said that when he himself first approached his own

[8]From the *Varaha Purana* cited in Shri Jiva Goswami's comment on Rupa's *Bhakti-rasamrita-sindhu*, 1.2.118, and from the *Hari-bhakti-vilasa*, 8.457.

[9]Dhyanachandra Goswami, *Gaura-govindarchana-paddhati*, 48: *shuddham shubhra-navambaram.*

[10]ibid., 45: *shuklambara-dharam divyam.*

[11]ibid., 15: *shvetambaram gaura-rucim sanatanam.*

initiating guru with the intention of being instructed, Shrila Sakhicharan Das Babaji let him know that unless he completely surrendered to an authentic guru belonging to a proper, uninterrupted guru-lineage with an accompanying accomplished lineage, took full initiation from him and rendered service to him, it would not be possible to start the process. This is the only way by which one can enter the realm of *bhakti* practice. Receiving full initiation by itself is instrumental to the development of the seed of the vine of passion-pursuing *bhakti*.

In the *Chaitanya-charitamrita* it is mentioned:

> *brahmanda bhramite kono bhagyavan jiva*
> *guru-krishna-prasade paya bhakti-lata-bija*
> *mali hoiya kare sei bija aropana*
> *shravana-kirtana-jale koraye sechana*[12]

> While wandering throughout the universe [in different species of life], if a living being is fortunate, then by the [causeless] grace of the guru and Shri Krishna it receives the seed of the vine of *bhakti* for Shri Krishna. He [the living being] then becomes like a gardener who plants this seed and waters it with the water of hearing and chanting [of Krishna's names, forms, qualities and sports].

In his *Laghu-toshani* commentary on a *Bhagavata Purana* verse, Shri Jiva Goswami wrote:

> *sat-sangamena raty-ankura-rupaiva matir jayata iti*[13]

> The intention [to engage in *bhakti* towards Shri Krishna] that is the very seed of attraction (*rati*) [to Krishna] appears through association with the saintly.

Baba was also very clear on the necessity of receiving the initiation *mantra* from an authentic guru. For him, it could not be done otherwise and certainly not through the medium of letters, the phone, a recorded audio or video-tape, the internet, or in a dream and so forth. Corroborating the proper process, Shri Ishana Nagara, in his *Advaita-prakasha*, relates how even after receiving the *krishna-mantra* in a dream from

[12]Krishna Das Kaviraj, Cc., 2.19.133-4.

[13]Shri Jiva Goswami, *Laghu-toshani* on 10.51.35.

Shrila Madhavendra Puri, Sita Devi (Advaitacharya's wife) was still initiated with that same *krishna-mantra* by her husband.

> *sita kohe bahu bhagye toma painu dekha*
> *dehatma shodhana koro diya mantra-diksha*
> *tabe puri sitare krishna-mantra dila*
> *dekhite dekhite puna antarhita hoila*
> *jagi sita-mata kohe kiba chamatkare*
> *svapnaveshe puri-raja mantra dila more*
> *acharye kohila sita sarva-vivarana*
> *tinho kohe bhagye tuya khandila bandhana*
> *prabhu sei mantra puna vidhi-anusare*
> *shubha-kshane samarpila sva-bharya sitare*[14]

> Sita Devi told Madhavendra Puri: "I am very fortunate to meet you. Please sanctify my body and soul by giving me mantra initiation." Then Madhavendra Puri gave Sita the *krishna-mantra* after which he vanished. When Mother Sita awoke, she said: "How amazing! Madhavendra Puriraja gave me *mantra* in a dream!" Sita Devi told everything to Advaitacharya, who said: "You are so fortunate that now all your bondage is destroyed." According to the rules and on an auspicious moment, Advaita Prabhu then gave his wife Sita that *mantra* again."

In his book the *Siddhanta-ratna* (Jewel of Conclusion), Shri Baladeva Vidyabhushana wrote:

> *esha tu bhaktis tan-nitya-parikara-ganad arabhyedanintaneshv api tad-bhakteshu mandakiniva pracharati. atas tad-bhakta-kripayaiva labhyeti bhagavatadi-samvadah.*[15]

> [When the practitioner's hearts gets purified by the process of hearing and chanting,] the *prema-bhakti* [divine love for

---

[14]Shri Ishan Nagara, *Advaita-prakasha*, 8.118-122. In the Ghose edition, pp 32-3. See bibliography.

[15]*Siddhanta-ratna*, 1.54. In Baladeva's commentary on the same text he also says: *nitye dhamni sthita nitya-parshadah tebhyah paramparaya ganga-pravaha-vad ihapi bhakter agamad ity arthah.* "From the eternal companions located in the eternal abode comes *bhakti* even into this world through the disciplic succession, like a current of the River Ganges.

> the Lord] that is present in the Lord's eternal companions, descends to the material world through the uninterrupted succession of devotees [the *guru-parampara*] like the descent of the celestial Ganges. Thus, eternally perfect love for Krishna appears in the hearts of present day practitioners, [blessing them forever with bliss].

The transmission of the *krishna-mantra* from the mouth of a guru to the right ear of a disciple is the real nature of initiation and once it is received in a correct way the disciple should not accept any other initiating guru, even if the guru does not inform him of his guru-lineage, his accomplished lineage, and of his perfected body in the sports of Shri Radha and Krishna. In this regard, when Padma Ma, who was Baba's cook and the one who performed the rites of worship for his sacred images, told him that she had received *krishna-mantra* from a guru in her adolescence but that he did not give her her guru-lineage and accomplished-lineage, nor the details of her perfected body (considering it premature for her), Baba investigated, discovered the legitimate guru-lineage and perfected-lineage she was to follow, and she got the eleven details of her *manjari* identity from her instructing (*shiksha*) guru.

Shri Narahari Chakravarti writes about Shri Caitanya Mahaprabhu's receiving initiation *mantra* from Shri Ishvara Puri:

> *nija-diksha-mantra tanre karnete kohiya;*
> *loilena mantra bhumi pori pranamiya*[16]

> Shri Ishvara Puri spoke his own initiation *mantra* into the ear of Nimai who then fell on the ground in obeisance.

In verse 2109 of the same chapter he says:

> *sampradaya nivishta hoile karya siddhi hoy*
> *anyatra dikshite mantra nishphala nishchoy*[17]

> Success is achieved after entering an authentic community (*sampradaya*). By initiation in some other way *mantra* certainly will not bear fruit.

In verse 2110 it is said:

[16] *Bhakti-ratnakara*, 5. 2103.
[17] ibid., 5.2109.

> *shri brahma rudra sanaka sampradaya chari*
> *kalite vidita kohe purane vistari*[18]
>
> The *Puranas* elaborate on how in the age of Kali, four Vaishnava communities (*sampradayas*) exist: the Shri (Lakshmi), the Brahma, the Rudra and the Sanaka (Kumara) communities.

In *Brahma-vaivarta Purana* it is said:

> *guru-vaktrad vishnu-mantro yasya karne vishaty ayam*
> *tam vaishnavam mahaputam pravadanti manishinah*[19]
>
> The wise call a person into whose ear the Vishnu *mantra* enters directly from the guru's mouth a greatly sanctified Vaishnava.

The same scripture states: "there is no greater guru than the initiation guru."[20]

In his teachings to Shri Sanatan Goswami, Shriman Mahaprabhu said:

> *prabhu kohe vaishnaver deha prakrita kabhu noy*
> *aprakrita deha bhakter chid-ananda-moy*
> *diksha-kale bhakta kore atma-samarpana*
> *sei kale krishna tare kore atma-sama*
> *sei deha tare kore chid-ananda-moy*
> *aprakrita dehe tar charana bhajoy*[21]
>
> The Lord said: "The body of a Vaishnava is never material. He has a supernatural body full of consciousness and bliss. At the time of initiation the devotee offers himself, and Krishna at that time makes him the same as himself. He makes that [devotee's] body full of consciousness and bliss, and then the devotee serves his [Krishna's] lotus feet with that non-material body."

---

18 ibid., 5.2110.
19 *Brahma-vaivarta Purana, Krishna-janma-khanda*, 83.35.
20 ibid., 93.79: *na guror mantradat parah.*
21 Krishna Das Kaviraj, *Chaitanya-charitamrita*, Antya, 4.183-185.

In Shri Jiva Goswami's *Bhakti-sandarbha*, it is mentioned:

> *divyam jnanam hy atra shrimati mantre bhagavat-svarupa-jnanam tena bhagavata sambandha-vishesha-jnanam cha*[22]
>
> Initiation bestows on the disciple not only the *mantra* but also knowledge about the specific personal form of the Lord expressed by the *mantra* and knowledge about his specific relation with the Lord.
>
> *yatha chaike tadrisham upasanam sakshad-vraja-jana-vishesha-yaiva mahyam shri-guru-charanair madabhishta-vishesha-siddhy-artham upadishtam bhavayami*[23]
>
> I meditate on that form of worship that my guru taught me, as one of Krishna's direct companions in Vraja, so that I can attain my special desired goal [in *prema-bhakti*].
>
> *tad-etat paramartha-gurv-ashrayo vyavaharika-gurv-adi-parityag-enapi kartavyah*[24]
>
> One should give up mundane gurus [that is, mother, father, ritual priest, etc.] and take a spiritual guru [with an authentic initiation *mantra*].

In the *Hari-bhakti-vilasa*, a statement is found from the *Vishnu Yamala*, wherein Lord Siva says:

> *adikshitasya vamoru kritam sarvam nirarthakam;*
> *pashu-yonim avapnoti diksha-virahito janah*[25]
>
> All activities of a non-initiated person are in vain. A person who is without initiation will take birth as an animal.

---

[22]Shri Jiva Goswami, *Bhakti-sandarbha*, para. 283.
[23]ibid., 312.
[24]ibid., 210.
[25]*Hari-bhakti-vilasa*, 2.4.

In the *Advaita-prakasha* Advaitacharya instructs his own son Krishna Mishra Goswami:

> *vaishnaver madhye yei sampradaya-hine*
> *sampradayi madhye yei gauranga na mane*
> *krishna-bahir-mukha sei korimu niryasa*[26]
>
> Again, amongst the Vaishnavas I consider those who are not initiated and those who are initiated but do not accept Gauranga both to be averse to Shri Krishna and I shall oust them.

In the *Hari-bhakti-vilasa* the definition of a Vaishnava is expressed in this way:

> *grihita-vishnu-dikshako vishnu-puja-paro narah*
> *vaishnavo 'bhihito 'bhijnair itaro 'smad avaishnavah*[27]
>
> The learned say that a Vaishnava is someone who is initiated into the *vishnu-mantra* and is dedicated to worshiping Vishnu. All others are non-Vaishnavas.

3.4 Passionate *Bhakti*

Shri Vishvanath Chakravarti mentions in his *Raga-vartma-chandrika* (Moonlight on the Path of Passionate Bhakti: "It is passion-pursuing *bhakti* if it is prompted by sacred greed alone."[28] That sacred greed has in its turn as its root causes: "It is caused by the grace of God or the grace of another passionate devotee."[29] In this same text Shri Vishvanath explains that the mercy of another passionate devotee is of two kinds: *praktana* or grace bestowed in a previous life and *adhunika*, grace bestowed in the present life. Then he continues with the statement that a natural, concomitant behavior of the *praktana* type is: "he surrenders to the lotus feet of a passion-pursuing guru *after* feeling that sacred greed,"[30] but that the *adhunika* type of devotee, on the contrary,

[26] *Advaita-prakasha*, 21.153-154. Ghose edition, p. 98, second column.

[27] *Hari-bhakti-vilasa*, 1.55.

[28] Shri Vishvanath Chakravarti, *Raga-vartma-chandrika*, 1.3: *raganuga syach ched bhaktau lobha eva pravartakah.*

[29] ibid., 1.6: *sa ca bhagavat-kripa-hetuko 'nuragi-bhakta-kripa-hetukash cheti dvividhah.*

[30] ibid., *adye sati lobhanantaram tadrisha-guru-charanashrayanam.*

is "graced by sacred greed *after* surrendering himself at the lotus feet of a passion-pursuing guru."[31]

In Section Seven of the same work, Shri Vishvanath explains that any devotee who is greedy for the feelings of one of Krishna's eternal companions in Vraja is still dependent on the instructions of the revealed scriptures and on logical arguments in order to learn the practices of passion-pursuing *bhakti* which is the means through which such feelings are attained. Then he says: "this practice of passion-pursing *bhakti* can only be demonstrated through the rules set forth in the scriptures and by logical arguments presented in them, and there is no other way to learn about it."[32] In Section Eight, he repeats again finding shelter with a guru, "surrender at the feet of a [passion-pursuing] guru," to emphasize its crucial importance for commencing the practice of passion-pursuing *bhakti* in an authentic and concrete way. In Section Nine, Shri Vishvanath talks of a plurality of avenues to enlightenment through knowledge of the feelings of Krishna and his companions in Vraja, as it is received from the guru, from a learned devotee or directly from the inner (*chaittya*) guru. The inner guru is Shri Krishna himself in the purified heart of practicing, passionate devotees.

3.5 Gates to *Bhakti*

Obviously when Shri Vishvanath Chakravarti talks about surrender to the lotus-like feet of a passion-pursuing guru, it goes almost without saying that for a uninitiated candidate, initiation into the *krishna-mantra* and into the accomplished lineage along with instructions in practice will be the result of this surrender to the guru. As discussed previously, these things are important for the growth and development of the seed of the vine-like practice of passion-pursuing *bhakti*. Without initiation, any attempt to start such a practice will be like building a sand caste, or relying on a will-o-wisp, or a mere bluff or pretense of *bhakti*. Shrila Rupa Goswami mentions in his *Bhakti-rasamrita-sindhu*[33] three gates through which the faithful enter into the realm of devotional

[31] ibid., *dvitiye guru-caranashrayananantaram lobha-pravrittir bhavati.*

[32] ibid., 1.7: *shastra-vidhinaiva shastra-pratipadita-yuktyaiva cha tat pradarshanam nanyatha.*

[33] Shri Rupa Goswami, *Bhakti-rasamrita-sindhu*, 1.2.74.

practice: "taking shelter at the lotus-feet of a [passionate] guru;"[34] "being initiated by him with the *krishna-mantra* [along with the accomplished lineage for the passion-pursuing aspirants] and receiving his teachings about *bhakti* [both as practice and as goal];"[35] and "serving the guru with full confidence."[36] As receiving initiation from an authentic guru is the greatest goal of life for an aspirant before initiation, so after initiation, instruction in worship and service to the guru become his highest goals of life and the greatest causes of advancement in *bhakti* and beatification in divine love (*prema-bhakti*).

3.6 Service of the Guru

Shrila Jiva Goswami wrote about the supremacy of service to the guru in his *Bhakti-sandarbha*:

> *tatra yadyapi sharanapattyaiva sarvam sidhyati ... tathapi vaishishtya-lipsuh shaktash cet tatah bhagavac-chastropadeshtrinam bhagavan-mantropadeshtrinam va shri-guru-charananam nityam eva visheshatah sevam kuryat| tat-prasado hi sva-sva-nana-pratikara-dustyajyanartha-hanau bhagavat-prasada-siddhau ca mulam*[37]

> By surrender [to God] one can attain spiritual perfection, but if one wants to attain special perfection in enjoying the flavors of devotion one can have it by constantly serving in a special way [giving priority to such service even over the Lord's service] the initiating guru who is the giver of the *mantra* of the Lord and the instructing guru who teaches one the process of worship. Only by the guru's grace can one please the Lord and become freed from obstacles in spiritual life, which are difficult to overcome by all other means.

As far as accepting instructing gurus when necessary, Baba told us that it should suit our taste and satisfaction. As far as the initiating guru

[34] ibid.: *guru-padashrayah.*
[35] ibid.: *tasmat krishna-dikshadi-shikshanam.*
[36] ibid.: *vishrambhena guroh seva.*
[37] Shri Jiva Goswami, *Bhakti-sandarbha*, 237.

is concerned, however, there can only be one. In this regard Shri Jiva Goswami has written this in his *Bhakti-sandarbha*:

> *tad aparitosenaivanyo guruh kriyate. ato 'neka guru-karane purva-tyaga eva siddhih*[38]
>
> Only if one is not satisfied with one's initiating guru is another one accepted. In thus accepting another guru the previous guru is [automatically] rejected.

Here it is to be noted that although such a alternative exists in relation with the initiating guru, it is not a move to be made lightly. More on this delicate subject will be discussed later in this book.

3.7 External Symptoms of *Bhakti*

Often Baba taught me that none of the various internal expressions of *bhakti* were prompted by the material qualities in one's heart. Expressions of *bhakti* mean services based on heartfelt feelings for their Lordships and not services that ignore such feelings. The former represent the heart under the influence of *bhakti*, the essence of the Lord's internal power (*svarupa-shakti*) and the latter represent the heart under the threefold influence (consisting of the qualities or strands of goodness, passion, and darkness) of his external power (*bahiranga-shakti*). In the *Bhagavata Purana* it is written:

> *tad-ashmasaram hridayam vatedam*
> *yad-grhyamanair hari-nama-dheyaih*
> *na vikriyetatha yada vikaro netre*
> *jalam gatra-ruhesu harsah*[39]
>
> If while repeatedly chanting the holy names of Hari someone's heart does not melt in spite of manifesting ecstatic symptoms like tears in the eyes, the standing up of hairs on the body, and so forth, then that person's heart is as hard as iron indeed.

[38] ibid., 207.
[39] *Bhagavata*, 2.3.24.

Even not fully accomplished *bhakti* practice, when efficiently performed, is conducted through the influence of *bhakti* in one's heart, making one feel separation from Shriman Mahaprabhu and from Shri Radha and Krishna and a strong desire to serve them lovingly in one's accomplished body.

3.8 Real Renunciation

Regarding true renunciation of sense indulgence Baba said that it was not to be forced either but that it accompanied the development of *bhakti* and was arrived at by the mercy of the Lord. The *Bhagavata* teaches us this:

> *bhaktih pareshanubhavo viraktir*
> *anyatra chaisa trika eka-kalah*
> *prapadyamanasya yathashnatah syus*
> *tusthih pusthih ksud-apayo 'nughasam*[40]
>
> Devotion, experience of the Lord, and detachment from worldly enjoyment appear simultaneously in the devotee, just as a person who eats feels satisfied, nourished, and relieved of hunger.
>
> *jata-shraddho mat-kathasu nirvinnah sarva-karmasu*
> *veda duhkhatmakan kaman parityage 'pyanishvarah*
> *tato bhajeta mam pritah shraddhalur dridhanishchayah*
> *jushamanash cha tan kaman duhkhodarkamsh cha garhayan*
> *proktena bhakti-yogena bhajato masakrin muneh*
> *kama hridayya nashyanti sarve mayi hridi sthite*
> *bhidyate hridaya-granthish chidyante sarva-samshayah*
> *kshiyante chasya karmani mayi drishte 'khilatmani*[41]
>
> [Shri Krishna told Uddhava:] "A devotee who listens with faith to my divine sports and who has lost all interest in ritual activities recognizes that sense desires lead only to sorrow. Still such a person is sometimes unable to give them up. Therefore, such a one should worship me with heartfelt love

[40] ibid., 11.2.42.
[41] ibid., 11.20.27-30.

> [by means of hearing, chanting and recollecting my divine names, forms, attributes and sports] full of faith and firm in the conviction [that everything will be accomplished by my grace and devotion to me alone].
>
> Although such a person sometimes enjoys those sensual desires, still he condemns them as attended by misery. All the material cravings embedded in the heart of a sage constantly worshiping me through the discipline of *bhakti* disappear when I am personally present in his heart. The knot in his heart is split apart, all his doubts are sundered, and his entire stock of *karma* is exhausted the moment I, the [Supreme] Self of the universe, am seen in person."

In his comment on verse twenty-eight of the passage above, Shri Jiva Goswami has written:

> If a faithful person is unable to give up sense desires immediately, he indulges his appetites and condemns them too, knowing that his indulgence will culminate in suffering. Here the word sense desire is not to be understood as something creating sin, because the scriptures never prescribe activities that cause sin. It is said:
>
> "Shri Hari is satisfied with one who does not desire others' wives or others' wealth, and who has no wish to commit violence to others."
>
> This verse from the *Vishnu Purana* [3.8.14] forbids the sinful intent even before it is put into action ...
>
> "If someone dear to Hari, someone exclusively engaged in the worship of his lotus feet, somehow performs some misdeed, Shri Hari, who is situated within his heart, will destroy its resultant sinful reaction."
>
> The word "somehow" (*kathanchid*) is used in this verse from the *Bhagavata* [11.5.42] to indicate that such votaries do not engage in sin on purpose.
>
> "Those who sin on strength of chanting the holy name will not be purified by so many other rules and regulations [other than by repenting and chanting],"

> and other praises of the destruction of offenses to the holy name clearly proclaim that sinning on strength of chanting the holy name is an offense. In the *Bhagavad-gita* verse [9.30]: *api cet suduracarah*, the Lord says that if a person who commits sins worships him he is still to be counted among the good (*sadhu*), but that statement does not condone the committing of sins --- it disdains sin and defines it as faulty, for in the next verse [of the *Gita*] it is mentioned: "He will swiftly become righteous," and that statement makes clear that it is better not to be a sinner. [42]

This is what Baba meant by saying: "It is not by force!" relating to devotion and renunciation of sensual desires.

3.9 Ajamila

On the subject of the depraved *brahmin* Ajamila, Baba once told me that although he was saved by Narayana's messengers from an imminent fall into the hells because he unintentionally invoked Narayana's clemency by calling desperately at the time of his death his son's name, which happened to be the same as Narayana's [thus becoming freed from all of his sins], that was not enough for him to get promoted to Narayana's eternal abode. He instead had his death postponed, so that

[42] Shri Jiva, *Bhakti-sandarbha*, 172:

> *sahasa tyaktum asamarthatvat kaman jushamanash cha garhayamsh cha. garhane hetuh duhkhodarkan shokadi-krid-uttara-kalan iti. atra kama apapakara eva jneyah. shastre kathanchid api anyanuvidhanayogat. pratyuta ---*
>
> *parapatni-paradravya-parahimsasu yo matim*
> *na karoti puman bhupa toshyate tena keshavah* (Vi. Pu., 3.8.14)
>
> *iti vishnu-purana-vakyadau karmarpanat purvam eva tan-nishedhat ...*
>
> *vikarma yacchotpatitam kathancit*
> *dhunoti sarvam hridi sannivishtah* (*Bhagavata*, 11.5.42.)
>
> *ityatrapi kathanchit-shabda-prayogena labdha-bhaktinam cha svatas tat-pravritty-ayogat*
>
> *namno balad yasya hi papa-buddhir na vidyate tasya yamair hi shuddhih*
>
> *iti padma-padye namaparadha-bhanjana-stotradau hari-bhakti-balenapi tat-pravrittav aparadhapatac cha. "api chet suduracharah" iti tu tadadadaradosha-parah eva, na tu duracaratavidhanaparah, "kshipram bhavati dharmatma" ity anantara-vakye duracaratapagamasya shreyas tv anirdeshad iti*

he could have recourse to God's system of surrender to an authentic initiation guru in preparation for the practice of *bhakti-yoga*. Only after reaching the level of divine love (*prema-bhakti*), which is the fulfillment of such a practice, did he gain his eternal identity as a servant-companion of Narayana and find residence in his eternal dwelling place.

> *sa tasmin deva-sadana asino yogam asthitah*
> *pratyahritendriya-gramo yuyoja mana atmani*
> *tato gunebhya atmanam viyujyatma-samadhina*
> *yuyuje bhagavad-dhamni brahmanyanubhavatmani*
> *yarhyuparatadhis tasminn adrakshit purushan purah*
> *upalabhyopalabdhan prag vavande shirasa dvijah*
> *hitva kalevaram tirthe gangayam darshanad anu*
> *sadyah svarupam jagrihe bhagavat-parshva-vartinam*
> *sakam vihayasa vipro mahapurusha-kinkaraih*
> *haimam vimanam aruhya yayau yatra shriyah patih*[43]

> Settling down at that holy place [Haridvara], Ajamila undertook the practice of [*bhakti*] yoga, withdrawing his senses from their objects by firmly thinking of God [Narayana]. Attaining the state of trance [*samadhi* or beatific divine love for Narayana] he became separated from the material qualities and situated in the light of God [Narayana], in Brahman, the very self of experience. When his intellect became quiet he beheld again in front of him the same divine messengers of Narayana seen before and he bowed his head to them. Immediately after seeing them, Ajamila left his body at that holy spot on the Ganga [Haridvara] and acquired an immortal [four-armed yet human-like] form of one of the companions of the Lord. Mounting a golden aerial car he ascended with those servants of Lord Narayana through the material heavens to the spiritual realm of Narayana, who is the husband of Shri [the goddess of beauty and prosperity].

3.10 Guidance in the Holy Sites

Baba was a perfect spiritual guide to all the main holy sites in the regions of Mathura, Navadvip, and Puri. Since he knew about the sports

[43] *Bhagavata Purana*, 6.2.40-44.

of Shri Radha and Krishna and of Shri Krishna Chaitanya Mahaprabhu related to those various places, he could describe them to the lucky pilgrims who came under his loving care.

3.11 Hearing Discussions about Krishna (*Krishna-katha*)

When a lecture on Hari was to be given by someone (especially by Pandit Shri Ananta Das Babaji Maharaja), Baba was always eager to attend. By the spiritual law of contagion some of his sacred passion was also infused from him into us. As we did not know Bengali such lectures were of little educational use for us. Still, by Baba's grace we found ourselves sitting among the venerable, saintly attendees, being showered by the lecturer's sweet discourse on Shriman Mahaprabhu and Shri Radha and Krishna's sports in Vraja. Often Baba reminded us that merely being present in such a gathering even without understanding a word of the lecture was of great spiritual benefit for us. Not only that, even simply feeling a desire to come to such a lecture was greatly beneficial, even if for some reason one was not able to do so. In the *Bhagavata* from which verses are inevitably quoted during such lectures it is written:

> *ishvarah sadyo hridy avaruddhyate*
> *'tra kritibhih shushrushubhis tat-kshanat*[44]

> The Lord becomes captured at once within the heart of persons who feel even the slightest desire to hear [the words of the *Bhagavata*].

So Baba encouraged his western visitors to go to the Bengali and Sanskrit lectures all around Radhakund, saying: "Even if you don't understand Bengali, you should still go and hear, just to get purified by the sound of the recital and by the sight of the Vaishnavas."

---

[44]ibid., 1.1.2.

3.12 Wondrous Radhakund

In January, 1988, during the cleansing of Shri Radhakund, when almost all of the water was pumped out and we could clearly see the numerous flowing sources of the pond, one of them started to turn out water as white as milk. Baba said it was milk from the cosmic Ocean of Milk, which was also present in the pond. He then told me to keep some of it in a bottle as a reserve for distribution to our future guests. One month later, when I opened the bottle, it amazingly enough smelled of curds, confirming Baba's previous assertion. He also said that during the summer of 1983 so much milk came out that Shri Radhakund's surface turned almost wholly white, and with clear nostalgia he remembered his dear deceased disciple Mukunda Das, who swam up to the middle of the pond, where the milk was more concentrated, to bring him back a bucket full of it.

One morning during that same period we accompanied Baba to take a bath in Shri Radhakund and after completing his bath, he sat down on one of its stairs. A nearby local resident, who was drawing the mud from the pond with a bucket, felt something on the bottom of the bucket and took it out with his hand. After he had cleaned off the mud, it turned out to be a beautiful whitish stone, which he ecstatically gave to Baba, exclaiming "This is Shri Radhika!" Later Baba gave it to me along with a small rock from Mount Govardhan, so I may worship them as Shri Radha and Krishna respectively, after he first initiated the worship himself.

At about the same time, as I was helping Baba shop at the little fruit and vegetable market situated just across from the western bank of Shri Radhakund, a motor rikshaw suddenly stormed into the bazaar, carrying a couple of devotees, who were from the USA, followed by some local priest-guides (*pandas*). They had come with the sole purpose of meeting Baba who had shown hospitality to one of them thirteen years earlier. Baba had received him so warmly that when he went back to his country he and his wife affectionately named their newly born daughter `Radhakund Dasi.' This devotee, whose name was Shrinath Das, was very glad to meet Baba again, but he was also overcome by grief because of the death, a few months earlier, of that very daughter, Radhakund Dasi, at the young age of twelve, as the result of a malignant brain tumor. Immediately after that tragedy Shrinath Das had been irresistibly drawn towards Radhakund, bringing the ashes of his daughter`s cremated body with him. Baba had them deposited on the local cremation ground near Shiva Khor. Wanting to know the whereabouts of his daughter's departed soul, Shrinath inquired about it from Baba, who answered after spending some time in meditation with his eyes closed, that her soul had become a young maidservant at Shri Radhakund (Shri Radhakund Dasi). On another occasion, when Shrinatha Das returned, he held a small festival in memory of Radhakund Dasi, arranged by Baba at the Shri Radha and Govinda temple where the food offered to the sacred images was distributed to the *babajis* as grace-food (*prasada*).

3.13 Vaishnava Marriage

As far as the concepts of Vaishnava marriage are concerned, Baba instructed my wife and me on the day of our marriage, Gaura Purnima, 1994, that the real purpose behind marriage is not the gratification of one's senses, but the worship of Shriman Mahaprabhu and Shri Radha and Krishna. A husband and wife who are both natural devotees of their Lordships accept each other as friendly helpers for that glorious purpose. Regarding having children, the main idea is to give a living being the chance to learn how to become a devotee of their Lordships. Baba used to say that according to what he heard from his parents and received through their family tradition, if a child is conceived on the fourteenth or sixteenth day starting from the beginning of the menses, it will be male and on the fifteenth day it will be female. The *Bhagavata* teaches:

loke vyavayamishamadyaseva
nityastu jantor na hi tatra codana
vyavasthitis teshu vivaha-yajna-
suragrahair asu nivrittir ishta
dhanam ca dharmaika-phalam yato vai
jnanam sa-vijnanam anuprashanti
griheshu yunjanti kalevarasya
mrityum na pashyanti duranta viryam
yad ghrana bhaksho vihitah surayas
tatha pashor alabhanam na himsa
evam vyavayah prajaya na ratya
imam vishuddham na viduh sva-dharmam
ye tv anevamvido 'santah

stabdhah sadabhimaninah
pashun druhyanti visrabdhah
pretya khadanti te ca tan[45]

In this world a human is naturally inclined towards the enjoyment of sexual pleasure, meat, and wine. No rules enjoin him to indulge in them. Rather restrictions are provided for these tendencies [by the scriptures] allowing for sexual intercourse with one's wedded wife, for meat-eating at the end of an animal sacrifice, and for drinking wine during a *sautramani* sacrifice [to those who are addicted to these]. The real purpose of the scriptures is, however, to turn man away from these pleasures.

The only real fruit of wealth is its use for *dharma* [devotion to the Supreme Lord], which gives real knowledge and direct realization of that knowledge [which in turn leads to the supreme grace of divine love for the Supreme Lord]. Those who use their wealth for their own comfort or for their family forget about death, that formidable enemy of the body.

They do not understand the pure nature of their duty (*svadharma*). To tell the truth, in reality, only smelling the aroma of wine is sanctioned [in a *sautramani* sacrifice] and only the touching of animals not their killing. Similarly, sexual intercourse with one's wife is for having children and not for sexual pleasure.

Those who are ignorant of this are wicked, stubborn, and yet consider themselves virtuous. They harm animals without feeling any remorse or fear of punishment and after they die are themselves devoured by those very animals [in their next births].

The *Manu-samhita* teaches:

na mamsa-bhakshane dosho na madye na ca maithune
pravrittir esha bhutanam nivrittis tu mahaphala[46]

[45]ibid., 11.5.11-14.
[46]*Manu-samhita*, 5.56.

> "There is no fault in eating meat, in drinking alcohol, or in having sex; these are inclinations of all living beings. But stopping these activities will yield great rewards."

And again in the *Bhagavata* it is stated:

> *labdhva sudurlabham idam bahu sambhavante*
> *manushyam arthadam anityam apiha dhirah*
> *turnam yateta na pated anumrityu yavan*
> *nihshreyasaya vishayah khalu sarvatah syat*[47]
>
> A wise person, who after many births has attained this very rare human body, which in spite of being temporary, [frail and subject to constant annihilation], bestows an opportunity to reach the highest spiritual welfare [*prema-bhakti* or divine, beatific love of God] should not delay, but should endeavor for it before death arrives. Sense pleasure is available also in all species [but spiritual perfection is not possible in any other body than the human body].

3.14 Dowry and Women's Rights

Concerning the crimes committed in the name of the Hindu dowry system, Baba remembered that when his previous parents-in-law asked him what they should give him as dowry, he replied that whatever they could give (just symbolically) according to their means would be all right and that they should not worry about it at all.

About women's rights Baba said that women are equally entitled to practice the same religious practices as men. He remarked also that in the visualization parts of such practices, which consist of sometimes envisioning oneself as a young, *brahmin* male follower of Shriman Mahaprabhu in his sport in Navadvip and then later as that same male envisioning himself as a *manjari* of Shri Radha in her sport in Vraja, it may be more difficult for women to play the young, male *brahmin* role (as it is in reverse for male practitioners to play the *manjari* role), but they cannot avoid its practice because it is an integral part of this form of worship. In *Bhagavad-gita* (9.32) Shri Krishna says to Arjuna:

[47] *Bhagavata Purana*, 11.9.29.

mam hi partha vyapashritya ye 'pi syuh papa-yonayah
striyo vaishyas tatha shudras te 'pi yanti param gatim[48]

Partha, whoever surrenders to me, though born of sinful wombs [such as *mlecchas* (barbarians, non-Aryans), *yavanas* (foreigners, esp. Greeks), and so forth], women, merchants or laborers, they will attain the supreme abode.

It is also mentioned in the *Chaitanya-charitamrita*:

shri-krishna bhajane hoy sabe adhikari
kiba vipra kiba shudra ki purusha nari

Everyone [endowed with faith] is eligible to worship Shri Krishna, whether they are *brahmins, shudras*, men or women.

3.15 Humility

Once, when we were walking near the milk-man's shop at Radhakund, Baba suddenly stopped and said in a deep ecstatic mood of humility, with tears in the eyes, that we were very, very far from the goal (*prema-bhakti*), and it would take a long time to reach it, but at least we were fortunate enough that we knew what the goal is by the grace of Shri Guru-deva and the Vaishnavas. On other occasions he said in the same mood that he will have to take birth again, but if that would be in Vraja-dhama, he would have the chance to associate with the resident saints there already from birth. Once he humbly said: "You know, I cannot do any worship, but let me just live and die here at Radhakund, then she [Shri Radha] will have to show me her grace." This attitude is echoed by Shrila Raghunath Das Goswami in his *Stavavali*:

udanchat-karunyamrita-vitaranair jivita-jagad
yuvadvandvam gandhair guna-sumanasam vasita-janam
kripam chen mayyevam kirati na tada tvam kuru tatha
yatha me shri-kunde sakhi sakalam angam nivasati[49]

[48] *Bhagavad-gita.*, 9.32.
[49] Raghunath Das Goswami, *Prarthanashraya-chaturdashaka*, 3.

> Friend [Rupa Manjari]! If the youthful divine couple --- who revive the whole world with a shower of ambrosial grace and who perfume all people with the fragrance of their jasmine-like attributes --- is not merciful to me, then please arrange it so that I can live my whole life at Shri Radhakund [and that I leave my body there]!

Another time, when I asked Baba to say something about his accomplishments in the worship of their Lordships, he replied that to have been able to pass all these years on the bank of Shri Radhakund and serve the Vaishnavas there was already the greatest perfection. About remembering the sports and mental service, he said that in his case it was possible to start practicing it while constantly serving the Vaishnavas engaged on this path. He came to this decision while thinking that if he was unable to do it himself, at least let him serve those who were doing it. The power of serving the Vaishnavas is mentioned in the *Shandilya-smriti*:

> *siddhir bhavati va neti samshayo 'chyuta-sevinam*
> *na samshayo 'tra tad-bhakta-paricharyaratatmanam*

> One may doubt whether or not the perfection of divine love for God (*prema-siddhi*) will be attained through the service of Shri Achyuta (God), but there can be no doubt that it will be attained through serving his devotees.

It is also said in the *Adi Purana*:

> *ye me bhakta-janah partha na me bhaktash cha te janah*
> *mad-bhaktanam cha ye bhaktas te me bhaktatama matah*[50]

> [Shri Krishna told Arjuna:] "Partha! Those who are only devoted to me are not really my devotees. You should know, however, that those who are devoted to my devotees are my greatest devotees.

[50]Cited in Rupa Goswami's *Bhakti-rasamrita-sindhu*, 1.2.218, with slight variation of the last quarter (*mama bhaktas tu te narah*).

Chapter 4

Teachings and Practices (III)

4.1 Shri Radhakund

Due to his powerful loving attachment to Shri Radhakund, Baba's hospitality was enormous. During our last meeting in March, 1998, he said that at Shri Radhakund the environment is such; it is a divine place, the topmost of divine places. Here Shri Radha and Krishna play during the middle of the day (*madhyahna*, from 10:48 A.M. to 3:36 P.M.). They really play here daily and only if we are sincere will we have a spiritual vision of them. But if we are not sincere we will not see them. At present we may not see them because our psyches are so clouded, but actually Shri Radha and Krishna come to Radhakund to enjoy their spiritual sports. Shri Sanatan Goswami teaches in his *Brihad-bhagavatamrita*:

yatha kridati tad-bhumau goloke 'pi tathaiva sah
adha-urdhvataya bhedo 'nayoh kalpyeta kevalam
kintu tad-vraja-bhumau sa na sarvair drishyate sada
taih shri-nandadibhih sardham ashrantam vilasann api
shri-suparnadayo yadvad vaikunthe nitya-parshadah
goloke tu tatha te 'pi nitya-priyatama matah
te hi sva-prana-nathena samam bhagavata sada
lokayor eka-rupena viharanti yadricchaya
shri-golokam gantum arhanty upayair

yadrigbhis tam sadhakas tadrishaih syuh
drashtum shakta martya-loke 'pi tasmins
tadrik-kridam suprasannam prabhum tam[1]

Just as Krishna plays here [in the earthly Vraja] he also plays in Goloka. People only imagine there is a difference, since the former is below [on earth] and the latter above [beyond Vaikuntha]. Although the Lord plays here, in this land of Vraja, with Nanda and his companions, this is not always perceived by everyone. Just as Garuda and the others are the Lord's eternal companions in Vaikuntha, so are they [Nanda and the others] in Goloka. Nanda and the people of Vraja are forever freely playing with the Lord of their lives in both [Gokula and Goloka]. Practitioners are able to see the same sports and compassionate Lord in Gokula [on earth] through the very same means [the practices of *bhakti*] as those by which they become worthy to go to Goloka.

Elated by this confidence [*vishvasa*, faith nourished by experience] Baba said that his door was open to everyone, so that he can serve them with spiritual instructions, irrespective of their stage in spiritual life or *sampradaya* [spiritual tradition-bearing community]. Everyone was welcome, even his enemies. He insisted that he was not advocating any particular religion such as Hinduism or Christianity. He simply recognized that we are all infinitesimal, conscious beings (*jivas*). He said that he followed the natural religion of that conscious being [*jaiva-dharma*] and that we have to accept the existence of such an eternal, conscious being because without it our psycho-physical body would be inactive. Stressing the importance of going to Shri Radhakund, he concluded by saying that only if we go there, will we realize the whole path vividly. In his view there was no alternative.

He used to say:

Whether believers or non-believers, when they come here they will get a chance to know what is in Shri Radhakund and to realize the sanctity of this place.

Shrila Vishvanath Chakravarti has mentioned in his *Raga-vartma-chandrika*:

[1] Sanatan Goswami, *Brihad-bhagavatamrita*, 2.5.168-172.

tatra bhaktanam karmi-prabhritinam siddha-bhaktanam ca pravesha-darshanenaivanubhuyate sadhaka-bhumitvam siddha-bhumitvam ca[2]

Because practitioner-devotees, performers of religious ritual, and accomplished devotees are all seen to enter there [the earth-like, manifest Shri Vrindavan], it is perceived as both a place for practitioners [*sadhaka-bhumi*] and a place for the accomplished [*siddha-bhumi*].

4.2 Bathing in Shri Radhakund

Baba favored our practice of bathing in Shri Radhakund as long as it is done with gentleness, respect, and the awareness that the *kund* is identical with Shri Radha. He said that in such a spirit we could bathe as many times as we wanted to.

Shrila Raghunath Das Goswami has written:

vraja-bhuvi mura-shatroh preyasinam nikamair
asulabham api turnam prema-kalpa-drumam tam
janayati hridi bhumau snatur ucchaih priyam yat
tad ati-surabhi radha-kundam evashrayo me[3]

That very fragrant, dear and beautiful Radhakund is my only shelter, since it quickly makes the desire-tree of love of God [love as found among the *manjaris*] sprout in the soil of the hearts of those who bathe there, though that love is very difficult to attain even for Krishna's dear ones in Vraja!

4.3 Service of the Vaishnavas

Baba used to say jokingly that he was like the potato that can mix with every *sabji* (vegetable). He loved everyone unconditionally and considered himself everyone's servant. He so liked serving the Vaishnavas that when he would take his walk he was always ready to break

[2] Shrila Vishvanath Chakravarti, *Raga-vartma-chandrika*, 2.7.
[3] Shri Raghunath Das Goswami, *Radha-kundashtaka*, 2.

into a run in order to render even the most menial service for a Vaishnava. Because I was afraid that due to his unbalanced walking he would stumble over something, he always let me stay with him, like his shadow, and he would support himself by holding onto my arm.

4.4 The Path-showing Guru

Baba wanted his disciples to be sincerely respectful and grateful to their path-showing gurus (*vartma-pradarshaka-gurus*), even if it should happen that those gurus may have been, or still were, offensive in many ways or supported by ill-gotten gains. He liked to give the example of Bilvamangal Thakur, who in the opening verse of his *Shri Krishna-karnamrita*, offered his grateful obeisance to his path-showing guru, a prostitute by the name of Chintamani. Once when he told us this story, he added that Chintamani became so impressed by the radical change in Bilvamangal that she consequently left her profession to dedicate herself solely to worship.

4.5 The True Nature of the Living Being (*Jiva*)

Baba's simple and pragmatic straightforwardness in answering spiritual questions lovingly satisfied the heart with a taste for the soul's natural function. Once I asked him what the soul was made of and he replied: "The living being (*jiva*) is an eternal servant of Krishna (the Supreme Person)." As I was reformulating the question Baba cut in and said: "If we do not accept it and do not do service to the Lord then we are cheating ourselves. We are eternal servants of Krishna and for us we are even more, because we are Shri Radha's *manjaris*." I joyfully wondered at his sweet call for devotion to Shri Radha and Krishna which is the final spiritual truth (*tattva*) about the living being, even beyond the truth relating to its constituent nature. In the *Shri Chaitanya-charitamrita* we find:

> *jiver svarupa hoy krishner nitya-das*
> *krishner tatastha shakti bhedabheda prakash*
> *suryamsha-kirana yaiche agni-jvalay chay*

> *svabhavika krishner tin shakti hoy*[4]
>
> The true nature of the living being is to be Krishna's eternal servant. As Krishna's marginal power it is both different and non-different from him. It is comparable with the sun [Krishna] and its rays [the living beings] or with the fire [Krishna] and its flames [the living beings]. Krishna by his very nature has three powers [the internal, marginal and external powers].

And again it is said there:

> *krishna-nitya-das jiva taha bhuli gelo*
> *ei doshe maya tar golaya bandhilo*
> *tate krishna bhaje, kore gurur sevana*
> *maya-jala chute pay krishner charana*[5]
>
> The living being has[, since time immemorial,] forgotten that it is an eternal servant of Krishna. This failing causes *maya* [the illusory power] to bind it around the neck. As a result, if it worships Krishna and serves its guru, it will escape the net of *maya* and attain Krishna's feet.

Again it is said in the same work:

> *nitya-baddha krishna hoite nitya bahirmukh*
> *nitya-samsari bhunje narakadi dukh*
> *sei doshe maya-pishaci danda kore tare*
> *adhyatmikadi tapa-traya jari tare mare*
> *kama-krodher das hoy tar lathi khay*
> *bhramite bhramite yadi sadhu-vaidya pay*
> *tar upadesha-mantre pishaci palay*
> *krishna-bhakti pay tabe krishna-nikate jay*[6]
>
> The beginninglessly bound living being has been forever turned away from Krishna. Dwelling in the material world from

[4]Krishna Das Kaviraj, *Chaitanya-charitamrita*, 2.20.101-102. (Radhagovinda Nath's edition, see the bibliography.)
[5]ibid., 2.22.17-18.
[6]ibid., 2.22.10-13.

time immemorial, it suffers in the hells and elsewhere. For the fault [of being turned away from Krishna] the witch *maya* punishes it with the three kinds of suffering headed by *adhyatmika* [psycho-physical] pain. Being a servant of lust and anger it is beaten up by *maya*. If the living being, in its wanderings around the material universe, encounters a doctor-like saint [*diksha-guru*] and follows his prescription, the witch will flee. Once it attains *bhakti* for Krishna the living being will draw close to him.

In the *Paramatma-sandarbha* Shri Jiva Goswami says:

tad-etat tasya paramatmamsha-rupataya nityatvam shri-gitopa-nishadbhir api darshitam:

mamaivamsho jiva-loke jiva-bhutah sanatanah
manah-sashthanindriyani prakriti-sthani karshati[7]

The eternity of the living being as a [small] part of the Supreme Self [Paramatma, Mahavishnu] is also shown in the *Bhagavad-gita* [15.7]:

But in the world of living beings, my own part, the [infinitesimal and] eternal living being (*jiva*), draws to itself the six material senses including the mind.

And in Jiva Goswami's *Priti-sandarbha*:

vaikunthasya bhagavato jyotir-amsha-bhuta vaikuntha-loka-shobha-rupa ya ananta murtayah tatra vartante, tasam ekaya saha muktasyaikasya murtir bhagavata kriyata iti vaikunthasya murtir iva murtir yesham ity uktam[8]

There are unlimited forms there [in the spiritual realm] that are forms of the splendor of the world of Vaikuntha and that are parts of the light of the Lord himself. The Lord makes a form for each liberated being with one of those [forms of light]. Thus [Shridhara Swami says] "whose form is like the form of Vaikuntha.

[7] Shri Jiva Goswami, *Paramatma-sandarbha*, 37.

[8] Shri Jiva, *Priti-sandarbha*, para. 10. Also, Shri Jiva's commentary on *Bhagavata*, 3.15.14.

In the spiritual realm there are two types of companions of the Lord; each type is endless in number: There are those eternally engaged in the Lord's direct service and those that are from beginningless time in an inactive state. The bodies of both kinds of companion are portions of the Lord's divine luster and are the treasures of the splendid spiritual realm. Each of the countless, deluded, infinitesimal living beings is an eternal servant of the Lord and simultaneously exists in the spiritual realm as an inactive eternal companion, with a body that is suitable for rendering service to the Lord. By the power of *bhakti*, the living being becomes eligible for the Lord's service and by the Lord's grace attains its companion-body which then becomes animated.

shri-radha-padapadma-cchabi-madhura-
tara-prema-chijjyotir-ekambodher
udbhuta-phena-stavakamaya-tanu-
sarva-vaidagdhya-purna
kaishora-vyanjitas-tad-ghana-rug-apa-
ghana-shri-chamatkara-bhajo
divyalankara-vastra anusarata
sakhe radhika-kinkaris tah[9]

Friend! Follow after Shri Radhika's adolescent servant-friends, whose bodies are clusters of foam that arise from the single ocean of the consciousness-light of the sweeter divine love that is the luster of Radha's lotus feet. These servant-friends are filled with every kind of cleverness, their complexions are of pure gold, they are the objects of beautiful astonishment, and they are divinely dressed and ornamented!

4.6 Song of the Cowherd Girls (*Gopis*)

Baba liked to recite the "Song of the Gopis" (Chapter 31 of the 10th Canto of the *Bhagavata Purana*) in a forgotten Orissan melody. During the last months of his earthly life he asked Shri Pranakrishna Das Babaji to come to him regularly to recite it for him.

[9]Prabodhananda Saraswati, *Vrindavana-mahimamrita*, 2.86.

4.7 The Krishna Initiation *Mantra*

One time Baba made a remark about the superiority of the Krishna initiation *mantra*[10] over the *brahma-gayatri mantra*,[11] saying: "When we have received the Krishna initiation *mantra* and the *kama-gayatri mantra*[12] why should we remember the *brahma-gayatri mantra*?" He added that he gave up meditating on the *brahma-gayatri* as soon as he received the Krishna initiation *mantra*. And when he took renunciation (called *bhekh*, the rite of becoming a *babaji*), in conformity with the traditional Gaudiya Vaishnava rules for renunciation as exemplified by the Vrindavan Goswamis (Sanatan, Rupa, Lokanath, and so forth), he also gave up wearing his sacred thread.

4.8 The Two Gopal Mantras

For Baba, the ten-syllable and eighteen-syllable Gopal *mantras* were intrinsically related to Bhakti Devi who is transcendentally universal and beyond any karmic, material designations. He said that the former *mantra* was only a shorter version of the latter *mantra*, and anyone, regardless of that person's caste, could receive either or both of them from a *sadguru*. The model for this view is found in the case of Shri Narottama Das Thakur who was initiated into the Gopal *mantra* by Shri Lokanatha Goswami who was a *brahmin* and who himself was initiated into it by Shri Advaita Acharya, also a *brahmin*. But Shri Narottama Das Thakur who was not a *brahmin* initiated many *brahmins*. Some offensive and stubborn *brahmins* criticized Narottama Das Thakur because of this. They were later, by his causeless mercy, freed from their offensive feelings and they repented heartily. They were also initiated by him in the end.[13] In the case of this fallen self, after initiating me with the eighteen-syllable Gopal *mantra*, to eradicate any of my doubts on this matter, Baba Shri Guru Maharaj (i.e, my Gurudeva, Shri Krishna Das

[10]The Gopal *mantra* of eighteen syllables.

[11]The Vedic *mantra* given to male members of the upper three classes in Hinduism at the time of the beginning of their study of the Veda. It is a single verse in the *gayatri* meter from the *Rig Veda* (III, 62, 10).

[12]A formulaic prayer to Kama-deva, the god of love, who is identified with Krishna, also composed in the *gayatri* meter.

[13]References to this are found in the *Shri Narottama Vilasa* of Shri Narahari Chakravarti Thakur and the *Shri Prema Vilas* of Shri Nityananda Das.

Baba) also gave me the ten-syllable Gopal *mantra*, despite the fact that I was neither born in India and nor belonged to any of the castes in its social system.

4.9 Worship of the Sacred Image

Regarding ritual worship (*archana*) of the sacred image, Baba wanted his initiated disciples mainly to worship a Giriraja stone (a stone taken from Mount Govardhan in Vraja) as Krishna. He insisted that his disciples should strictly stick to the etiquette of receiving the stone from an authentic Gaudiya Vaishnava holy person. They should not take the stone independently and start worshiping it just like that. The same went for Tulasi[14] chanting beads and neck beads, or any other sacred article related to religious practice. The idea is that behind any of these sacred articles the blessings of a genuine holy person in person is the vital factor. Once Baba told me that when we become completely pure-hearted, our sacred images of Krishna will talk with us and we shall see the sacred images really accepting our offerings. Such things will really happen. For example, the following testimonies are found in the *Shri Chaitanya-charitamrita*:

krishna kohe pratima chole kothao na shuni
vipra kohe pratima hoiya koho keno vani
pratima naho tumi sakshad vrajendranandana[15]

Krishna said: "I have never heard of an image walking anywhere." The *brahmin* replied: "If you are just an image why are you speaking? You are not an image. You are really the son of the king of Vraja!"

yadyapi gopal sab anna vyanjana khailo
tar hasta-sparshe anna puna taiche hoilo
iha anubhava koilo madhava gosai
tar thai gopaler luka kichu nai[16]

Although Gopal [the image installed by Madhavendra Puri] had eaten all the rice and curries, by the mere touch of his

[14]The sacred basil plant.
[15]Krishna Das Kaviraja, *Chaitanya-charitamrita*, Madhya 5.94-95.
[16]ibid., Madhya 4.77-78.

hand the food became again as it was before. Madhavendra Goswami perceived it; Gopal kept nothing hidden from him.

4.10 Eligibility for and Responsibilities of Worship

In the *Bhakti-sandarbha* it is said:

dvijanam anupanitanam svakarmadhyayanadishu
yathadhikaro nastiha syacchopanayadanu
tathatradikshitanam tu mantra-devarchanadishu
nadhikaro 'sty atah kuryad atmanam shiva-samstutam[17]

Just as *brahmin* are not eligible to perform rites, study the Vedas, and so forth without initiation [into the *gayatri mantra*] but are eligible after initiation, similarly those who are not initiated [into the *vishnu-mantras*] are not eligible to recite the *mantras*, worship the sacred images, and so forth. Therefore, one should make oneself praised by Shiva [that is, become properly initiated].

dikshitanam tu sarvesham tad-akarane naraka-patah shruyate. yatha vishnu-dharmottare:

ekakalam dvikalam va trikalam pujayed dharim
apujya bhojanam kurvan narakani vrajen narah

It is heard that all those who are initiated into the *vishnu-mantra*, whether they are students, householders, forest dwellers, or renunciants, but who do not perform ritual worship fall into hell. It is said for instance in the *Vishnu-dharmottara*:

> One should ritually worship Hari once, twice or three times a day. A person who eats without worshiping [Hari] will go to the hells.

[17] Shri Jiva Goswami, *Bhakti-sandarbha*, para. 283, and Gopal Bhatta Goswami, *Hari-bhakti-vilasa*, 2.3, a citation from the Agama shastras.

4.11 A Christian at Radhakund

In February, 1988, Baba was shocked that during a circumambulation of Shri Radhakund and Shyamakund, a westerner who accompanied him avoided seeing and offering his respect to each and every sacred image of God that they visited on the way. When Baba questioned him about his strange behavior, he replied that as a Christian he only worshiped God, not stones and idols. Baba asked him if he believed in the omnipresence of God and the young man answered that he did. To this Baba replied that if God is omnipresent then he should give respect to him also in the 'stones' and 'idols,' especially if they are God's representations.

In the *Padma Purana* it is mentioned:

archye vishnau shila-dhir gurushu
nara-matir vaishnave jati-buddhir
vishnor va vaishnavanam kali-
mala-mathane pada-tirthe 'mbu-buddhih
shuddhe tannamni mantre sakala-
kalushahe shabda-samanya-buddhir
vishnau sarveshvareshvare tad-
itara-sama-dhir yasya vai naraki sah[18]

A person who considers the image of Vishnu to be a mere stone, his gurus to be mere human beings, Vaishnavas (devotees of Vishnu) to belong to a certain caste, water that has washed the feet of Vishnu and the Vaishnavas to be mere water, although it is holy water that destroys all the filth of the age of Kali, Vishnu's pure names and initiation *mantras*, that destroy all sins, to be ordinary words, and Vishnu himself, who is the Lord of all Lords, to be similar to all other gods, is indeed a resident of hell.

4.12 Absence of Pride

Baba did not manifest the least bit of pride when he was addressed respectfully by others. Once we were together near the temple of Shri

[18]Cited in Shri Jiva's *Bhakti-sandarbha*, para. 248.

Kundeshvar Mahadev when a holy man dressed in saffron clothes called him 'Maharaj,' to which Baba jokingly replied: "I don't have a peacock tail to be a Maharaj" (meaning: I don't have the self esteem to be a `Maharaj' at all), making the fellow burst into laughter. Shrila Narottam Das Thakur wrote:

> *abhimani bhakti-hin, jaga-majhe sei din,*
> *vritha tar ashesha bhavana*[19]

> The proud are always bereft of *bhakti* and they are the lowest people in the world. All their endless conceits are in vain.

In the *Udyoga Parva* of the *Mahabharata* it is written:

> *mado 'shtadasha-doshah syat purah yah sa prakirtitah*
> *loka-dveshyam pratikulyam abhyasriya mrisha-vachah*
> *kama-krodhau paratantram parivado 'tha paishunam*
> *artha hani-vivadash cha matsaryam prani-pidanam*
> *irshya moho'tivadash cha samjna nasho 'bhyasuyita*
> *tasmat prajno na madyeta sada hy etad vigarhitam*

> Eighteen faults can be found in a proud person. A person who is overcome by pride is disliked by people. He imagines himself to be opposed by others and therefore acts in negative ways towards them. He finds fault with the virtuous, engages in different kinds of slander, and does not hesitate to lie in different ways, so that no one will be as honored as him. He becomes very attached to and eager for the object in which his pride lies and if anybody speaks against his desired object his anger ignites like fire. He becomes submissive to those who kindle the fires of his pride. Proud people constantly slander others and are vessels of various kinds of deception. In order to preserve his pride he wastes lots of wealth and is constantly engaged in quarreling. Envy of someone else's prosperity is always present in the heart of the proud and he inflicts pain on others. His heart always burns in the fires of envy and is thus bewildered by delusion and ignorance. A proud person always violates etiquette, is devoid of knowledge of good and evil, and is always engaged

[19] Shri Narottam Das, *Prema-bhakti-chandrika*, song 7.

in violence against others. Because of all these terrible vices an intelligent person always gives up false pride.

Baba called my attention to the futility and ridiculousness of assessing oneself as an advanced votary of the Lord, by saying: "I may think of myself as a great devotee who can do private worship, but when someone pricks me even slightly, I immediately react, feeling pain [feeling offended]."

pratishthasha dhrishta shvapaca-ramani me hridi natet
katham sadhu prema sprishati shuchir etan nanu manah
sada tvam sevasva prabhu-dayita-samantam atulam
yatha tam nishkashya tvaritam iha tam veshayati sah[20]

O mind! The desire for honor is dancing in my heart like a dog-eating witch! How can pure, saintly love then touch it? Therefore, constantly serve the Lord's dear, unequaled, devotee chieftains, so that they can chase that witch out and make saintly love enter!

4.13 Grace

On another occasion, in the course of one of Baba's readings of Shrila Narottam Das Thakur's *Prarthana*, he remarked that although it is our soul's inherent duty to practice with love our different devotional practices, it is presumptuous and wrong to think that *prema* will be reached because we practice such practices. The fact is that only when it reveals itself to us will we get it. We do not get it by practice but only by grace, and usually it appears in a heart that has been purified by practice.

nitya-siddha krishna-prema sadhya kabhu nay
shravanadi-shuddha-chitte karaye uday[21]

Since it is eternally existent, divine love for Krishna is not to be achieved by *bhakti* practices. It manifests itself in a mind purified by practices like hearing about, [repeating and remembering Krishna's divine names, forms, attributes and sports].

[20] Raghunath Das Goswami, *Manah-shiksha*, 7.
[21] Krishna Das Kaviraj, *Chaitanya-charitamrita*, Madhya 22.207.

4.14 Diagrams for Visualization

Baba possessed a drawing book filled with diagrams of different kinds which are used to help one's visualization of the different places in the spiritual worlds of Navadvip and Vraja. He had himself meticulously drawn, colored, and inscribed each picture copying the drawing book that his own guru-deva, Shri Sakhicharan Das Babaji Maharaja, had made for Vrajabhushan Das Babaji (Delhi Baba). He often showed us the diagrams and commented on them.

4.15 Snakes

On a rainy late evening of 1988 a small cobra crawled onto the veranda of the sacred image room of the Shri Radharaman temple, terrorizing the priests, who started to yell. Baba immediately rushed out of his room and using two wooden sticks, caught the reptile. As I lit his way with a flashlight, he carried the reptile outside the temple compound and deposited it back in nature. When we returned he confessed to me that he had never been afraid of snakes and had often dealt with them in such a way in the past whenever it was necessary.

The snake charmers of the neighborhood were objects of Baba's affection. They used to collect honey from the beehives in the trees and come to him to sell it. After having bargained for some time with them, he told me to get the scale from his cell and some plastic containers. First the honey was strained through a cloth and then it was poured into the plastic containers which were then weighed.

4.16 Spiritual Patrimony

As a matter of good practice in respecting one's guru-deva as a veritable manifestation of Krishna, Baba told us to preserve the spiritual patrimony inherited from him (the initiation *mantras*, the lineage of gurus, the spiritual identities of that lineage of gurus, the private worship manuals, and so forth). He said that the proper etiquette in this regard was not to omit or to correct any part of it, but instead we could add to it as much as we felt we wanted.

4.17 The *Vyashti* and *Samashti* Gurus

Baba told me once the reason why he always used to put at top of his letters two `Shri-s' before guru-deva. He said that one `Shri' was meant for his *vyashti-guru*, the individual or distributive guru (Shri Sakhicharan Das Babaji Maharaj in his case), and the other `Shri' was for the *samashti-guru*, the collective guru, who is energetically present within all *vyashti-gurus*.

He said that despite the recognition by the disciple of his *vyashti-guru* as an *avatar* (descent) manifestation of the Supreme Lord Shri Krishna and as an embodiment of his full grace, during formal worship, food, incense, ghee lamp, flowers, perfume, and so forth are presented to the guru only after first being offered to Krishna.[22] It is so because the *vyashti-guru* is a devotee of Krishna and subordinate to him, as is also the case with any of his other *avatar* manifestations.

> *eka-matra amsi krishna, amsa avatara*
> *amsi amse dekhi jyeshtha-kanishtha-achara*[23]
>
> Only Krishna the whole, the *avatars* are his parts. Between the whole and the part we see the behavior of elder towards younger.

In the process of formal worship, offerings are first given to Shri Krishna and companions and then gradually down the line through the line of gurus and siddhas to one's *vyasti-guru*. The other way around would have been unbelievably offensive towards the Supreme Lord Shri Krishna.

4.18 The Guru in Succession

In March, 1998, out of great concern for the leader of a non-traditional Vaishnava sect whom Baba knew and who came to visit his place at Radhakund, Baba felt compassion and wanted to talk to him in private. He asked me to invite him to come and meet him, explaining

[22]For references, please consult the Gaudiya Vaishnava manuals of worship like that of Shripada Gopalaguru Goswami, Shripada Dhyanachandra Goswami, and Shripada Siddha Krishna Das Baba.

[23]Krishna Das Kaviraj, *Chaitanya-charitamrita*, 1.6.98.

that, like his own guru-deva, Shrila Sakhicharan Das Babaji Maharaja, this votary had in his adolescence been initiated into the lineage of Śrī Narottam Das Thakur by an authentic lineage guru. Baba thought that being reminded of that would perhaps create a spiritual revival in him, resulting in his putting himself again under the guidance of his real guru who had an uninterrupted initiation and perfected lineage. Regarding the exalted spiritual status and gravity of the guru with the proper credentials, the following verse from the *Brahma-vaivarta Purana* is quoted in *Hari-bhakti-vilasa*:

> *upadeshtaram amnayagatam pariharanti ye*
> *tan mritan api kravyadah kritaghnannopabhunjate*[24]
>
> Even vultures will not eat the corpses of the ungrateful ones who abandon a guru who comes in proper succession (*amnayagata*).

Commenting on this verse, Shri Sanatan Goswami explains:

> *amnayagatam kula-kramayatam*
>
> An *amnayagata* [*guru*] is one who comes in a communal succession.

An *amnayagata* guru means a *guru* who is affiliated (by receiving initiation *mantras*) with an uninterrupted succession of initiating *gurus* (whether within or without the family lineages of, for example, Shri Nityananda Prabhu and Shri Advaita Prabhu).

The following verse from the *Aditya Purana* was also cited in the same scripture:

> *avidyo va savidyo va gurur eva janardanah*
> *margastho vapy amargastho gurur eva sada gatih*[25]
>
> Whether a guru [in proper succession] has knowledge of the scriptures or not, [for his disciples] he is still Janardana [the Supreme Lord]. Whether a guru is on the path [engaged in worship] or not, he is still always the goal of life [for his disciples].

[24]Gopal Bhatta Goswami, *Hari-bhakti-vilasa*, 4.363.
[25]ibid., 4.359.

4.19 Abandoning the Guru

Shrila Jiva Goswami has pointed out, in his *Bhakti-sandarbha*, the circumstances under which one's initiating *guru* should be honored from a distance or abandoned:

> *yo vyakti nyaya-rahitam anyayena shrinoti yah*
> *tav ubhau narakam ghoram vrajatah kalam akshayam*

> *iti narada-pancharatre. ataeva durata evaradhyas tadrisho guruh; vaishnava-vidveshi chet parityajya eva*

> *guror apy avaliptasya karyakaryam ajanatah*
> *utpatha-pratipannasya parityago vidhiyate*

> *iti smaranat tasya vaishnava-bhava-rahityenavaishnataya avaishnavopadishtena ityadi vacana-vishayac cha*[26]

> A person who speaks without propriety [that is, contrary to the teachings enunciated in the Vaishnava scriptures] and a person who hears such teachings without reasoning, both will live in a foul hell for undiminishing time.
>
> Thus is it stated in the *Narada-pancharatra*. Therefore, one should honor such a *guru* from a distance. If a *guru* is an enemy of Vaishnavas (*vaishnava-vidveshi*) it is better to give him up altogether. According to *smriti*:
>
> It is required that one give up a guru who is arrogant, who does not know what should be done and what should not be done and who [thus] is following the wrong path.
>
> Since such a guru lacks the nature of a Vaishnava he becomes the subject of the verse: "By a *mantra* taught by a non-Vaishnava one goes to hell."

The word *dvesha*, hatred or enmity, also includes *ninda*, calumny, as Sri Jiva says in his *Bhakti-sandarbhah*: "calumny is equal to hatred.[27] This enmity for Vaishnavas includes the six kinds of offenses to Vaishnavas from the *Skandha Purana*:

---

[26]The whole passage is from *Bhakti-sandarbha*, para 238. The last verse is cited in full in the *Bhakti-sandarbha*, verse 621.

[27]*nindapi dvesha-samah.*

hanti nindati vai dveshti vaishnavan nabhinandati
krudhyate yati no harsham darshane patanani shat[28]

One kills, calumniates, hates, does not welcome, becomes angry with, and is not happy to see Vaishnavas — these are the six falls [into hell].

4.20 Baba's Personal Habits

When I massaged Baba's body he would often jokingly say that it was not gratifying to me because he offered only his skin and bones for me to massage. He told me that he had never allowed anyone to do it before, even his own wife.

Baba's ideas about diet were to eat mainly greens, salads and fruit, and he was faithful to the directions of the Lakshman Sharma school of Naturopathy. As I learned more about his ideas on this matter he asked me to take care of his diet and for his pleasure and consequently also mine, I daily prepared grated coconut, green salads, and fruit as offerings for Giriraja. He also avoided white sugar as we discovered that bone-charcoal was used in the process of refining it. Regarding hot chili, Baba said that it hurt Krishna's soft lips and he should be spared this pain.[29]

4.21 Baba's Miraculous X-ray Image

When I went back to Europe I brought with me the x-ray image of Baba's fractured hipbone. Once while examining it I remarked that there appeared to be a human face in it. I thought it at first to be probably the fruit of my imagination, but looking at it again and again, a face was really there. I thought that maybe while taking the picture, Gurudev's face somehow had also entered into the field of vision. But then I remembered that I was present during the shooting, and the photo camera was situated just above the pelvis, away from the face. The resulting photo was only of part of the pelvis, not even the trunk, what

[28] Cited in the *Bhakti-sandarbha*, verse 800.

[29] Baba also used to eat grated raw carrots, light red in color, as a revitalizing medicine whenever he needed it.

to speak of the higher part. Puzzled, I showed it to some of my friends without telling them anything about it. After examination, each of them also identified a human face in it. Someone suggested that I show it to a lady living in Paris, who had a reputation as a mystic. Before the meeting, we first agreed between us not to give her any information or hint about the provenience and identity of the x-ray negative, nor of any of our personal opinions about it. At first her analysis detected the right hipbone fractured in two pieces and then the face which according to her was that of a male who was foreigner to this continent. She then also expressed her surprise at a face appearing in an x-ray negative of a pelvis. I then asked if she could also determine his age. She looked again and said: "I think it is of a boy of about 12 to 13 years old." When I told her that it belonged to my Gurudev she commented: "It is really a strange thing!"

As for myself, I was also pleasurably amazed, feeling really blessed to find Gurudev's glories recognized unexpectedly in such a manner. Being so closely associated with Gurudev when he was in his apparently critical condition of suffering, and being myself immature, I was probably underestimating his divine position. This episode contributed substantially to eradicating such eccentricities of mine. By Baba's mercy, things became tangibly clear to me that even during such a crucial period, his spiritual inner self remained strongly reflected on him, to the point of being even reproduced on an x-ray, clearly enough to be deciphered by some mystic who had no knowledge at all of the Chaitanya tradition and its esoteric aspect relating to the self's transcendental personality in relation to the divine Krishna.

4.22 In the Winter

In the winter, if Baba would wake up very early in the morning and see that I was still very tired, he would tell me to remain on the ground where I was resting near his bed. While reciting a set of his prayers he would often place his feet on my head. Sometimes entering into trance due to the influence of some verse, he would stop reciting. When he came back to external consciousness he would restart, repeating the same verse again and again with great eagerness. Often, due to his elation he would explain the meaning of the verse to me. I remember once during his recitation of the *Shri Radha-rasa-sudha-nidhi* ("Ocean of the Nectar of the Rapture of Radha"), he started recalling with aching heart, his association with the saint Pandit Shri Dinasharan Das Babaji Maharaj who told him that while reading this particular book, some verses would strike us in a very special way. Pandit Baba revealed to him also his particular attachment to verse eighty-five:

> *tat-saundaryam sa ca nava-nava-yauvana-shri-praveshah*
> *sa drig-bhangi sa ca rasa-ghanashcarya-vakshoja-kumbhah|*
> *so'yam bimbädhara-madhurima tat-smitam sa ca vani*
> *seyam lila-gatir api na vismaryate radhikayah||*[30]
>
> I cannot forget the beauty of Radhika, or her delightful entrance into the age of ever fresh youth, or the quirkiness of her eyes, or her jug-like breasts which are wonders of solidified *rasa*, or the sweetness of her red lips, or her smile, or her speech, or even her sportive gait.

4.23 Visions and Ecstasies

One early morning in the month of Kartika in 1987 as I entered his room I was caught unprepared when I found him completely devastated by ecstatic feelings of separation. With a choked voice that was nevertheless strong and sharp he said: "She (Shri Radha) was here! She was just here!"

During the lectures of Pandit Ananta Das Babaji Maharaj it was sometimes no longer possible for Baba to control his strong spiritual emotions and he would often burst into tears, making loud noises. Back in his room afterwards, he felt sorry that he had not been able to control himself, saying that it was beyond his power. He always tape-recorded the lectures and translated them for us into English afterwards. Once when he was going to read the *Shri Prema-bhakti-chandrika* to us he at first had wanted to answer nature's call and then start. But his strong eagerness to read the text made him forget all about it and he commenced reading immediately, continuing for nearly two hours. He told me later that when he read the scriptures his absorption in his spiritual body was such that he completely forgot his physical body and its needs.

---

[30] Shri Prabodhananda Sarasvati, *Shri Radha-rasa-sudha-nidhi*, verse 85.

4.24 Poor Man's Guru

Baba's disciples are mostly non-Indian westerners. He used to say with feelings of deep love for them that he was a poor-man's guru for westerners. Regarding this there is a verse from the *Padma Purana* that is cited in the *Bhakti-rasamrita-sindhu*:

> *mat-tulyo nasti papatma naparadhi na kashcana*
> *parihare'pi lajja me kim bruve purushottama*[31]
>
> Purushottam! I am such a sinful offender that you will not be able to find anyone equal to me. What can I say? I am even ashamed to ask you for forgiveness.

Baba said that if we recite this prayer it will attract Purushottam (the Supreme Person) to descend to help us, because it is a prayer composed by his eternal companion and has the power to attract him. When we repeat this prayer from the core of our hearts we can obtain anything we desire. This should be our prayer and we should always remember it. We should not utter it merely with our lips but with real fervor. He wanted each one of his disciples to memorize it.

[31] *Padma Purana* cited at Brs., 1.2.154.

Chapter 5

Teachings and Practices (IV)

5.1 Remembering (*Smaran*)

Baba also stressed the importance of serving, with feelings of deep love, from the identity of one's mentally envisioned, accomplished body (*siddha-deha*) as revealed to a disciple by his guru-deva. This should be done according to the appropriate times of the sports of Shri Gaura and Govinda, without neglecting to do loud singing (*kirtan*) of their names, sports, and such and private chanting of their holy names. Shrila Jiva Goswami wrote in his *Bhakti-sandarbha*:

> *atha sharanapattyadibhih shuddhantah-karanash chen nama-sankirtanaparityagena smaranam kuryat*[1]
>
> When one's mind is purified by the processes of surrender and so forth [that is by faith, surrender, service to one's guru and to the Vaishnavas, hearing and repeating Shri Radha and Krishna's names, forms, qualities and sports], one may practice recollection without giving up the singing of the holy names.

[1]Shri Jiva Goswami, *Bhakti-sandarbha.*, para 275.

Baba said that we should not chant just like parrots. Rather, we should always have some idea how to perform those mental services. For this reason we need *anugati*, or following the examples of the Goswamis of Vrindavan by learning from their books about the personal services they performed in their spiritual identities as *manjaris*. In this way we will be happier and the whole process will become even more beautiful. Thus he outlined the two sides of proper practice as a *manjari*, as it has been clearly described by Shrila Krishna Das Kaviraj Goswami in his *Chaitanya-charitamrita*:

> *bahya-antar ihar dui to sadhan*
> *bahya sadhaka-dehe kore shravan kirtan*
> *mone nija siddha-dehe koriya bhavan*
> *ratri-dine vraje radha-krishner sevan*[2]
>
> [Passion-pursuing] *bhakti*[3] is performed both externally and internally. Externally one engages one's physical body in hearing and repeating [Shri Radha and Krishna's names, forms, attributes, and sports in Vraja]. Internally one engages one's mind in imagining oneself in one's [guru-given] perfected body performing the service [that was given by one's guru] of Shri Shri Radha and Krishna in Vraja night and day.
>
> *ataeva gopi-bhav kori angikar*
> *ratri dine cinte radha krishner vihar*
> *siddha-deha cinti kore tahai sevan*
> *gopi-bhave pay radha-krishner charana*[4]
>
> Therefore, taking on the loving feelings of a cowherd girl, one thinks of Radha and Krishna's playful activities day and

[2]Krishna Das Kaviraj, *Chaitanya-charitamrita*, Madhya, 22.156-157.

[3]That is, the practice of *raganuga-bhakti*, a method of religious purification of the self in order to cultivate the self's eternally perfected or accomplished body called the *siddha deha*. Shrila Jiva Goswami has written in his *Bhakti-sandarbha* (para. 286): *tatra bhuta-shuddhir nijabhilasita-bhagavat-sevopayika tat-parshada-deha-bhavana-paryantaiva tat-sevaika-purusarthibhih karya nijanukulyat*, "Devotees whose only goal in life is to serve the Lord should meditate, as is suitable for them, on themselves as a companion of the Lord as the means by which they may serve him in the way they want to. That is their purification of the elements (*bhuta-shuddhi*)."

[4]ibid., Madhya 8.228-229.

night. Thinking of one's perfected body, one serves them there and attains the lotus feet of Radha and Krishna as a cowherd girl.

ragamayi-bhaktir hoy ragatmika nam
taha shuni lubdha hoy kono bhagyavan
lobhe vraja-vasir bhave kore anugati[5]

[The Vraja-vasis' (Krishna's eternal companions in Vraja)] devotion [to the Lord] is characterized by complete attachment [*raga*] to him and is called *ragatmika-bhakti.* If by hearing about that, a person becomes greedy for it, then that person is very fortunate. Prompted by such a holy greed, a person follows the feelings of those Vraja-vasis.

ragatmika-bhakti mukhya vraja-vasi-jane
tar anugata bhakti raganuga name[6]

Ragatmika-bhakti is mainly [found] in the residents of Vraja. The *bhakti* that follows after that *bhakti* is called *raganuga,* pursuant of holy passion.

5.2 Passionate and Passion-pursuing *Bhakti*

In his *Bhakti-rasamrita-sindhu* Shrila Rupa Goswami also makes a clear distinction between passionate (*ragatmika*) and passion-pursuing *raganuga*) *bhakti* and mentions who is eligible for the latter:

ishte svarasiki ragah paramavishtata bhavet
tanmayi ya bhaved bhaktih satra ragatmikodita
virajantim abhivyaktam vrajavasi-janadishu
ragatmikam anusrita ya sa raganugocyate[7]

Raga, or passion, is spontaneous, intense absorption in the object of one's desire [in this case, the Lord] and *bhakti* which is consists of that [kind of passion] is called *ragatmika-bhakti,*

[5] ibid., Madhya 22.152-153.
[6] ibid., Madhya 22.85.
[7] Rupa Goswami, *Bhakti-rasamrita-sindhu,* 1.2.272, 270.

passionate *bhakti*. The companions of Krishna in Vraja display such *ragatmika-bhakti* and *bhakti* which follows that [or, in other words, which is modeled on their actions and feelings] is called *raganuga-bhakti*, passion-pursuing *bhakti*.

ragatmikaikanishtha ye vrajavasi-janadayah
tesham bhavaptaye lubdho bhaved atradhikaravan[8]

One who is impatient to attain the feelings of the Lord's companions in Vraja, who are the only bastions of passionate love [for Krishna], is eligible for the practice [of passion-pursuing *bhakti*].

tat-tad-bhavadi-madhurye shrute dhir yad apekshate
natra shastram na yuktin cha tal-lobhotpatti-lakshanam[9]

The characteristic of the development of such impatience is that the mind, when one hears about the sweetness of the feelings of those [various companions of Shri Radha and Krishna in Vraja], no longer depends on scripture or argument [for motivation].

shri-murte madhurim prekshya tat-tal-lilam nishamya va
tad-bhavakankshino ye syus teshu sadhanatanayoh
purane shruyate padme pumsam api bhaved iyam[10]

After perceiving sweetness in the sacred images or hearing about the sports [in Vraja of Shri Radha and Krishna], those who long for those feelings [of the cowherd girls] become practitioners of those two types [of passion-pursuing *bhakti*, the one desiring direct enjoyment of Krishna or the one desiring to relish their various feelings]. We hear from the *Padma Purana* that this happens even to men.

Shrila Vishvanath Chakravartipada wrote in his *Raga-vartma-chandrika*:

yathojjvala-nilamanau tad-bhava-baddha-raga ye janas te sadhana-ratah. tad-yogyam anuragaugham prapyotkanthanusaratah

[8]ibid., 1.2.291.
[9]ibid., 1.2.292.
[10]ibid., 1.2.300.

> ... *anuragaugham raganuga-bhajanautkanthyam na tv anuraga-sthayinam sadhaka-dehe 'nuragotpatty-asambhavat*
>
> In [Shrila Rupa Goswami's] *Ujjvala-nilamani* [*Hari-priya-prakarana*, 49-50] it is said that those who are attracted to the feelings [of the cowherd girls of Vraja] and thus perform passion-pursuing worship (*raganuga-bhajan*), attain in course of time, an abundance of eagerness (*anuraga*) that is well suited for the practice of that kind. The words "abundance of eagerness" (*anuragaugha*) mean eagerness well suited for the performance of passion-pursuing worship. It does not refer to the permanent emotion (*sthayi-bhava*) of that same name (*anuraga*), because that permanent emotion of deep attachment cannot arise in a practitioner's [external] body (*sadhaka-deha*).[11]

Shrila Narottam Das Thakur Mahashay sang in his *Shri Prema-bhakti-chandrika*:

> *sadhan smarana-lila, ihate na koro hela,*
> *kaya-mane koriya susara*[12]
>
> The [main] practice is remembering the sports [of Shri Radha and Krishna]. Do not neglect this. Make it the essence of both body and mind.

And again:

> *maner smaran pran, madhura madhura dham,*
> *yugala-vilasa-smriti sar*
> *sadhya sadhan ei, iha boi ar nahi,*
> *ei tattva sarva vidhi sar*[13]
>
> The very life of the mind is remembering, and remembering the sports of the divine couple [Shri Radha and Krishna] is the sweetest. This is both goal and means; there is nothing other than this. This truth is the essence of all rules.

[11] Vishvanath Chakravarti, *Raga-vartma-chandrika*, 2.7.
[12] Shri Narottam Das, *Prema-bhakti-chandrika*, 14.
[13] ibid., 61.

It is also said there:

yugala-charana sevi, nirantara ei bhavi,
anuragi thakibo saday
sadhane bhavibo yaha, siddha-dehe pabo taha,
raga pather ei sei upaya[14]

Ceaselessly thinking of myself serving the lotus feet of the divine couple [in the imagined body given to me by Shri Guru-deva], I will ever remain enthusiastic. What I contemplate during my practice, I will attain in my accomplished form. This is the way of passion-pursuing *bhakti.*

sadhane ye dhan cai, siddha-dehe taha pay,
pakkapakka matra se vichar,
apakke sadhana-riti, pakile se prema-bhakti,
bhakati lakshan tattva-sar[15]

The treasure I desire in practice, I will get in my accomplished body. It is only a question of being ripe or unripe. The unripe stage is the stage of practice. When it ripens it becomes beatific love (*prema-bhakti*). That is the essential truth about *bhakti.*

5.3 Levels of Meditation

Shrila Jiva Goswami has delineated five levels of meditation that develop on the five stages of *bhakti*: 1) steadiness (*nishtha*), 2) taste (*ruchi*), 3) attachment (*asakti*), 4) feeling (*bhava*) and 5) divine love (*prema*) :

tadidam smaranam panchavidham yat-kinchid-anusandhanam smaranam, sarvatash chittam akrishya samanyakarena mano-dharanam dharana, vishesato rupadi-chintanam dhyanam, amrita-dharavad avichinnam tat dhruvanusmritih, dhyeya-matra-sphuranam samadhir iti.[16]

[14]ibid., 55.
[15]ibid., 56.
[16]Shri Jiva Goswami, *Bhakti-sandarbha*, para. 278.

> This remembering has five levels : 1) simple *smaran* or thinking to some degree [of serving with one's visualized form Shri Radha and Krishna in their divine sports], 2) *dharana* or drawing the mind away from everything else and placing it [on the sports of Shri Radha and Krishna] in a general way, 3) *dhyana* or contemplating in a particular way their forms, [names, qualities, and sports], 4) *dhruvanamriti* or uninterrupted contemplation [of those sports], which flows unbroken like a stream of nectar, and 5) *samadhi* or the appearance [of Shri Radha and Krishna] as soon as one begins to meditate.

5.4 The *Rasas*

In his explanation of the different *rasas* or forms of sacred rapture experienced when one is blessed by the awakening of divine love, Baba said that those who are in the *rasa* of peace (*shanta*) feel no sense of possessiveness (*mamata*) towards Shri Krishna. Although such devotees experience Shri Krishna's spiritual form, they prefer his supreme impersonal aspect (*param brahman*), sometimes thought of as the light from his body, or his super-self aspect (*paramatman*), his expansion as Vishnu who acts as the oversoul or inner witness in the material world. Once Baba expressed his surprise when he noticed some persons appreciating and cultivating this peaceful rapture (*shanta-rasa*) while living in Vraja.

A devotee in the rapture of servitude (*dasya-rasa*) regards Shri Krishna as his powerful prince and himself as his valet. Shri Krishna is great, he is small and therefore such a devotee must serve him for his pleasure without committing any offense. It contains reverence based on the fear that the Lord may not talk to him and may not let the devotee serve him. Such a devotee does not regard Shri Krishna as *ishvara* (God) but only as a mighty cowherd prince (the son of king of cowherds, Nanda) and for this reason he is afraid he may not be able to please Krishna. A devotee in the rapture of friendship (*sakhya-rasa*) thinks that he is equal to Shri Krishna and sometimes even superior to him. Though sometimes he quarrels with Shri Krishna, they still remain friends. A devotee in the rapture of parental love (*vatsalya-rasa*) thinks of Shri Krishna as a child who has to be educated and disciplined so he will not become spoiled. With the feelings of a protector such a devotee thinks that if she or he does not protect or correct him—who will do it? A devotee in the rapture of erotic love sees Shri Krishna as a lover whom she wants to serve by offering him her body (with the exception of those who are *manjaris*), thinking that if he wants enjoyment, then let him find pleasure with her. Shriman Mahaprabhu (Shri Chaitanya) taught Shrila Rupa Goswami about the different *rasas* in the following way, according to Krishna Das Kaviraj:

shanter svabhava—krishne mamata-gandha-hin
param-brahma-paramatma-jnana-pravin
kevala svarupa-jnana haya shanta-rase
purnaishvarya-prabhu-jnana adhika haya dasye
ishvara-jnana sambhrama gaurava-prachur
seva kari krishne sukha den nirantar
shanter guna dasye ache adhika sevan
ataeva dasya-raser haya dui gun
shanter guna dasyer sevana—sakhye dui hoy
dasye sambhrama gaurava seva sakhye vishvasa-moy
kandhe chade, kandhe chadaya, kare krida-ran
krishna seve, krishne karaya apana-sevan
vishrambha-pradhan sakhya—gaurava-sambhrama-hin
ataeva sakhya-raser tin guna chin
mamata-adhika, krishne atma-sama jnan
ataeva sakhya-rase vash bhagavan
vatsalye shanter guna, dasyer sevan
sei sei sevaner ihan nama palan
sakhyer guna asankocha agaurava sar
mamata-adhikaye tadana-bhartsana-vyavahar
apanake palaka jnana, krishne palya-jnan
chari-raser gune vatsalya amrita-saman
...
madhura-rase—krishna nishtha, seva atishay
sakhyer asankocha, lalana mamatadhikya hoy
kanta-bhave nijanga diya karen sevan
ataeva madhura-rase haya pancha-gun
akashadir guna yena para-para-bhute
eka dui tina krame pancha prithivite
ei-mata madhure saba-bhava-samahar

ataeva svadadhikye kare chamatkar[17]

In *shanta-rasa* [the rapture of peace] there is not even a whiff of feelings of possessiveness towards Shri Krishna. Knowledge of the Lord as Supreme Brahman [the impersonal absolute] and as Paramatma [the supreme self] prevail in this *rasa*. There is only knowledge of the Lord's bare essential nature in *shanta-rasa*. In *dasya-rasa* [the rapture of servanthood] there is a greater awareness of Shri Krishna's possession of all of the godly opulence. One regards him as a powerful Lord and feels awe and respect for him. Devotees in this *rasa* please Shri Krishna by serving him constantly. In *dasya-rasa* the quality of *shanta-rasa* is also found, but in addition there is the desire to serve. Thus in *dasya-rasa* we find two qualities.

The two qualities of *shanta-rasa* [knowledge the Lord's essential nature] and *dasya-rasa* [service] are both present in *sakhya-rasa* [the rapture of friendship]. In *sakhya-rasa*, however, there is more confidence. Sometimes during mock fights, Shri Krishna climbs on the shoulders of his cowherd friends and sometimes he makes them climb on his. Sometimes his cowherd friends serve Shri Krishna and at other times they make Shri Krishna serve them. In the fraternal relationship there is no awe and reverence but confidence is primary. *Sakhya-rasa* thus has three qualities [knowledge, service, and confidence]. In that *rasa* possessiveness for Shri Krishna is so great that his cowherd boy friends consider themselves equal to Shri Krishna. In that *rasa* the Lord places himself under their control. *Vatsalya-rasa* [the rapture of parental love] has the qualities of *shanta-rasa* and *dasya-rasa* but service here means protecting. Out of an increased sense of possessiveness [which is free of awe and reverence], such devotees sometimes scold and threaten Shri Krishna. They consider themselves Shri Krishna's guardians and Shri Krishna as in need of protection. With its four qualities, the *vatsalya-rasa* is like nectar.

...

---

[17] Krishna Das Kaviraj, *Chaitanya-charitamrita*, Madhya 19.177-192.

> In *madhura-rasa* [the rapture of sweetness] are present the qualities: steadfast devotion to Shri Krishna, an abundance of service, uninhibited friendship and the increased possessiveness of protectorship. The additional quality of this *rasa* is that the devotee serves by offering her body as a lover. Thus *madhura-rasa* has five qualities. Like the way the qualities of space and the rest exist also in each successive material element: one, two, three in order and all five in the element earth. In a similar way *madhura-rasa* is the totality of all the *rasas*. Therefore, because of the great abundance of [its] flavor one is astonished.

The experience of *shanta-rasa* by itself is not found amongst the living phenomena (human, animal, insect, fish, plant, flower, tree, stone, mountain, etc.) living in Vraja. It leads ultimately to the *sayujya-mukti* (the liberation of merging into the divine) of the living being, that is, to impersonal liberation in the Brahman or in Paramatma, which are locations that do not provide the living being with a capacity to express its constitutional nature as an eternal servant of *svayam-bhagavan* Shri Krishna. So, in his infinite compassion Shriman Mahaprabhu never distributes to anyone that *rasa* alone but the other four *rasas* which contain within themselves the quality of *shanta-rasa*. This can be clearly understood from Mahaprabhu's own words:

> *chari-bhava-bhakti diya nachaimu tribhuvan*[18]
>
> Giving them *bhakti* of the four moods [rasas], I made [the living beings of] the three worlds dance.

Baba once said that if one had lived in medieval times when Shriman Mahaprabhu was on earth with his personal companions, one would by their incredible spiritual influence instantly become a devotee fully endowed with divine love on meeting them. Since one would concomitantly learn of his (or her) eternal identity (as a cowherd girl) and with that understanding experience an uninterrupted flow of remembrance of Shri Radha and Krishna's erotic sports in Vraja and a pure meditational concentration on them, there would be no need any longer for him (or her) to practice the method of cultivation of the *Chaitanya-charitamrita* described above, the passion-pursuing cultivation of the feelings and identity of a *manjari*).

---

[18]ibid., Adi 3.17.

5.5 Success (*Siddhi*)

The accomplished level of *bhakti* (that is, acquiring the feelings of the cowherd girls) can be immediately reached by the power of their grace. As nowadays that is very rare because the Lord has ended his manifest sports with his personal companions, religious cultivation (*sadhana*) to improve one's skill, which he left behind through his devotees as a token of his matchless magnanimity, is the means to gradually become fit to receive self-manifesting *bhakti* of divine love. First one reaches the the budding state of divine love:

> *sadhanabhiniveshena krishna-tad-bhaktayos tatha*
> *prasadenatidhanyanam bhavo dvedhabhijayate*
> *adyas tu prayikas tatra dvitiyo viralodayah*[19]

> Love's first blossom, called *bhava* [or *krishna-rati*], is attained either by intentness in practice or for the very fortunate by the grace of Krishna or his devotee. The former is usually the case; the latter is very rare.

Shrila Jiva Goswami comments on this verse as follows:

> *athasyah prapanca-gata-bhaktesu avirbhava-nidanam aha sadhaneti ati-dhanyanam prathamika-mahat-sanga-jata-maha-bhagyanam. bhavapavargo bhramato yada bhaved ity adeh rahu-ganaitat-tapasa na yat ity adesh cha vichara-visesas tu bhakti-sandarbhe drishyah.*[20]

> Now the cause of its manifestation in devotees in the material world: either through intentness in practice or by the grace of Krishna or his devotee. What does 'very fortunate' [in Rupa's verse] mean? He who has attained the personal company of great devotees [either in this life or in a previous one] is very fortunate. [As it is said in the *Bhagavata*:]
>
> > When a person who is wandering about is freed from worldly existence then he attains the association of the holy, [Bhag. 10.51.53]

[19] Rupa Goswami, *Bhakti-rasamrita-sindhu*, 1.3.6.

[20] Jiva Goswami, on *Bhakti-rasamrita-sindhu*, 1.3.6.

and

> O Rahugana! One does not attain this by austerities ... without being sprinkled by the dust of the feet of the holy [that is, without association with the holy one] [Bhag. 5.12.12].

Its subsequent stage is called *prema.*

bhavottho 'tiprasadotthah sriharer iti sa dvidha[21]

Divine love is of two kinds: that arising from love's first blossom, *bhava*, and that appearing from Shri Hari's extraordinary grace.

5.6 The Stages in the Cultivation of *Bhakti*

On passing through the stages of developing faith in the Chaitanya Vaishnava scriptures (*shraddha*), gaining association with recognized Chaitanya Vaishnava holy persons (*sadhu-sanga*) and finding shelter at the feet of an authentic guru, the practice of cultivating of the feelings of a *manjari* is commenced by receiving the Shri Krishna initiation *mantras* (the Gopal *mantra* and emphkama-gayatri) and the lineage of gurus, including their accomplished identities (*siddha-svarupa*), from one's guru (in the way discussed before). Along with those initiations the guru gives his specific instructions on how to practice devotion to Shriman Mahaprabhu and Shri Radha and Krishna. The process of practice continues through the successively evolving stages of unstable execution of such practice (*bhajana-kriya*), elimination of the different obstacles to proper practice (*anartha-nivritti*), firmness in practice (*nishtha*), strong taste for proper practice (*ruci*) and attachment (*asakti*) to Shriman Mahaprabhu and Shri Radha and Krishna.

When the stage of divine love (*prema*) is reached one is a an accomplished devotee, and a direct vision of Shri Mahaprabhu and Shri Radha and Krishna occurs. Then, after death, one takes birth in one's accomplished body, that of a cowherd girl, from an eternally accomplished

[21] Rupa Goswami, ibid., 1.4.4.

cowherd woman in an earth-like Vraja somewhere in the material universe where Shri Radha and Krishna are revealing their divine sports. One is thus able to become properly familiar as a cowherd girl with the human-like sports that take place there. One is also able to reach successively higher levels of love, a development that could not be attained in one's previous body.[22]

After that life is over one is finally transferred to one's final form and identity as a cowherd girl in the earth-like Goloka-Vraja located at the summit of the spiritual world where Shri Radha and Krishna are eternally engaged in human-like sports.[23]

The passion-pursuing cultivation of the feelings of a *manjari* of Radha is in practice interwoven with the worship of Shriman Mahaprabhu in an imagined body of a young, *brahmin*, male servant-companion of Mahaprabhu in his divine sports continuing through the eight periods of the day and night. Therefore, after one is blessed with *prema* for Shriman Mahaprabhu, one is also born in one's next life as a young *brahmin* male in a Navadvipa-dham of the some universe in which Shriman Mahaprabhu is engaged his divine sports.

After that, one is transferred to a spiritual body in the spiritual abode of Goloka-Navadvip which is located near Goloka-Vraja. In this way, by inconceivable divine power, one and the same self (*atman*) participates simultaneously in Navadvip and Vraja's divine sports in the feeling (*bhava*) of a young, *brahmin*, male servant-companion of Mahaprabhu and a *manjari* of Radha. Shrila Narottam Das Thakur Mahashay wrote in his *Prarthana*:

> *mano vancha siddhi tabe hao purna trishna*

---

[22]Those higher levels are discussed in Rupa Goswami's *Ujjvala-nilamani* (Blazing Sapphire), Chapter 14. They are compared with the gradually thickening and hardening of sugarcane juice. They, like thickening sugarcane juice, become more and more intensely sweet. The levels are softness of heart (*sneha*), pique in love (*mana*), deep confidence (*pranaya*), delight (*raga*), ever refreshed delight (*anuraga*), a self-aware, group-shared love (*bhava*) and the highest love that absorbs the mind entirely into itself (*maha-bhava*).

[23]This abode is not to be confused with the Maha-vaikuntha Goloka, filled with godly opulence, described in the *Brahma-samhita*. That Goloka is located beneath the Goloka-Vraja mentioned here. There Shri Radha and Krishna are eternally engaged in majestic, awe-inspiring sports. That lower abode is reached by those devotees who have attained success by worshiping Shri Radha and Krishna through the path of rule-motivated devotion (*vaidhi-bhakti*). They do not distinguish between the marital and extra-marital forms of the relationship between Shri Radha and Krishna. See *Raga-vartma-chandrika*, 2.6: *atra vidhi-margena radha-krishnayor bhajane maha-vaikunthastha-goloke khalv avivikta-svakiya-parakiya-bhavam aishvarya-jnanam prapnoti.*

hethay chaitanya mile setha radha-krishna[24]

> When one attains one's heart's desire, one's thirst is quenched. Here [in Navadvip] we meet Shri Chaitanya and there [in Vraja] Shri Radha and Krishna.

In the *Skanda Purana* it is mentioned:

ya yatha bhuvi vartante puryo bhagavatah priyah
tas tatha santi vaikunthe tat-tal-lilartham adritah

> All the dear residences of the Supreme Lord that are found on earth are also present in Vaikuntha, for the purpose of the Lord's various sports [with His devotees].

5.7 Obstacles to Progress

About obstacles on the path of *bhakti* Baba said once, during one of his public readings of Shri Narottam Das Thakur's *Prarthana*, that lust, anger, greed, illusion, pride and envy, these six things will not allow us to do private worship and stay in Vraja. Also, although we may hear (or read of) Shri Radha and Krishna's sports in Vraja, if our hearts are not pure but instead are contaminated by lusty desires and not ready to melt with feelings from our positions as *manjaris*, we will not be able to practice private worship internally in the footsteps of the eternally perfected *manjaris* of Radha. Shrila Jiva Goswami has written in his *Bhakti-sandharba*:

nama-smaranam tu shuddhantah-karanatam apekshate[25]

> But recollection of the holy names depends on having a purified mind. [That is, an impure mind which is polluted by sensual craving has no power to concentrate and thus cannot carry out recollection of the holy names.]

In his dealings with different devotees and disciples, Baba discussed Shri Radha and Krishna's erotic sports only with those who were predisposed to it and had the proper eligibility. Otherwise, he talked about the other divine sports of Shri Radha and Krishna.

[24] Narottam Das Thakur, *Prarthana*, 43.
[25] Shri Jiva, *Bhakti-sandarbha*. para. 276.

> *tatrapi parama-shrestha-shri-radha-sambalita-lilamaya-tad-bhajanam tu paramatamam eveti svatah sidhyati. kintu rahasya-lila tu paurusha-vikaravad-indriyaih pitri-putra-dasa-bhavaish cha nopasya sviya-bhava-virodhat*[26]
>
> The private worship of Shri Krishna in his [erotic] sports with his most beloved Shri Radha is the highest form of worship. Still, those whose senses are sexually aroused [while hearing or reading about such sports] and also those who are devotees in the relationships of parents, sons or servants should not engage in this type of meditation, as it is in opposed to their relationships.

Baba once told me that the experiences I may have of Shri Radha and Krishna's sports in my private worship while living outside of the earthly Vraja (located in the District of Mathura, Uttar Pradesh, India) are in reality coming from there because it is the only doorway for such sports. And he made me understand, too, that without mentally living there while physically away from it, the experiences of such sports are not at all possible. Shri Rupa Goswami mentioned in the chapter on *bhakti* as practice of his *Bhakti-rasamrita-sindhu*:

> *krishnam smaran janam chasya preshtham nija-samihitam*
> *tat tat katha ratash chasau kuryad vasam vraje sada*
>
> A passion-pursuing practitioner remembers his beloved Shri Nandanandan Krishna and someone most dear to Krishna who appeals to him and being engaged in stories about them, always lives in Vraja.[27]

In his *Raga-vartma-chandrika* Vishvanath Chakravartipada has written:

> *vraje vasam ity asamarthye manasapi*[28]
>
> If one cannot live in Vraja physically, one should at least live there mentally.

---

[26] ibid., para 338.
[27] Shri Rupa Goswami, *Bhakti-rasamrita-sindhu*, 1.2.294.
[28] Shri Vishvanath Chakravarti, *Raga-vartma-chandrika*, 1.11.

5.8 The Seven Day Recitation of the *Bhagavata*

Baba supported the practice of hearing the *Bhagavata Purana* for seven days, saying it is a spiritual practice meant for those initiated into the worship of Vishnu through the Vishnu (i.e. Krishna) initiation *mantra* received from an authentic guru. In the section of the *Padma Purana* called the *Bhagavata-mahatmya* (The Greatness of the Bhagavata) the practice is confirmed:

> *saptaha-vratinam pumsam niyaman shrinu narada*
> *vishnu-diksha-vihinanam nadhikarah kathashrave*[29]
>
> Narada, hear from us [the Kumaras] about the rules of conduct to be followed by those who have vowed to listen to the *Bhagavata* for a week. Those who have not received the *vishnu-mantra* initiation are not eligible to hear the recitation.

5.9 The Stature of the *Bhagavata Purana*

On occasion Baba cited verse 28 of the Third Chapter of the First Canto of the *Bhagavata Purana*:

> *ete camsha-kala-pumsah krishnas tu bhagavan svayam*
> *indrari-vyakulam lokam mridayanti yuge yuge*[30]
>
> Of the different forms of God, some are parts and some are parts of parts, but Krishna is the Supreme Person himself [in his fullness]. All these forms of God descend [from the spiritual realm] from age to age to protect this world when it is oppressed by the enemies of Indra [the king of the material heavens].

He thus sought to remind us that according to the view of deeply realized *acharyas* [those who teach by their actions] this verse is the

[29] *Padma Purana, Bhagavata-mahatmya*, 6.44.
[30] *Bhagavata Purana*, 1.3.28.

definitive rule not only of the entire *Bhagavata Purana*, but also of all the other scriptures based on the Vedas.

That the *Puranas* (old lore) and *Itihasas* (epics or histories) are considered parts of the Vedas is demonstrated by the following verse from the *Atharva Veda*:

> *ricah samani chandamsi puranam yajusha saha*
> *ucchishtaj jajnire sarve divi deva divi-shritah*

> The Rig hymns, the Sama hymns, the meters, and the Purana along with the Yajur Veda were born out of the remainder [that is, out of the Supreme Lord himself] as were all the gods residing in the heavens.[31]

And from the *Chandogya Upanishad*:

> *rig-vedam bhagavo 'dhyemi yajur-vedam samavedam atharvanam*
> *caturtham itihasa-puranam panchamam vedanam vedam*[32]

> Lord, I [Narada] have studied the Rig Veda, the Yajur Veda, the Sama Veda and the fourth, the Atharvan. I have studied the fifth [Veda], the Itihasa [history] and Purana [ancient lore] and the Veda of the Vedas [grammar].

And from the *Garuda Purana* we hear about the *Bhagavata Purana* in particular:

> *purnah so 'yam atishayah*
> *artho'yam brahma-sutranam bharatartha-vinirnayah*
> *gayatri-bhashya-rupo 'sau vedartha-paribrimhitah*
> *purananam sama-rupah sakshad-bhagavatoditah*
> *dvadasha-skandha-yukto 'yam shata-viccheda-samyutah*
> *grantho 'shtadasha-sahasram shrimad-bhagavatabhidhah*[33]

> This is the most complete [Purana]. It is the meaning of the *Brahma-sutras*, the illuminator of the meaning of the *Mahabharata*, a commentary on the *Gayatri* verse [the mother of

[31] *Atharva Veda*, 11.7.24.
[32] *Chandogya Upanishad*, 7.1.2.
[33] *Garuda Purana* cited in the *Tattva-sandarbha* of Shri Jiva Goswami, verses 56-58.

all Vedic knowledge] and enriched by the meanings of the Vedas as well. It is like the Sama Veda among the Puranas and is spoken by the Supreme Lord himself. It has twelve cantos, hundreds of chapters, eighteen thousand verses and is called the Shrimad Bhagavata.

And in the *Padma Purana*:

> *puraneshu tu sarveshu shrimad-bhagavatam param*
> *yatra pratipadam krishno giyate bahudharshibhih*[34]
>
> Among all the Puranas the *Shrimad Bhagavata* is the best. In every line great sages glorify Lord Shri Krishna in many ways.

Furthermore, this fundamental spiritual truth, that Shri Krishna is the Supreme Person, is equally supported by the post-Vedic religious scriptures containing teachings taken from the Vedas. One might claim as an example, the New Testament of the Bible where we find: "In the beginning was the Word, and the Word was with God and the word was God,"[35] which has the appearance of being borrowed from the following Vedic utterances:

> *prajapatir va idam eka asit*[36]
>
> [In the beginning] the creator [God] indeed alone was this.
>
> *tasya vag eva svam asit, vag dvitiya*[37]
>
> Only his speech was his own. Speech was his second.
>
> *vag vai paramam brahma*[38]
>
> Speech indeed is the highest Brahman [God].

---

[34] *Padma Purana, Uttara-khanda*, 193.3.
[35] The Gospel of John, 1.1.
[36] *Pancavimsha Brahmana*, 20.14.2. Or, *Kathaka Samhita*, 12.2 (167.15).
[37] ibid.
[38] This line is not found with the two preceding passages in the *Panchavimsha Brahmana*. It is not an implausible statement. Perhaps it is in the *Kathaka Samhita* version which I was unable to check. [Ed.]

5.10 Baba's Blessings

Often Baba gave us the verbal blessing:

> Chant Hare Krishna [the *maha-mantra* of thirty-two syllables, known also as the *brahman* that saves one (*taraka-brahman*)] and weep.

He intended by this that such a practice results in intense feelings of separation from Shri Radha and Krishna and eternal service of them in our *manjari* forms. His teaching about chanting was that it should be done with the sole purpose of giving pleasure to Shri Radha and Krishna. The word "Hare" (pronounced: ha-ray) is the vocative case of either "Hara" (Shri Radha) or "Hari" (Shri Krishna), Baba made us understand that the *maha-mantra* can be used in a plurality of contexts. For example, when Shri Radha suffers feelings of separation from Shri Krishna the practitioner *manjari* can try to relieve some of her pain by chanting to her only the names of Krishna, intending then Hare as "Hari" (Krishna).[39] Or, when Shri Radha and Krishna are together the practitioner as *manjari* can intend both of their names (in this case Hare is Hara, Radha).

5.11 Baba's Letters

Even when he was uncomfortable and constantly bedridden, Baba used to write tirelessly to his disciples and to non-disciples, encouraging them in worship.

We could understand from Baba's neat calligraphy that his health was all right and this made us feel reassured. But on seeing the contrary, shaky or scrawled writing, we became worried. We became specially anxious when we did not receive his letter at the usual scheduled time. At each letter's arrival, the spiritual presences of the worlds of Navadvip and Vraja were present in our beings and in our surrounding atmosphere, even before we retrieved the letter from the mailbox. Baba always inscribed "Jaya Shri Shri Radhe! Radhe!" on both sides of the aerogramme, and from 1993 onwards, he started to inscribe the first

[39]For this case consult Shrila Ragunath Das Goswami's explanation of each word of the *maha-mantra*.

half of the following verse from the third prayer of Shrila Narottam Das Thakur's book *Prarthana*:

> *jaya radhe jaya krishna,*
> *jaya jaya radhe krishna,*
> *krishna krishna jaya jaya [shri] radhe*
>
> Glory to Radha! Glory to Krishna!
> Glory, Glory to Radha and Krishna!
> Krishna! Krishna! Glory, Glory to [Shri] Radha!

Each year he took the trouble to make a list of the main fasts and feasts to be observed from the almanac and sent it to us. In the last letter that he wrote, on Shri Gopashtami (October 28, 1998), he emphasized complete surrender to Shri Radha. He also mentioned that he would have to leave the Shri Radharaman temple and would await our arrival.

5.12 Parting Submission

> *anipuna vani apane nachite na jane*
> *yato nacailo tato nachi karilo vishrame*
> *shab shrota-ganer kari charana vandana*
> *ya sabar charan kripa shubher karana*[40]
>
> My unskilled words do not know how to dance by themselves, but they have danced as much as the grace of my guru has made them dance. Now they rest. I venerate the lotus feet of my audience whose grace is the cause of all good things.

[40] *Chaitanya-charitamrita*, Antya 20, 149-150.

Appendix A

Shri Sakhicharan Das Babaji

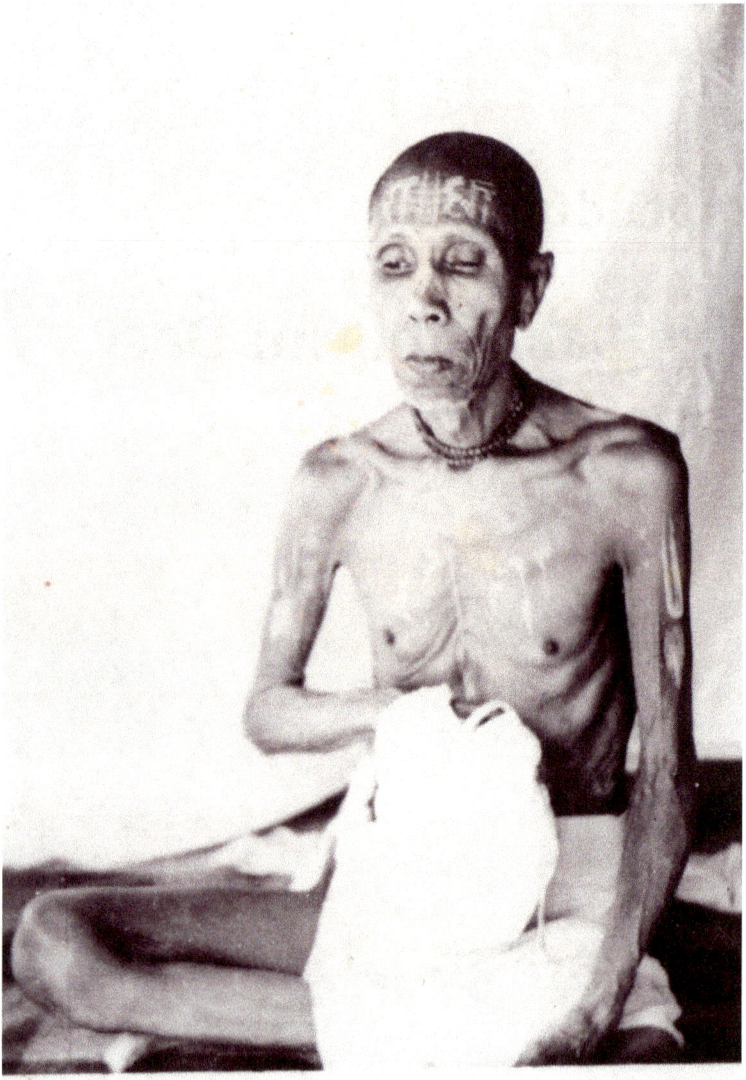

A.1 Foreword

Auspicious Invocations

ajnana-timirandhasya jnananjana-shalakaya
chakshur-unmilitam yena tasmai shri-gurave namah

I offer my humble obeisance to my initiating spiritual teacher (*guru*), who has opened my eyes by treating them with the balm of divine knowledge, dispelling in this way the darkness of my ignorance.

vande 'ham shri-guroh shri-yuta-pada-
kamalam shri-gurun vaishnavamsh ca
shri-rupam sagrajatam sahagana-
raghunathanvitam tam sajivam
sadvaitam savadhutam parijana-
sahitam shri-krishna-chaitanya-devam
shri-radha-krishnapadan sahagana-
lalita-shri-vishakhanvitamsh ca

I praise the lotus-like feet of my initiating guru; I also praise my other gurus (instructing, hearing, Holy Name, and path-showing gurus), the Vaishnavas, Shri Rupa Goswami and his elder brother Shri Sanatan Goswami, as well as Raghunath Bhatta, Raghunath Das and Shri Jiva Goswami. I praise Shri Krishna Chaitanya-deva with Shri Nityananda and Shri Advaita as well as Shri Radha and Krishna with their companions, headed by Lalita and Vishakha.

After writing the hagiography of my guru-deva, 108 Shri Krishna Das Madrasi Babaji, I felt like writing about his guru-deva, 108 Shri Sakhicharan Das Babaji. I have based my account on information given to me by my guru-deva and on that gathered by Dr. O.B.L. Kapoor from some of Shri Sakhicharan Das Babaji's other disciples. Dr. Kapoor's account can be found in his Hindi book *Vraja ke Bhakt.*[1] Let me thank Shri Advaita Das for his kindness in translating it to English for me.

[1] This work has been partially translated into English under the title *The Saints of Vraja*. The biography of Shri Sakhicharan was not among those translated. See the Bibliography.

My guru-deva always spoke of his guru-deva with profound love and veneration and made it clear to us that there was not a shadow of a doubt regarding his accomplishments in devotion to Shriman Mahaprabhu and Shri Radha and Krishna with respect to divine love (*prema-bhakti*). The spiritually faithful and introspective reader will surely realize this by reading through the following account.

Although I am not at all worthy to write about the immaculate life of Shri Sakhicharan Das Babaji, still I am doing it out of loving affection for him. I beg for just a tiny drop of his grace which I think is more than is necessary to be blessed with divine love.

I am also confident that Shri Guru-deva, his guru-brothers, and all the great, compassionate, rasa-tasting devotees of the Lord, who are expert in extracting the spiritual essence of things, who are like those swans who are able to drink only the milk in a mixture of water and milk, will find delight in reading it and pour their blessings on such a poor wretch as me. With such aspirations in my heart let me welcome you to the story of the life of Shri Sakhicharan Das Babaji.

A.2 The Life of Srila Sakhicharan Das Babaji

My guru-deva's guru,108 Shri Shrimad Sakhicharan Das Babaji made his appearance in the state of Manipur in India, on Phalguni Krishna Trayodashi (the thirteen day of the dark half of the month of Phalgun, which occurs from the middle of February to the middle of March) of 1886, while the Shravan constellation was predominant. His parents were initiated by a guru coming in the guru succession of one of the branches in the lineage of Shri Narottam Das Thakur Mahashay (16th cent. C.E.).

Their son was a spiritual prodigy who surprised everyone with his highly developed natural inclination for associating with saints, doing *sankirtan* of the holy names of Hari, studying the holy scriptures and other devotional practices. His natural inclination was amplified in an incredible manner when, in his budding adolescence, his parents had him initiated by the great Chaitanya Vaishnava saint and scholar, Shri Hemeshvar Thakur, who was also in the lineage of Shri Narottam. It is still the custom today in Manipur that Chaitanya Vaishnava parents have their children initiated into the tradition between the ages of ten and twelve. In this way, in case it is needed, their offspring can also take care of the ritual worship of the sacred images which is a practice strictly followed in every house in Manipur.

Due to his strong inclination for the *bhakti* of Vraja, young Shri Sakhicharan Das's aspiration was to go and reside in the sacred land of Vraja, and in particular to reside at Shri Radhakund which was and still is of special importance to the Vaishnava community in Manipur. Because of such a deep attraction to it, the people of Manipur have even recreated in Imphal two idyllic ponds representing Shri Radhakund and Shri Shyamakund. This keen interest in Vraja's most important sacred site is in part due to the grace of their former king, Shri Kulachandra Maharaja.

In the sixteenth century, two of the foremost disciples of Shri Narottam Das Thakur, namely Shri Ganganarayan Chakravarti and Shri Ram Krishna Acharya, went to Manipur, and by their grace the king and his subjects were initiated into Chaitanya Vaishnavism. From then on all the successive kings and the majority of the citizens of Manipur have been Chaitanya Vaishnavas.

There is no doubt that Kulachandra Maharaja was touched by the grace of Shri Radhika, since she allowed him to reside at her most dear pond. He had been born and raised in the royal family of Manipur and in time became the king, but circumstances forced him to leave everything behind and spend his final days at Shri Radhakund. For him, destiny was directly touched by Shri Radha who allowed him to remain eternally in her spiritual realm of Vraja.

Shri Kulachandra Maharaja's tenacity in not allowing his kingdom to fall under British domination was frustrated when after he had repeatedly humiliated them in combat, the British beguiled him by keeping a herd of cows and calves in front of their troops. Because of his devotion to the cow, the king did not want to risk hurting them and so it was a child's game for the opponent's armies to conquer him. When he was imprisoned in Delhi the British allowed him choose his place of exile. As he expressed a desire to live at Radhakund, they built a temple for him there with a mansion near Gopi Kuwa, where he was then transferred. From this time on, the Manipuri community started to flourish at Radhakund. Many of them still live there, engaged in devotional practices with determination. Throughout the year, excursion buses full of pilgrims regularly arrive from Manipur.

Amongst all those Manipuri devotees our Shri Sakhicharan Das was to become a particularly blessed soul. Although his body was in Manipur, his heart was in Vraja, always pondering the twenty-sixth song of Shri Narottam Das Thakur's book *Prarthana*, which he sang with a very sweet and emotional voice:

> *ar ki eman habo,*
> *sab chadi vrindavan yabo*
> *ar kabe shri rasa-mandale*
> *gadagadi dibo kutuhole*
>
> *kabe govardhan giri*
> *dekhibo nayan bhori*
> *shyamakunde radhakunde snan kori*
> *kabe judabo parana*
>
> *ar kabe yamuna jole*
> *majjane hoibo niramale*
> *sadhu-sange vrindavan-vas*
> *narottam das kore ash*[2]
>
> And when shall I become such that I will leave everything behind and go to Vrindavan? And when will I roll around in ecstasy at the site of the Circle Dance (*Shri Rasa-mandala*)? When will I fill my eyes with the sight of Mount Govardhan? When will I bathe in Radhakund and Shyamakund and calm my heart? When will I plunge into the immaculate water of the Yamuna? When shall I reside in Vrindavan in the association of holy? These are the aspirations of Narottam Das.

The devotional vine of Shri Sakhicharan Das's spirituality grew healthily day after day, diffusing its intoxicating aroma of sweet devotion to the lotus-feet of Shriman Mahaprabhu and Shri Radha and Krishna. Consequently, he was engaged in devotional practices like the congregational chanting of Shri Shri Radha and Krishna's holy names, listening to spiritual discourses given by erudite saints, studying the *Bhagavata Purana* and related Chaitanya Vaishnava scriptures, worshiping the sacred images, meditating (*smaran*) and so forth. He became famous for his expertise in singing songs describing the spiritual sports of Shriman Mahaprabhu and Shri Radha and Krishna. His heart radiated

[2]Similar to some verses from Song 27 of the *Prarthana* in Niradprasad Nath's edition, pp. 327-8.

so much devotion for their Lordships with the natural increase in the quality and quantity of the above mentioned devotional practices, that his attention to eating and sleeping became considerably reduced; he almost forgot about them.

In the *Shri Chaitanya-charitamrita* it is said:

mali hoiya kore sei bija aropan
shravan kirtan jale koroye sechan
upajiya barhe lata 'brahmanda' bhedi jay
'viraja' 'brahmaloka' bhedi 'paravyoma' hoy
tabe jay tad upari 'goloka vrndavan'
krsna charana-kalpa-vriksha kore arohana
taha vistarite hoiya phale prema phala
iha mali sece sravana kirtanadi jala

> A votary becomes a gardener and plants the seed of passionate *bhakti* [in his heart]. He then waters it by hearing and chanting [and remembering the names and sports of Shri Radha and Krishna]. Consequently that seed sprouts into a vine which breaks through the shell of the universe and pushes through the Viraja ocean, the plane of Brahman, and reaches the higher heaven. Then it continues growing upward to Goloka-Vrindavan [which is situated at the highest point of the higher heaven]. It then begins to climb the wish-granting tree of Shri Krishna's lotus-like feet. There, this vine blossoms and fructifies in the fruit of *prema* [divine love for Shri Radha and Krishna]. Meanwhile, here in the material world, the gardener continues to sprinkle it with hearing and chanting.[3]

At one point his eagerness to travel to Vraja and to remain there to do private worship increased to such a degree, that in 1921 when he was thirty-five years of age, he left home and went to Radhakund never again to leave it. Finding a place to stay in Shri Jiva Goswami's Ghera (by the side of Shri Shyamakund and Shri Lalitakund), he continued his private worship with even more eagerness and dispassion. Firm in his conviction that without taking initiation into the order of hermit-like *babajis*, he would not be able to advance quickly in his private worship,

---

[3]Shri Krishna Das Kaviraj, *Shri Chaitanya-charitamrita*, *Madhya*, 19.152-5.

he started to search for a guru to perform the renunciation rites for him. A long period of time passed, but Shri Sakhicharan Das was unable to make up his mind on whom to choose and so he became very desperate. To solve his dilemma he began praying day and night to Shri Radhika, so that she might give him some kind of guidance. But though his plea was heart-rending and long lasting, it was not successful in invoking any response from Shri Radha whatsoever. He then felt so miserable and dejected that he decided to end his life by fasting.

As he was already eating less than the minimum required, when he completely stopped eating and drinking, his physical and mental conditions became greatly weakened. After a fews days there was no difference for him between sleep and wakefulness and his body was extremely weak. On the seventh day, when he was on the verge of giving up his spirit, Shri Radhika appeared to him in person and told him to take the vows from Shri Bhagavan Das Babaji, the head priest of the Shri Radha and Gopinatha temple at Radhakund.

The divine love of Shri Radha and Krishna which is usually granted only after practicing the discipline of *bhakti* for a long time is instantly granted by seeing Shri Radha. That was the case for our lucky Shri Sakhicharan Das. Shrila Sanatan Goswami has written in his *Shri Brihad-bhagavatamrita*:

sa radhika bhagavati kvacid ikshyate chet
prema tadanubhavam ricchati murtiman sah
shakyeta ched gaditum esha taya tadaiva
shruyeta tattvam iha ched bhavati sva-shaktih

chet krishna-chandrasya mahavataras
tadrig-nija-prema-vitanakari
syad va kadachid yadi radhikayah
premanubhutim tad-upaity athapi[4]

If one sees the goddess Shri Radha sometime, then divine love becomes visible as if it had form. And if one were able to speak with her, then one would hear of it [prema] as it is, provided one had the ability [to understand it].

If there were a great descent of moon-like Shri Krishna who distributes that kind of love for himself, or if there were a

[4] Shri Sanatan Goswami, *Brihad-bhagavatamrita*, 2.5.233-234.

great descent of Shri Radhika, then, too, that divine love would become perceptible.

So following Shri Radha's order, he took the cloth and vows of a *babaji* from Shri Bhagavan Das Babaji and from then onwards became known as Shri Sakhicharan Das Babaji. Although he automatically became a devotee perfected in love by seeing Shri Radha personally, without practicing, in a strict, systematic and elaborate way, the remembering of the sports of Shri Gaura and Govinda in the eight periods of the day, Baba desired to engage in the full-fledged practice of that important devotional form. So he approached his renunciant guru with the intention of learning how to practice it from him.

Shri Bhagavan Das Babaji, however, was too busy with his services in the Shri Radha and Gopinath temple and had no spare time in which to teach him. He told him to study it instead from Shri Narottam Das Babaji and Shri Radhika Das Babaji, two highly advanced devotees from Manipur who were living in Shri Lokanath Goswami's private worship hut near Kadamba Khandi at Khadira-van.

Thus for the sake of enjoying the remembering form of *bhakti* as practice in the identity of a *manjari* of Shri Radha, Baba started his apprenticeship, with an ideal advantage, since instead of being an ordinary practitioner who had not yet reached success, he was a saint already beatified by divine love.

All this was the wish of Shri Radhika who, out of her infinitely concentrated grace, let him remain living in Vraja for the benefit of those not yet accomplished practitioners, blessing them in this way through his spiritual association and exemplary demonstration of this important form of *bhakti*.

From the accounts that follow it can be understood that Baba was a realized soul, with a completely spiritualized psycho-physical body, capable of doing feats not possible for ordinary votaries.

Shri Rupa Goswami gives the definition of a devotee successful in accomplishing divine love:

> *avijnatakhila-kleshah sada krishnashrita-kriyah*
> *siddhah syuh santata-prema-saukhyasvada-parayanah*[5]

> Those who are unaware of mental and physical sufferings, whose actions are always dependent on Shri Krishna, are the perfected or accomplished devotees (*siddha*). They are intent on constantly tasting the joy of divine love [for Shri Radha and Krishna].

So Baba engaged in his sport of learning from his two Manipuri instructing gurus how to systematically remember the daily sports of Shri Gaur and Govinda. The source of knowledge for this type of meditational practice was a manual based on the style of private worship propounded by the famous 19th century saint, Shri Krishna Das Baba of Govardhan.

The distance from Radhakund to Khadira-van is about twenty-five kilometers, and although Baba was like a walking skeleton, he walked that far as many times as it was necessary for him to completely memorize the manual. Since he had taken a vow to not spend even one night away from Radhakund, he had to walk back the same day to return before nightfall. Dissatisfied with the practice of remembering according to that manual, he started to search eagerly for a more detailed manual and came to know that in Kamya-van a grand-disciple of Govardhan's Shri Krishna Das Baba was in possession of a more ancient one. He

[5]Shri Rupa Goswami, *Bhakti-rasamrita-sindhu*, 2.1.280.

immediately walked all the way to Kamya-van, a distance of forty-two kilometers from Radhakund, to get that manual. At first the Baba in possession of it was reluctant to lend it to him, but when Baba begged him to allow him to keep his vow of not spending a night anywhere outside of Radhakund, the Baba consented, asking him to bring the manual back after three days. This Shri Sakhicharan Das Baba did.

After mastering this second manual Baba still felt dissatisfied and went back to ask for another one. But not even this third manual made him happy, and so he again walked back to Kamya-van to inquire if there was not an even better one. At this point the Baba of Kamya-van had no other choice but to give him his best manual, although he had never lent it to anyone before. This manual he considered to be his life and soul. It was only because that Baba was struck by Shri Sakhicharan Das Baba's unusual ascetic disposition and boundless devotional enthusiasm, demonstrated so evidently by his numerous long walks between Radhakund and Kamya-van, that he allowed him to take it, on the condition that he bring it back after fifteen days. Shri Sakhicharan Das Baba happily returned to Radhakund, copied it within twelve days, and again walked all the way back to Kamya-van to return it to the Baba.

Finally satisfied, he memorized completely this manual and became absorbed in the practice of remembering day and night. To keep his body and soul together he depended only on *madhukari*, that is, he followed the rule of begging for his daily food from only seven houses. When he was lucky he received the customary piece of *roti* (flat bread) usually given to the mendicants by the inhabitants of Vraja. But sometimes he would come home with an empty bag. In this latter case he would not bother with eating at all but instead gladly take it as Shri Radha's grace in providing him with some more time to spend in the remembrance of Shri Gaura and Govinda's divine sports. He would only drink some water from Shri Radha 's pond (*kund*), or perhaps just fast completely. Later, he told his disciples that when he only drank Shri Radhakund water, or abstained even from that, the visions of divine sport were even more vivid.

Baba's body was quite emaciated, frail, and almost as light as a feather. Although he was on the level of uninterrupted mental service in the visualization of the sports of Shri Gaur and Govinda, he also continued all of his external practices, like paying respectful visits to his two instruction gurus in Khadira-van, worshiping his stone from Govardhan, and so forth.

When Shri Chudachanda of Manipur built a temple at Radhakund, Shri Sakhicharan Das Baba, at his request, installed the sacred images of Shri Radha and Vrajamohan in it and also started serving them daily according to the prescribed rules of worship.

In 1930, on the ninth day of the bright fortnight of the month of Bhadra (August/September), Baba's instruction guru Shri Narottam Das Babaji passed away to join Shri Gaur and Govinda's manifest spiritual sports. Baba's other instruction guru, Shri Radhika Das Babaji, was so close to his friend Shri Narottam Das Babaji, that out of complete dejection from losing him, he gave up all food and drink and consequently joined him after only two days. Deprived of his two instruction gurus, Shri Sakhicharan Das Babaji's heart started now to burn with a luminous fire of divine love-in-separation from them. Thinking that they had left him because he was an offender, he too gave up eating and drinking and started imploring Shri Radha to let him also join her. For an entire month he daily sipped only one spoon of Giriraja's foot-wash-nectar.[6] His already emaciated body became now but skin and bone and seeing that he soon would pass away, his companions started to arrange for singing of the holy names of Hari.

At that time Shri Karunamayi [the infinitely merciful Shri Radhika] appeared in his meditation hut, holding a golden tray with the most delicious types of grace-food (*prasada*). She told him: ``Resume your eating by eating this grace-food." Baba replied: "Dear Swamini! I am an offender and I do not want to maintain this body any longer; please take me with you." But Shri Radha answered: ``Not now. For the moment you remain and perform worship." Then she personally fed him with her lotus-hand and left. Complying with Shri Radhika's wishes, Baba recommenced eating and continued with his private worship as before.

The next year, during the anniversary of the disappearance of his two instruction gurus, the fire of his divine love-in-separation for them increased so much that it became impossible for him to extinguish it. As a result he again stopped eating food and drinking, resolute in his decision to join them. One month passed in this way and when he was about to give up his spirit, Shri Vraja-mandala-bhumi, the very land of Vraja in its divine, lovely aspect, revealed itself to him. He then saw again graceful Shri Radha coming to him holding in her lotus-hands a

[6]Giriraja, King of Mountains, refers to a small stone from Mount Govardhan, believed to be an incarnate form of Shri Krishna and thus often ritually worshiped by Chaitanya Vaishnavas.

golden tray with grace-food. With her delightful, cuckoo-like voice she told him: ``Stop fasting. Go on with your worship for a little while more, before I come back to take you along with me." Baba replied: ``Dear Swamini! How shall I continue in such a desperate condition? My body is so weak that I do not even have the strength to go and fetch water from the neighboring well and there is no one to help me. Please just take me to your lotus-feet." But Swamini told him: ``You don't have to worry about that. A servant will come to assist you and a well will be dug just in front of your meditation hut." Baba said, astonished: "But I don't have money for the digging of a well." "Don't worry the least about that, Dhumra-ray will come and provide for it." After reassuring Baba in this way, Shri Radhika then fed him with her own lotus-hand and vanished.

As predicted by Shri Radhika, Dhumra-ray, who was Baba's nephew and a railway commissioner, came to see him. A long period of time had passed since his last meeting with his uncle and just at that particular required time he was urged by some unknown force to leave everything and come to meet him. When he saw that Baba had no nearby water facilities he immediately had a well dug just in front of his meditation hut, although Baba did not request to have it done. It was impossible to get sweet water from any other well of the zone, but by Shri Radha's sweet kindness the water from Baba's well turned out to be very sweet. A servant also came to him and in this way by Shri Radha's grace there was no obstacle to disturb his private worship.

Baba's scheduled time for sleeping was from 11 P.M. to 2 A.M. and the number of holy names he chanted in a day was over three hundred thousand (192 rounds on a string of one hundred and eight *tulasi* beads). He was constantly engaged in remembering the divine sport while chanting and counting the number of Hare Krishna *maha-mantras* he chanted on his string of beads. Even when he put the beads in their bag down somewhere to do something else the beads continued to move in the bag. This was witnessed by many who saw and heard Baba's string of beads moving along in his bag even when he was separated from it.

The *Bhagavata* had such a spiritual effect on him that once he told his disciple Shri Krishna Das Madrasi Baba that he was really sorry that he was no longer able to read it privately in his meditation hut because he always would have outbursts of tears that would spoil the book. Anytime he opened the book and started to read from it, this would happen. To remedy it he had no other choice than to close the book and put it away. So, he was compelled to give up his attempts to read it.

At the beginning of his renunciation Baba kept his body and soul together by begging from seven houses. Later he reduced that to five houses and then to three houses. Once during such an outing for begging, it happened that at the first house he visited the flat breads (*roti*) were not yet baked, and although Baba was asked to come back later, he did not do so because he had vowed to go only once to each house. At the second house he did not get anything because it was impure. At the third house there was a feast going on and since the food-offering had not been made yet to the sacred image, the owner of the house invited him to be his guest and come back a little later to eat at the feast.

Baba told him that he never accepted invitations from anybody. The owner informed him that the offering of the food was just going on and that very soon he would have some grace-food to take along with him. But Baba replied to him: ``It has become late now and I have not yet performed my noon-time duties. I shall come back to your house another day." The owner was mortified and told him: ``Baba, I cannot let you leave my house without grace-food!" So somehow Baba submitted to his request and took the grace-food with him.

It was late when he came back to his meditation hut and he still had to perform his noon-time duties. He, therefore, immediately sat down to start them. But usually at this time he had already completed them and was eating the grace-food. So out of habit, his strictly programmed mind was thinking of eating and was focused on the grace-food *puas* (a kind of soft cake deep-fried in clarified butter). Becoming angry at his mind for being more attracted to the *puas* than to his worship, Baba took the *puas* and threw them to the monkeys outside of his meditation hut. He addressed his mind: ``You wanted to eat instead of doing worship. Now what will you eat?"

Baba sat down again, performed his midday service with great vigor, and later only drank some Radhakund water.

Shri Satya Narayana of Kolkata came as usual to Radhakund to observe Niyam-seva (in October-November) and upon seeing Baba's skeletal appearance, he was moved and became worried about him. He somehow convinced him to accept a contribution for a daily supply of half a liter of cow's milk, thinking that in this way Baba will get more nourishment. But taking it as an opportunity to devote more time to his private worship, Baba completely stopped his outings for begging and started to subsist only on this milk. He used to boil it, sometimes putting a little tapioca and raisins in it. He drank half of the milk after completing his daily mental service of the divine sport at Radhakund (around 3 P.M.) and the other half at 10 P.M. With such a diet he used to move his bowels only every three or four days. He maintained that standard of living till the end of his life, finding it really suitable for his private worship.

For a time his private worship became disturbed when he found out that the milkman sometimes diluted the milk with water. This made him a little worried and he wondered how to remedy such mischief. But this problem was solved as one of his new disciples, Shri Madanmohan Das Babaji, took charge of it, personally going to the milk-man's house at milking time to collect the milk.

As an accomplished adept in the devotional form of remembering the divine sports of Shri Gaur and Govinda, Baba attracted many candidates who came to him in order to learn how to practice this type of religious discipline. He used to give them spiritual guidance by patiently drawing for them colored diagrams (with detailed annotations) of the different locations of divine sport in the spiritual worlds of Shri Navadvip and Shri Vrindavan.

Shri Vrajabhushan Das Babaji, who was a disciple of Shri Radhagovinda Das Babaji of Vrindavan's Harabari, took renunciation vows from Shri Sakhicharan Das Babaji after settling his residence at Radhakund and also took instructions from him in how to conduct his private worship. Baba was so kind that he drew for him an entire book full of diagrams which my Shri Guru-deva Krishna Das Babaji reproduced for himself with Baba's approval.

Once Baba announced to Shri Madanmohan Das Babaji that he would soon go to Shri Radha but that this should remain a secret. Moved to tears Shri Madanmohan Das Babaji pleaded with him to stay, telling him that as a young disciple he had still many doubts regarding the performance of the remembering form of worship. Knowing in advance the moment of his disappearance, Baba told him that he would pass on in two years and that over this period of time he should resolve all of his doubts.

Shri Sakhicharan Das Babaji spent these two last years of his life in seclusion. He no longer received visitors. He locked himself inside his meditation hut and even his own disciples would rarely see him. He would not even open the door for them. His intense, spiritual feelings of separation from Shri Radhika would not let him do so.

When two years had passed, he announced to Shri Madanmohan Das Babaji that he would soon leave as he had foretold. Although Shri Madanmohan Das Baba begged him to remain, Baba did not answer, knowing that his spiritual destiny was entirely in the hands of Shri Radha to whom he was completely surrendered. Such a decision was ultimately hers to make. She had already made up her mind about the moment when he would join her and now that moment was very close.

The following day, Baba started to reduce the quantity of milk he was drinking. Within a month his body became even more emaciated and he then just lay on his bed, deeply absorbed in remembering the sports of Shri Gaur and Govinda, unconscious of the external world. Shri Gopal Dasji was at that time his personal servant and from time to time he would softly ask him, speaking close to his ear, about which divine sport he was seeing at that time. Baba would always describe it for him, precisely and vividly.

Sometimes his state of divine love-in-separation became so intense that it entirely scorched him, and he would exclaim out of deep humility: ``*Jvale gelo; jvale gelo!.* My body is burning; my body is burning!"

A day before his disappearance, knowing that he was on the verge of leaving, he asked all of his disciples to come to him. Summoned by him through a disciple, my guru-deva Shri Krishna Das Baba, who was at that time at the Vrindavan's Ramakrishna Mission Hospital, came also.

By Baba's wish a party of singers was gathered and the singing of the holy names of Shri Hari was begun.

While Baba was meditating on the divine mid-day sports (those occurring between 10:48 A.M. and 3:36 P.M.) of Shri Radha and Krishna, he suddenly saw, in a vision, the girlfriends helping him dress up as a *manjari* before accompanying Shri Radhika to Shri Radhakund for her meeting with Shri Krishna. Seeing him in such a state of deep trance, completely unconscious of the external world, the singers brought the singing to a climax in a thrill of ecstatic devotional joy. The tremendous, supernatural power of Shri Radha and Krishna's divine holy names from the singing attracted Baba's consciousness outward once again, making him leave his state of deep meditation.

Shri Sanatan Goswami mentions in his *Brihad-bhagavatamrita* that the group-singing of the holy names of Shri Radha and Krishna is the most powerful form of passion-pursuing worship:

krishna shravana-pasat tvam niryato dhyana-rajjubhih

grahyas tabhyas cha niryato nama-kirtana-srinkhalaih
tvad-bhakti-lalitenadya na maya jatu mokshyase
vrito dhrito 'si gadham tvam pita-kauseya-vasasi[7]

Krishna! Escaped from the cords of hearing, you are caught by the ropes of meditation. Escaped from those, too, you are captured by the chains of the singing of your holy names. I, perturbed by love for you, will no longer let you go now. Wearer of yellow silk, you are surrounded now and tightly held!"

At the loss of the vision Baba started to weep, his heart over-flooded with love-in-separation from Shri Radhika. He yearned for the service of accompanying her to Shri Radhakund to meet the lord of her life, Shri Krishna. In his intensely blissful suffering he addressed the singers: ``I was going to finish dressing with the help of the girlfriends and then go to Shri Radhakund, but by the powerful sound of your singing you forcibly brought me back here. Please, stop singing the names of Shri Hari for now and let me adjust my visualization of the sports. When it is all right to sing again, I will give you a signal to start!"

The following morning, which was the first day of the bright lunar half of the month of Ashadha (the 30th of June) in 1965, he asked them to lay him down in the dust. At 1 P.M., just when Shri Radha and Krishna were sporting in the water of Shri Radhakund, Shri Sakhicharan Das Baba left his body to join Shri Gaura and Govinda's manifest sport, in the midst of an assembly of devotees who were singing the holy names of Shri Hari with deep feeling.

Shri Sakhicharan Das Baba's main disciples are Shri Krishna Das (Madrasi) Babaji, Shri Achyuta Das Babaji, Shri Vrajamohan Das Babaji and Shri Madanmohan Das Babaji.

[7]Shri Sanatan Goswami, *Brihad-bhagavatamrita*, 2.1.1. This verse does not appear in all the manuscripts or editions of the text. Puridas's edition has it only in a footnote at the end of the first part of the text. In Puridas's opinion that it is not by Shri Sanatan but one of the text's copyists. [Ed.]

Appendix B

Images

Shri Krishna Das Babaji Maharaj

The samadhi tomb of Shri Krishna Das Babaji
and his Gurudev
Shri Sakhicharan Das Babaji

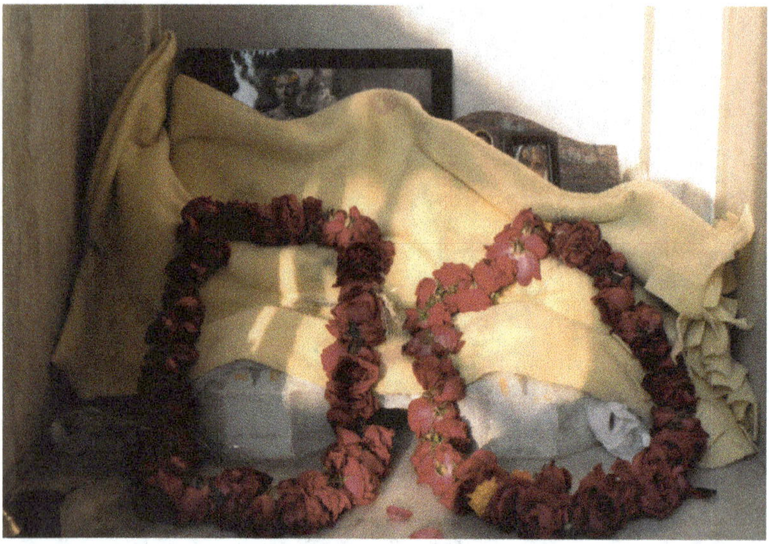

Garlands on the samadhi tombs of
Shri Krishna Das Babaji
and
Shri Sakhicharan Das Babaji

Feast on the disappearance day of
Shri Krishna Das Babaji

Appendix C

Glossary of Terms and Names

Ajamila (Ajāmila) Ajamila is the name of a fallen *brāhmaṇa* whose story is told in the *Bhāgavata Purāṇa* (6.1-2). He is a prime example of someone who was saved from his sins by a semblance of the holy name (*nāmābhāsa*). On his deathbed he called for his beloved son whose name was Nārāyaṇa, one of the many names of Viṣṇu. Though he was calling his son, not Lord Nārāyaṇa, he was, as the story goes, freed from the cycle of birth and death and after a short delay was welcomed into Viṣṇu's heaven, Vaikuṇṭha (see below). This is the primary meaning of semblance of the holy name: uttering a name of Kṛṣṇa in some other context and with some other purpose than calling on Kṛṣṇa.

bhajan (bhajana) In this work, *bhajana* is translated as "private worship." Private worship refers to various religious practices performed by an individual alone, apart from participation in group or communal practices and rites. In the Caitanya community, private worship consists of repetition of the names of Rādhā and Kṛṣṇa, called *nāma-japa*. *Nāma-japa* has three levels of recitation: vocal, whispered, and mental. Vocal *japa* is loud enough to be heard by others nearby is thus sometimes considered to be a form of *kīrtana* (See *japa* and *kīrtana* below). The mental form of *japa* is also known as remembering (*smaraṇa*) the holy names.

Some practitioners combine repetition of the holy names with remembering (*smaraṇa*) the daily sports of Rādhā and Kṛṣṇa as they are described in some of the meditation/visualization texts of the tradition. Others, however, focus entirely on repeating the holy names in the belief that when the time is right, the sports of Rādhā and Kṛṣṇa will appear before them without any extra effort. These two forms of practice are referred to as multiple-form and single-form *bhakti* cultivation, respectively. The division is derived from the discussion of *bhakti* in Rūpa Gosvāmin's *Bhakti-rasāmṛta-sindhu* (1.2.264-8) and is discussed in greater detail in Manindranath Guha's work, *Nectar of the Holy Name.* Refer to those works for more detail.

Private worship is performed on a daily basis by practicing members of the Caitanya tradition and is dependent on the instructions of the practitioner's gurus (both initiating and instructing). It also often includes simplified ritual for the worship of private images of the practitioner's desired deities (in this case, Caitanya and Nityānanda, Giridhārī, and Rādhā and Kṛṣṇa).

An example group practice as distinct from private worship is *saṅkīrtana*, the festive singing of the holy names and songs about the qualities and sports of Rādhā and Kṛṣṇa to the accompaniment of musical instruments (see below). Though generally performed in a group, it can be performed by an individual alone. Another example of a communal or group practice would be the worship of sacred images of Rādha and Kṛṣṇa in an established temple. Such worship is performed by one individual on behalf of a group or community of believers who look on and participate by singing or dancing or contributing money or materials to the worship.

bhajan kutir (bhajana-kuṭīra) A *bhajana-kuṭīra* is a small hut meant for private worship. It may also be the place where a practitioner lives, but it is thought of as having its main purpose fulfilled in allowing the practitioner to concentrate on his or her private worship without being adversely affected by the weather or other outside conditions. *Bhajana kuṭīras* are generally built in secluded places preferably in one of the places considered holy or sacred by the tradition. One can then sit quietly apart in one's *kuṭīra* and concentrate on the performance of private worhip.

bhakti *Bhakti* is the main term in Indic religion for the recognition of one's dependence on and desire to cultivate love for the supreme being. *Bhakti* comes from the Sanskrit root $\sqrt{bhaj}$ which means "to partake in," "to divide or share with," "to resort to," "to honor or worship." While *bhakti* can be felt for and practiced towards one's parents, other elders, and teachers, it has come to refer primarily to the cultivation and eventual experience of powerful feelings of love for a given deity. In the case of *bhakti* directed to Kṛṣṇa, it is connected with the development of a particular kind of intimate relationship with Kṛṣṇa and with all the complex feelings that go with that relationship.[1] A multivalent term, it is applied to the set of practices that are undertaken as part of the cultivation, to the end result of that cultivation, also called *preman* or love, and in the form of *bhakti-rasa*, to the tasting or enjoyment of the flavor of that love. Thus, the path of *bhakti* usually begins with a set of practices like hearing the sacred texts and singing or chanting the names of Kṛṣṇa, say, undertaken out of a desire to gain intimacy with him and his dear companions; it then passes through the appearance of genuine feeling for or attraction (called *rati*) to the deity in the heart of the practitioner, and culminates in the experience of sacred rapture (*bhakti-rasa* or *preman*). This last is the point at which the love that previously appeared in the heart rises fully into consciousness and becomes relished by the one who possesses it. All of these stages (practice, appearance, and tasting) are referred to as *bhakti* and one who has it in any of its forms is called a *bhakta*.

Gaura(hari) "Golden Hari," Hari or Viṣṇu with a golden complexion. This is one of the many names of Śrī Caitanya. Sometimes he is called Gaura, "Golden," Gaurāṅga, "Golden-limbed," and Gauracandra, "Golden Moon."

Goloka/Gokula World of Cows/Herd of Cows. This is Kṛṣṇa's paradisiacal world located far beyond the borders of the material realm. There he lives with his loving companions as an eternal cowherd

[1]There are five recognized relationships according to Rūpa Gosvāmin: peaceful appreciation (*śānta*), servitude (*dāsya*), friendship (*sakhya*), parental affection (*vātsalya*), and erotic attraction (*madhura*, lit. sweet). The degree of intimacy increases with each successive form.

boy. The Caitanya tradition believes this cowherd form to be Kṛṣṇa's highest form and cowherding his eternal activity. The pastoral planet on which this takes place for all eternity is called Goloka. The basis for these ideas is probably the *Brahma-saṃhitā*, the fifth chapter of which Śrī Caitanya is said to have found and copied during his tour of South India. The second verse of that text reads:

> Like a lotus with a thousand petals
> is the great abode called Gokula.
> Its pericarp is his residence
> produced by a portion of his Ananta.[2]

Gokula is practically synonymous with Goloka. There might be a slight distinction made in some texts, but in the *Brahma-saṃhitā* the two seem to be the same. Later, in verses 46 and 52, the name Goloka is used instead of Gokula. Gokula means a herd of cows or a village of cowherds with a herd of cows.

Govinda A name of Kṛṣṇa: "Possessor of cows." *Go* can have a number of meanings. Cow is the most common meaning and the word "cow" is in fact etymologically related to the Sanskrit word *go*. *Go* has also been used to mean the senses and the rays of the sun. The *vinda* part of the name is said to come from the root $\sqrt{vid}$, "to find, acquire, procure, possess." Interestingly, some scholars think the name Govinda may have been brought back into Sanskrit from Prakrit where is was a corrupted form of Gopendra, King of the Cowherds.

Hari A name of Viṣṇu or Kṛṣṇa. The name probably comes from the root $\sqrt{hṛ}$, "to take, bear, carry in or on, carry off or away, steal." Thus, it is often thought to mean the one who carries away one's sins or who steals one's heart. It also means the color yellow or

---

[2] *Brahma-saṃhitā*, 5.2:

sahasrapatraṃ kamalaṃ gokulākhyaṃ mahatpadam|
tatkarṇikāraṃ taddhāma tadanantāṃśasambhavam||

Ananta is, according to Śrī Jīva, Baladeva, Kṛṣṇa's brother, who on the higher plane is the first expansion of Kṛṣṇa, often depicted as a huge snake with unlimited heads called Ananta or Śeṣa, and who acts as the facilitating force, manifesting and arranging Kṛṣṇa's eternal abode for Kṛṣṇa's sport. The portion out of which this abode is produced is light, says Jīva.

green and might be a reference to the color of the complexion of Viṣṇu or Kṛṣṇa. See the entry for Kṛṣṇa for more details. The root *hṛ* also means "to master, overpower, subdue, conquer, win, win over" and thus the qualities of victory and mastery are applied to Hari. It might be from this set of meanings that *hari* also came to mean "lion," thus also suggesting that Viṣṇu/Kṛṣṇa occupies the same place among gods and men as lions do in the animal world. A last set of meanings center around ideas like "to enrapture, charm, and fascinate." These powers of fascination too are attributed to the great god Viṣṇu/Kṛṣṇa.

japa Muttering, whispering, repeating. *Japa* is from the root $\sqrt{jap}$ which means "to utter in a low voice." It is one of the ways in which the holy name and the usual way in which other mantras are recited. It is said to be of three types: silent or mental (*mānasika*), whispered (*upāṃśu*), and vocal (*vācika*. In actuality, however, only the second one is really *japa*. The first falls under the scope of "remembering" (*smaraṇa*) and the third is part of *kīrtana*. See Sanātana Gosvāmin's commentary on the *Hari-bhakti-vilāsa* (Play of Devotion to Hari) (11.472).

Kali-yuga This is the last of the four ages that make up a complete cycle in the Hindu conception of time. It lasts 432,000 years according to later Hindu calculations (originally it was only 1200 years) of which approximately 5,000 years have already passed. The complete cycle begins with the Kṛta-yuga or "Age of Fours." It is also called the Satya-yuga, the Age of Truth or "the Golden Age" and represents a time when the world is new and fresh. Peace, prosperity, and religious practice are found in full measure. Life is long and people are good and happy. The Kṛta-yuga lasts four times as long as the Kali-yuga. The next age after Kṛta is the Tretā-yuga, the "Age of Triads." It is three times as long as the Kali-yuga and contains three-fourths of the goodness and truth of the Kṛta-yuga. Then comes the Dvāpara-yuga, the Age of Deuces. It has half of the goodness and truth of the Kṛta-yuga and is twice as long as the Kali-yuga. The Kali-yuga, the Age of Ones, is the last and the worst of the four ages. When it is over the world will be partially destroyed and remade and the cycle will start over again at the top. All together these ages last ten units of time, a unit being equal to the duration of the Kali-yuga. Thus, the whole cycle is

4,320,000 years long. The names of the ages come from the Indian game of dice, the best throw being *kṛta* (four dots), the next best *tretā* (three dots), then *dvāpara* (two dots), and last *kali* (one dot), the losing die. Kali is not to be confused with Kālī, the dark, ferocious goddess of death and protection popular in Bengal and other parts of India, the anger-manifestation of the goddess Durgā.

kirtan (kīrtana) "Mentioning, repeating, saying, telling, praising." It comes from the root $\sqrt{kīrt}$, "to mention, make mention of, tell, name, call, recite, repeat, relate, declare, communicate, commemorate, celebrate, praise, glorify," and is related to the word *kīrti*, which means "fame." Thus, it means to make famous or spread the fame of someone. Mentioning, repeating, saying, telling, etc. are all ways of doing this. In the context of Vaiṣṇava practice it means to mention, repeat, say, tell of, or praise Kṛṣṇa's names, qualities, forms, and activities. As *saṅkīrtana*, or "complete telling," it means to sing of those things to musical accompaniment and according to the Gosvāmins, in groups. Śrī Jīva says that among all the forms of *kīrtana*, loud *kīrtana* of Kṛṣṇa's names is the best.[3] About *saṅkīrtana* he says: "*kīrtana* performed by many people gathered together is called *saṅkīrtana*. And because it leads to a special, astonishing delight it is better than the former (ie. *kīrtana*)."[4] The musical connection is made by Sanātana Gosvāmin when he says that *saṅkīrtana* means the complete or sweet sounding, loud singing of the names of the enjoyer of the Rāsa dance (Kṛṣṇa) with melody, rhythm, and so forth.[5] Thus, for the purposes of this text *kīrtana* is the loud repeating or telling of Kṛṣṇa's names, qualities, forms, and activities and *saṅkīrtana* is the loud and musical repeating or telling of Kṛṣṇa's names, qualities, forms, and activities as part of a group.

Krishna (Kṛṣṇa) Kṛṣṇa is the primary name of the god worshipped in the Caitanya tradition. The word *kṛṣṇa* is quite ancient. It is found many times in the oldest of the Vedas, the Rig Veda (15th-10th

[3] Śrī Jīva Gosvāmin, *Bhakti-sandarbha*, para 265: *nāmasaṅkīrtanañcedamuccaireva praśastam*

[4] ibid., para 269: *atra ca bahubhirmilitvā kīrtanaṃ saṅkīrtanamityucyate| tattu camatkāraviśeṣapoṣātpūrvato 'pyadhikamiti jñeyam|*

[5] Śrī Sanātana Gosvīmin, comm. on Bb, 2.1.21: *saṃkīrtayantīti| tasya śrīrāsarasikasya nāma ye samyak susvaraṃ gāthābandhādinoccairgāyantītyarthaḥ|*

cents. BCE), but it rarely occurs there as a name. There it means "black, dark, dark-blue" and is often found in opposition to *śukla* and *śveta* which mean "white." It may come from the root $\sqrt{kṛṣ}$ which means "to draw, draw to one's self, drag, pull, drag away, tear; to lead or conduct; to draw into one's power, become master of, overpower." Thus, Kṛṣṇa is often invested with a power of attraction. Kṛṣṇa draws the hearts and minds of all beings away from all else and brings them to himself. The word *kṛṣṇa* may be from another root, however, the root $\sqrt{kṛś}$ which means "to become lean or thin, emaciated; to cause the moon to wane." This would fit better with the word's meaning as "dark" and its common usage in referring to the dark half of the lunar month (*kṛṣṇa-pakṣa*) when the moon wanes.

Śrī Jīva in his commentary on the *Brahma-saṃhitā* discusses the meaning of the name "kṛṣṇa" after demonstrating on the basis of the construction of certain passages of the *Bhāgavata Purāṇa* that it is the predominant or primary name of the supreme being. Predominance means that all other names are included in it and that it refers to the primary and highest agent of all divine actions and expansions. He cites a verse of unknown original that gives a meaning of the name as follows:

> "Kṛṣ" is a word that means `being' (*bhū*) and `ṇa' means delight (*nirvṛti*). The oneness of those two is the supreme *brahman* conveyed by the word kṛṣṇa.[6]

Jīva then quotes another, verse from the *Gautamīya Tantra* that has almost the same meaning:

> The word "kṛṣ" means existence (*sattā*) and `ṇa' has the nature of joy (*ānanda*). Therefore, happy is the self that consists of being and joy.[7]

---

[6]Śrī Jīva's comm. on *Brahma-saṃhitā.*, 5.1:

kṛṣirbhūvācakaḥ śabdo ṇaśca nirvṛtivācakaḥ|
tayoraikyaṃ paraṃ brahma kṛṣṇa ityabhidhīyate||

[7]ibid.:

kṛṣśabdasya sattārtho ṇaścānandasvarūpakaḥ|
sukharūpo bhavedātmā bhāvānandamayastataḥ||

After dwelling on some hermeneutic issues, Jīva provides the following explanatory summary:

> The verse from the *Gautamīya* should be explained in this way. In the first half [of the verse] Kṛṣṇa is [defined as] joy that has the power of attracting all. In the second half [it is said that] since he is the joy that attracts all therefore the self [the supreme self, *paramātman*] and the living being find pleasure in him. The reason for that is that the self [both the supreme self and the living being self] consists of the joy of *bhāva* [being, feeling] which is divine love (*preman*). Therefore, the word kṛṣṇa refers to the greatest joy of all that attracts all by its beauty and qualities. And that word applies by convention only to the son of Devakī [Devakīnandana]. His ability to give joy to all is seen in the *Vāsudeva Upaniṣad*: "the son of Devakī gives pleasure to all."[8]

Thus, according to this argument, the fundemental nature pointed to by the name Kṛṣṇa is pleasure or joy that attracts all.

madhukari (madhukarī) *Madhukarī* means the "maker of honey," in other words, the honey bee. In this context *madhukarī* means going from house to house, the way a honey bee moves from flower to flower, collecting alms-food for one's meals. This is the way that most renunciants in modern Caitanya Vaiṣṇavism get the food on which they live. They depend on the charity of others which they regard as an avenue of Kṛṣṇa's grace on them. What they get varies from day to day depending on the houses they go to. Some days they get enough food and some days they do not. In both cases it is regarded as the grace of Rādhā and Kṛṣṇa.

manjari (mañjarī) *Mañjarī* means "cluster of blossoms, flower, bud" and is the word applied to what is envisioned in the Caitanya tradition as the eternal, feminine identity of those followers who seek

[8]ibid.: *gautamīyapadyañcaivaṃ vyākhyeyam| pūrvārddhe sarvākarṣaṇaśaktiviśiṣṭa ānandaḥ kṛṣṇa ityarthaḥ| uttarārddhe yasmādevaṃ sarvākarṣakasukharūpo 'sau tasmādātmā jīvaśca tatra sukharūpo bhavet| tatra hetuḥ| bhāvaḥ premā tanmayānandatvāditi| tadevaṃ rūpaguṇābhyāṃ paramabṛhattamaḥ sarvākarṣaka ānandaḥ kṛṣṇaśabdavācya iti jñeyam| sa ca śabdaṃ śrīdevakīnananda eva rūḍhaḥ| asyaiva sarvānandakatvaṃ vāsudevopaniṣadi dṛṣṭam| devakīnandano nikhilamānandayediti|*

to become the servants of Rādhā and assist her in her amorous love affair with Kṛṣṇa. A *mañjarī* is a young cowherd girl (12-13 years old) who is both a friend and a servant of Rādhā and who favors Rādhā even over Kṛṣṇa. It is not known who first used the term in this special sense, but it may have been Rūpa Gosvāmin. There is a description of such a female cowherd identity in the *Padma Purāṇa*,[9] but it is not known how early or authentic that passage is. The *mañjarī* identity was later picked up and used extensively by Raghunātha Das Gosvāmin, Kavikarṇapūra, Gopālaguru Gosvāmin, and Kṛṣṇadāsa Kavirāja.

One might view the *mañjarī* metaphorically as a "bud" or "sprout" on the vine of Rādhā. A verse from the great poem of Kṛṣṇadāsa Kavirāja, the *Govinda-līlāmṛta* (Ambrosia of the Sports of Govinda), suggests that there is such a symbiotic relationship between Rādhā and her friends. Kṛṣṇa embraces Rādhā and shivers and goose-bumps appear on the bodies of her *mañjarī* friends.[10] As both a friend and a servant, the *mañjarī* enjoys a certain degree of intimacy with Rādhā that the other girlfriends (*sakhīs*), who are just friends of Rādhā, don't. The *mañjarī* is also typically a year or so younger than Rādhā and the other *sakhīs* (who are eternally 14-15 years) and thus is able to play a subservient role to them.

The kind of love that a *mañjarī* feels for Rādhā and Kṛṣṇa is defined by Rūpa as *tat-tad-bhāvollāsa-rati*, a love that rejoices in their (Rādhā and Kṛṣṇa's) feelings for each other and pleasures derived from each other. Rūpa defines it in his *Bhakti-rasāmṛta-sindhu* (Ocean of the Ambrosia of the Rasa of Bhakti).[11] See also *preman*.

prema (preman) Sacred or divine love, *preman* or *prīti*, is considered in the Caitanya tradition to be the fifth and highest goal of human life, beyond even liberation from rebirth (the fourth).[12] *Preman* is defined by Rūpa Gosvāmin in this way: Attraction (ie. delighting in Kṛṣṇa, *kṛṣṇa-rati*), when it becomes condensed or intensified such that it completely melts the heart of its possessor and creates

---

[9] *Padma Purāṇa*, 5 (Pātāla-khaṇḍa), Chapter 83.

[10] Kṛṣṇa Dāsa Kavirāja, *Govinda-līlāmṛta*, 10.12-3.

[11] Śrī Rūpa Gosvāmin, *Bhakti-rasāmṛta-sindhu*, 2.5.128.

[12] Hindu tradition recognizes four goals of human life (*puruṣārtha*): wealth, pleasure, piety, and liberation. Caitanya Vaiṣṇavism has added to those four a fifth, divine or sacred love.

in that person a strong sense of possessiveness towards Kṛṣṇa, is called sacred love. It is a selfless love that is concerned more for the welfare and pleasure of the one loved than for the pleasure of the one loving. It, thus, stands in opposition to lust or selfish love (*kāma*) which seeks self-gratification.

Radha (Rādhā) Rādhā is Kṛṣṇa's divine lover. She is the highest example of sacred love (*preman*). She among all the cowherd women pleases Kṛṣṇa the most and though not wishing it, she derives the greatest pleasure from loving him. Theologically, she is Kṛṣṇa's pleasure power (*hlādinī-śakti*) in person. By connecting with her as her friends and servants (i.e. as *mañjarīs*, see above), others also become capable of pleasing Kṛṣṇa and through her of deriving pleasure from loving Kṛṣṇa. Though not mentioned explicitly in the 10th Canto of the *Bhāgavata Purāṇa* she is considered to be the one *special* cowherd woman Kṛṣṇa took with him when he disappeared from the rest of the cowherd women who had come to dance with him in the forest of Vṛndāvana during the episode of the circle dance.

Radhakund (Rādhākuṇḍa) Rādhākuṇḍa is the pond of Rādhā. It is the pond in which she likes to bathe and at which Rādhā and Kṛṣṇa meet during the middle of the day. There is a famous verse about Rādhā and Rādhākuṇḍa from the *Padma Purāṇa*:

> Just as Rādhā is dear to Viṣṇu, so is her pond dear to him. Among all the cowherd ladies, she alone is the most extremely beloved to Viṣṇu.[13]

The pond in the District of Mathura that is currently recognized as Rādhākuṇḍa was discovered by Śrī Caitanya at the village of Āriṭa during his visit to Vṛndāvana. That is described by Kṛṣṇadāsa Kavirāja in his *Caitanya-caritāmṛta* (18.1-11). The land around the pond was later acquired by Śrī Jīva Gosvāmin and since then Rādhākuṇḍa has remained one of the most important sacred sites in the Caitanya tradition.

---

[13] *Padma Purāṇa*, cited in Rūpa's *Ujjvala-nīlamaṇi*, 3.5:
yathā rādhā priyā viṣṇostasyāḥ kuṇḍaṃ priyaṃ tathā|
sarvagopīṣu saivaikā viṣṇoratyantavallabhā||

Radharaman (Rādhā-ramaṇa) The "enjoyer of Rādhā," a name of Kṛṣṇa that indicates his special erotic relationship with the cowherd woman Rādhā. The Rādhāramaṇa Mandira is one of the main temples in Rādhākuṇḍa.

raganuga bhakti (rāgānugā-bhakti) "Passion-pursuing" or "passion-following," specially as an adjective for the kind of *bhakti* taught by Śrī Caitanya according to his followers. *Rāgānugā-bhakti* is a form of *bhakti* cultivation that receives its impetus from a different source than the "rule-motivated" *bhakti* or *vaidhī-bhakti* of older forms of Vaiṣṇavism. Passion-pursuing *bhakti* is motived by a desire to develop the same kind of passionate love for Kṛṣṇa that his beloved servants, friends, parents, and lovers have. It is impelled, therefore, by a strong desire or greediness (*lobha*) to love Kṛṣṇa the way they do. For this kind of *bhakti* Kṛṣṇa's dear servants, friends, parents, and lovers become the models. Their actions motivated by their love for Kṛṣṇa become the sources of the practices adopted by the practitioner in the cultivation of their kind of *bhakti.*

Rule-motivated *vaidhi-bhakti,* on the other hand, is performed out of a sense of duty, duty instilled by respect for the accepted scriptures or by one's family traditions and other social institutions. One worships Kṛṣṇa because one's father or mother or earlier ancestors did or because the scriptures one trusts say one should. It is almost the opposite of passionate *bhakti* in which one worships or undertakes practice because one has a strong desire to do so.

rasa Aesthetic rapture. In this text *rasa* is used as shorthand for *bhakti-rasa,* sacred rapture. *Rasa* was a concept developed in Sanskrit aesthetics to describe the aesthetic experience of the connoiseur in enjoying plays and poetry. Though first discussed in the *Nāṭya-śāstra* of Bharata Muni (4-5th cents. C.E.), Abhinavagupta (10th cent. C.E.) is probably most responsible for bringing the idea of *rasa* to its highest level of sophistication in his commentaries on the *Dhvanyāloka* and on the *rasa-sūtra* of the *Nāṭya-śāstra.* Bhojarāja (11th cent. C.E.), king of Dhārā, developed the idea of *rasa* independently and in a different way. Each writer has his distinct areas of influence, but Abhinavagupta's understanding of *rasa* came to be regarded as the mainstream tradition. Rūpa Gosvāmin, following the lead of several predecesors, took the idea of *rasa* and applied it to religious experience, surprisingly relying more on Bhojarāja's understanding than on Abhinavagupta's. The result was his version of the idea of *bhakti-rasa*, sacred rapture, which became dominantly influential in the later Caitanya Vaiṣṇava tradition and in other Vaiṣṇava traditions as well.

One experiences sacred rapture when one's feeling (*bhāva*), that is, delight in Kṛṣṇa (*kṛṣṇa-rati*), is brought to the level of enjoyment or tastiness by means of the excitants (*vibhāvas*), consequents (*anubhāvas*), and transient emotions (*vyabhicāribhāvas*). The feeling of delight in Kṛṣṇa is, according to the Caitanya tradition, outside the natural world (*alaukika*), and it which consists of pure being or goodness (*śuddha-sattva-viśeṣātmā*) appears in the mind of a practitioner at some point in his or her development in *bhakti* and becomes part of the mind. Then when the practitioner encounters the excitants, consequents, and transients in literature, drama, or song, that delight is transformed into full-fledged joy or bliss. Since *preman* is an intensified or condensed form of delight in Kṛṣṇa, the threshold for the transition of delight into joy becomes dramatically lowered in *preman*. Then the mere sight of a peacock feather or a bluish rain cloud can send a person with *preman* into the throes of sacred rapture.

sankirtan (saṅkīrtana) See *kīrtana*.

smaran (smaraṇa) Remembering or recollecting. This refers to a Caitanya Vaiṣṇava practice that is more of a form of meditation or visualization than it is a "remembering," as remembering is commonly understood. The practitioners have never really experienced what they are "remembering." So, for them, it is not remembering at all. What they are really doing is focused or guided thinking about Kṛṣṇa and what he and his various companions are doing at any particular moment of the day. Thus, remembering is based on the idea that Kṛṣṇa is engaged in an eternal series of actions or sports which is taking place daily in Kṛṣṇa's otherworldly paradise, Goloka. The day is divided into eight periods and Kṛṣṇa's activities in each of those periods is "remembered" in the corresponding period of the practitioner's day. Thus, when Kṛṣṇa is in the forest bower with Rādhā at the end of the night and must be awakened and returned to his home before his mother and other elders discover he is missing, the practitioner "remembers" or visualizes it, placing himself or herself in the action in a mentally conceived or imagined body (usually but not always that of a *mañjarī*) given to him or her by the guru. A number of poetic works have been composed by followers of Caitanya to help the practitioner in this process of creative envisioning or remembering. The longest and most detailed is the *Govinda-līlāmṛta* (Ambrosia of the Sports of Govinda) by Kṛṣṇa Dāsa Kavirāja.

sattvika-bhavas (sāttvika-bhāvas) The *sāttvika-bhāvas* are a group of eight autonomous, physical reactions or conditions. They are regarded as outward physical manifestations of powerful, inner religious emotions. Those emotions, called *bhāva*, when heightened, enhanced, and relished, become known as *bhakti-rasa*, or sacred rapture. (See above)

Rūpa gives the standard list of physical reactions from the tradition of Sanskrit aesthetics:

> They are becoming stunned [immobilized], sweating [profusely], standing of hair on end, cracking of the voice, violent trembling, losing or changing color, tears, and fainting.[14]

The members of the Caitanya tradition generally regard the presence of some of the *sāttvika* reactions as indications of a high level of religious development in a particular practitioner. The manifestation of all eight simultaneously or at various times is considered a sign that the practitioner has reached the highest level of spiritual attainment, the level of feeling or tasting divine love (*preman*). This need not necessarily be so, however. One of the great Chaitanyite aesthetician-theologians, Śrī Rūpa Gosvāmin, devotes a whole chapter to the eight *sāttvikas* in his work on the nature and expressions of *bhakti* towards Kṛṣṇa.[15] Śrī Rūpa is not the inventor of the eight *sāttvika* conditions. He adapted them from the

[14]ibid., 2.3.16:

te stambhasvedaromāñcāḥ svarabhedo 'tha vepathuḥ|
vaivarṇyamaśru pralaya ityaṣṭau sāttvikāḥ smṛtāḥ||

[15]The *Bhakti-rasāmṛta-sindhu* (The Ocean of the Nectar of the Flavors [Raptures] of Bhakti)

older tradition of Sanskrit aesthetics and dramaturgy.[16]. There, they are understood as part of the actor's craft. In other words, good actors are able to fake them, to incorporate them into their acting in order to bestow the aura of reality on whatever part they are playing. In Rūpa's adaptation they are understood to be produced autonomously out of one's power feelings of love for Kṛṣṇa. Rūpa says:

> The mind when overrun by feelings connected with Kṛṣṇa, either directly or somewhat indirectly, is called the *sattva* by the wise. And those conditions which are produced from that *sattva* are called the *sāttvikas*. They are of three varieties: moist, anointed, and dry.[17]

The word *sattva*, therefore, refers to the mind when it is overrun by or overcome with emotion relating to Kṛṣṇa.[18] Those emotions are felt either in direct connection with Kṛṣṇa or indirectly. The physical conditions or reactions that are produced from the *sattva* are called the *sāttvika*, that is, conditions born out of the *sattva*. Thus, the physical conditions called *sāttvika* are produced when the mind (or heart) of a person is overrun by emotions relating to Kṛṣṇa. They are the external manifestations of powerful inner emotional experiences relating to Kṛṣṇa. Rūpa divides them into three varieties not by the kind of condition they are (i.e. tears, trembling, etc), but by how they are produced. He gives them names indicating a decreasing order of "moistness" or affection (*sneha*). The first, the *snigdha*, are the "moist ones." This group refers to the physical reactions of a person who has developed feelings of love for Kṛṣṇa and who experiences or tastes those feelings

[16]They are mentioned for the first time in the *Nāṭya-śāstra* (Treatise on Drama) (4th-5th cents. C.E.) attributed to Bharata Muni

[17]Brs., 2.3.1-2:

> *kṛṣṇasambandhibhiḥ sākṣātkiñcidvā vyavadhānataḥ|*
> *bhāvaiścittamihākrāntaṃ sattvamityucyate budhaiḥ||*
> *sattvādasmātsamutpannā ye ye bhāvāste tu sāttivikāḥ|*
> *snigdhā digdhāstathā rukṣā ity amī trividhā matāḥ||*

[18]The word *sattva* which ordinarily means "being, existence, entity" is used in a technical sense here to mean mind in a special state of emotional arousal. This idea, too, is borrowed from the earlier Sanskrit aesthetic tradition.

in direct connection with Kṛṣṇa. They have two sub-varieties depending on whether they arise from the five main forms of love for Krishna[19] or the seven minor forms of love for Kṛṣṇa.[20]

The second group, the "anointed ones" or *digdha*, are the physical reactions of a person who also has developed feelings of love for Krishna, but whose reactions do not occur in direct connection with Kṛṣṇa. In other words, they occur in situations influenced by that person's love for Kṛṣṇa but not in direct connection with Kṛṣṇa himself. The example Rūpa gives is that of Mother Yaśodā, Kṛṣṇa's foster mother in Vraja, who hears in a dream the demon Pūtanā, the ogress who tried to kill Kṛṣṇa by smearing poison on her beasts. Yaśodā wakes up twisting about in her bed and trembling like a leaf. Immediately, she goes to look for her son. Yaśodā's trembling is, according to Rāpa, a *sāttvika* reaction that results from her love for Kṛṣṇa, but it is aroused by a nightmarish vision, not the direct perception or presence of her son. Her reaction, as a result of her love for Kṛṣṇa, derives its moistness or affection from that love and thus it is considered "anointed."

The last type is the dry or arid (*rukṣa*) group of *sāttvikas*. Arid *sāttvikas* occur sometimes in those who seem like they are true *bhaktas* who have developed love for Kṛṣṇa but who actually have not yet reached the level of having developed love for Kṛṣṇa. Those *sāttvikas* appear as a result of the joy or wonder or other powerful emotions that is produced by hearing stories about Kṛṣṇa's sweetness or his amazing acts and so forth. Thus, it sometimes happens that even those who have not yet developed genuine love for Kṛṣṇa may exhibit some of the *sāttvika* physical reactions. While these *rukṣa-sāttvikas* are considered genuine, they demonstrate that it is unreliable to judge a person's spiritual advancement on the basis of the presence or absence of the *sāttvikas*.

shravan (śravaṇa) Hearing or listening. Hearing is the first stage in

[19]Peacefulness, servitude, friendship, parental love, and erotic love. These are the five main forms of *kṛṣṇa-rati*, attraction or love for Kṛṣṇa.

[20]The seven minor forms of attraction for Kṛṣṇa are: the comic, wonder, the heroic, compassion, fury, terror, and disgust. These are minor or secondary because, though blended with love for Kṛṣṇa, that love contracts itself and takes a secondary place, allowing the other emotions to be dominant. In the main forms, it is love for Kṛṣṇa that dominates.

the practice of *bhakti*. It means hearing from the guru, the scriptures, and other Vaiṣṇava about Kṛṣṇa, his names, his qualities, his forms, and his activities. Hearing if done well, it is said, will destroy the impurities or diseases of the heart and mind and clear the way for the descent of *bhakti* into them.

vaidhī (bhakti) See *rāgānugā* above.

Vaikuntha (Vaikuṇṭha) Kṛṣṇa's lower heaven. Vaikuṇṭha is the place where Kṛṣṇa's majestic aspect is manifested. Vaikuṇṭha is from the word *vikuṇṭha* which means "sharp, keen, penetrating, irresistible." Complementing his majesty is his sweetness (*mādhurya*) or intimate aspect which is manifest in his higher heaven called Goloka (see above). In Vaikuṇṭha Kṛṣṇa reigns as Viṣṇu with four arms and possesses all the majesty and opulence of a super-cosmic king. Those who worship Kṛṣṇa by means of rule-motivated *bhakti* (*vaidhi-bhakti*) are said to go to Vaikuṇṭha after gaining success. Those who worship by passion-motivated *bhakti* (*rāgānuga-bhakti*) instead go to Goloka.

Vrajendranandana The son of the king of Vraja, another name of Kṛṣṇa. The king of Vraja, the pasture lands, is Nanda the cowherd and Yaśodā is his wife. Kṛṣṇa is referred to as Nanda's son, though according to the story of his birth, Kṛṣṇa was actually born as the son of Vasudeva because of which he was known as Vāsudeva. To protect him from the evil king Kaṃsa, Vasudeva carried him on the night of his birth to the village of Nanda and swapped him for Nanda's new-born daughter. Along these same lines, Kṛṣṇa is also often called Nandanandana and Yaśodānandana.

Bibliography

Bābā, Ananta Dāsa. *Śrī Guru Tattva Vijñāna & Śrī Bhakta Tattva Vijñāna.* Rādhākuṇḍa, India: Śrī Ananta Dāsa Bābājī Mahārāja, 2003, 1st edition. Two essays by Paṇḍita Ananta Dāsa Bābājī Mahārāja. English translation by Advaita Das.

Bharati, Premananda. *Sree Krishna: the Lord of Love.* London: William Rider & Son, Ltd., 1905, 1st edition.

Cakravartipāda, Śrīla Viśvanātha. *Rāga Vartma Candrikā: a Moonray on the Path of Rāgānuga Bhakti.* Rādhākuṇḍa, India: Śrī Ananta Dāsa Bābājī Mahārāja, 2003, 1st edition. With the commentary of Śrī Ananta Dāsa Bābājī Mahārāja. Translation into English by Advaita Dasa.

Chakravartipada, Srila Vishvanatha. *Madhurya Kadambini.* Rādhākuṇḍa, India: Śrī Ananta Dāsa Bābājī Mahārāja, [n.d.], 1st edition. With the commentary of Srila Ananta Dasa Babaji Maharaja. English translation by Advaita Dasa.

Dāsa, Haridāsa. *Śrī Śrī Gauḍīya Vaiṣṇava Jīvana, Dvitīya Khaṇḍa.* Navadvīpa, India: Haribol Kuṭīra, 489 GA [1975], 3rd edition.

Ṭhākura, Narottama Dāsa. *Sri Sri Prema Bhakti Candrika.* Rādhākuṇḍa, India: Śrī Ananta Dāsa Bābājī Mahārāja, [n.d.], 1st edition. With the commentaries of Vishvanatha Chakravartipada and Srila Ananta Dasa Babaji Maharaja. Translated into English by Advaita Dasa.

Ghose, Shishir Kumar. *Lord Gauranga or Salvation for All,* volume 1-2. Calcutta, India: Piyush Kanti Ghose, 1923, 3rd edition.

Gosvāmin, Gopāla Bhaṭṭa. *Śrī Hari-bhakti-vilāsaḥ.* Mayamanasiṃha (now in Bangla Desh): Śacīnātharāya-caturdhurīṇa, 1946, 1st edition. Edited by Purīdāsa Mahāśaya with the commentary of Sanātana Gosvāmin. In Sanskrit.

Gosvāmin, Jīva. *Śrībhakti-Śrīprīti-nāmaka-sandarbha-dvayam.* Vṛndāvana, India: Haridāsa Śarmā, 1951, 1st edition. Edited by Purīdāsa Mahāśaya. In Sanskrit.

Gosvāmin, Raghunātha Dāsa. *Stavāvalī.* Mūrśidābād (West Bengal, India): Rādhāramaṇa Yantra, 1329 [1923], 2nd edition. In Sanskrit with the commentary of Vaṅgeśvara Vidyābhūṣaṇa and a Bengali translation.

Gosvāmin, Rūpa. *Ujjvala-nīla-maṇi.* Varanasi, India: Chaukhamba Sanskrit Pratishthan, 1985, reprint edition. Edited with the commentaries of Jīvagosvāmin and Viśvanātha Chakravarty by M. M. Pandit Durga Prasad & Vasudev Lakshaman Shastri Panashikar. In Sanskrit.

———. *The Bhakti-rasāmṛta-sindhu of Rūpa Gosvāmin.* New Delhi, India: Indira Gandhi Center for the Arts, 2003, 1st edition. Translated with introduction and notes by David L. Haberman.

———. *Śrī Śrī Bhakti-rasāmṛtra-sindhuḥ.* Mathurā, India: Śrī Kṛṣṇajanmasthāna, 495 [1981], 3rd edition. Edited with the commentaries of Śrī Jīva, Mukundadāsa, and Viśvanātha Cakravartin and a Bengali translation by Haridāsa Dāsa. In Sanskrit and Bengali.

———. *Ujjvala-nīla-maṇiḥ.* Navadvīpa, West Bengal, India: Mukundadāsa, Ga. 478 [1964], 2nd edition. Edited with the commentary of Viṣṇudāsa Gosvāmin by Haridāsa Dāsa, In Sanskrit with a Bengali translation.

Gosvāmin, Sanātana. *Bṛhad-bhāgavatāmṛta.* Mayamanasiṃha (now in Bangla Desh): Śacīnātharāya, G458 [1944], 1st edition. Edited with the author's own commentary by Purīdāsa. In Sanskrit.

Guha, Manindranath. *Nectar of the Holy Name.* Kirksville, MO, USA: Blazing Sapphire Press, 2006, 1st edition. An English translation of the author's Bengali work, *Śrīman-nāmāmṛta-sindhu-bindu.*

Kapoor, Dr. O. B. L. *The Companions of Sri Chaitanya Mahaprabhu*. Radhakunda, India: Srila Badrinarayana Bhagavata Bhushana Prabhu, 1997, 1st edition.

———. *Experiences in Bhakti: the Science Celestial*. Kirksville, MO, USA: Blazing Sapphire Press, 2006, 2nd edition.

Kapoor, O. B. L. *The Saints of Vraja*. New Delhi, India: Aravali Books International (P) LTD, 1999, 2nd edition.

Kavirāja, Kṛṣṇadāsa. *Caitanya-caritāmṛta*, volume 1-6. Kalikātā: Sādhanā Prakāśanī, [1963], 4th edition. Edited with commentary by Dr. Rādhāgovinda Nātha. In Bengali and Sanskrit.

———. *The Caitanya Caritāmṛta of Kṛṣṇadāsa Kaviraja*. Cambridge, MA: Department of Sanskrit and Indian Studies, Harvard University, 1999, 1st edition. A translation and commentary by Edward C. Dimock, Jr. Edited by Tony K. Stewart.

Mahāprabhu, Śrī Caitanya. *Śrī Śrī Śikṣāṣṭakam*. Rādhākuṇḍa, India: Śrī Ananta Dāsa Bābājī Mahārāja, 2003, 1st edition. With the commentary of Śrī Ananta Dāsa Bābājī Mahārāja. Translated into English by Advaita Das.

Nāth, Nīradprasād. *Narottama o Tāñhār Racanāvalī*. Kalikātā (Kolkata), India: Kalikātā Viśvavidyālaya, 1975, 1st edition. In Bengali. On the life and works of Narottama Dāsa Ṭhākura. Contains editions of all his major works and many attributed to Narottama Dāsa.

Purīdāsa, editor. *Śrīmad-bhāgavatam*, volume 1-3. Mayamanasiṃha, Bangla Desh: Śacīnātharāya-caturdhurīṇa, 1945, 1st edition. In Sanskrit. No commentaries.